What critics and readers have said about other books by Daniel Will-Harris

Nobody knows more about desktop publishing with IBM PCs than Daniel Will-Harris—nobody. And he knows type, graphics, design. And he can even write; he's funny, interesting, and informative.

—Steve Roth, Editor
Personal Publishing

In terms of understanding computers, Daniel Will-Harris is something of a genius. I can think of no safer hands to place you in.

—Peter McWilliams, author,
syndicated columnist

Daniel Will-Harris' engaging and informal style turns this treatise into a treat . . . it's an entertaining and informative romp through desktop publishing. **The author's advice is clear, sound, and practical.**

—Alfred Poor, *PC Week*

Will-Harris makes desktop publishing understandable, unintimidating, and fun. The book is worth the read not least for the comfortable way its author wears his considerable knowledge.

—Richard Barber, *Publish*

I have learned much from your book. It's well written and fun to read.

—Russ Heggen, Eugene, OR

If you are edging into desktop publishing, **this book could be a lifesaver.**

—L. R. Shannon, *New York Times*

Pithy, honest, unpretentious advice . . . it's hard to see how anyone could top this effort or do a better job.

—Gord Graham, *Quill & Quire*

I have been reading your book and I've found it **informative and helpful.** Since I am barely computer literate, I need all the help I can get at a reasonable cost. Thanks for the support.

—Stanley Beacock, London, ON

Daniel Will-Harris is the very best. He holds your attention, teaches, knows PCs and different brands of printers better than anyone I have ever read. Daniel Will-Harris *is* style—this is an AUTHOR.

—Anne Tuminello,
Canyon Lake, TX

As a typesetter I am particularly grateful for the pleasant way you ease the transition for me from commercial to desktop publishing. **I really appreciate your guidance and all this information.**

—Alice Bernstein, New York, NY

Daniel Will-Harris is a genius with a huge literary talent. What a superb book. Many thanks for each and every zinger.

—Cheryl Ryshpan,
Thornhill, ON

I am finding your book enormously helpful (and of course, delightful)! Thank you for putting together such a comprehensive and useful piece of work!

—Melody M. Brinkman,
Spencerport, NY

I just wanted you to know how much I enjoyed reading your book. Your sense of humor is great! You provided wonderful ideas that I have used very successfully.

—Susan Perry, Tustin, CA

I have really enjoyed your book and *Designer Disk*. They have been very helpful.

—Juan de Luis Camblor,
Madrid, Spain

Your book is absolutely sensational! I loved the way you made everything so simple and you did it humorously.

—Lucile Cheng, San Diego, CA

Daniel Will-Harris really did a great job. The book is tremendously helpful, full of great examples, suggestions, and tips.

P.S. I am not his mother, agent, or publisher. I just think an outstanding job deserves recognition.

—David Vandagriff,
CompuServe

I would like you to know how much I enjoyed your book. **Thank you for a most enjoyable and useful book.**

—Henry Milne, Rockville, MD

I want to personally thank you for all the great advice in your book, and all the great humor, too!

—Theresa Wiener,
Des Plaines, IL

An absolutely superb book.

—Douglas Myall,
Dorset, England

Love your book! Love your humor! Love your *Designer Disk!*

—C. G. Williams,
Lake Hughes, CA

I found your book to be very entertaining and an invaluable source of information on desktop publishing. Thank you and keep up the good work.

—Patricia Dickinson,
Bridgeport, CT

Your book has been very entertaining and informative, and I can now produce a passable newsletter, including columns and graphics, even on my dot-matrix printer.

—Jane Bliss, Santa Ana, CA

Fabulous. If you have a mailing list for future publications, please put me on it!

—L. S. Wagner,
Grand Junction, CO

Please notify me if Daniel Will-Harris writes any more books, on any subject; I'd like to buy them. I like his style very much.

—Peter Maston, Davis, CA

TYPE*Style*

TYPE*Style*

How to choose & use type on a personal computer

Daniel Will-Harris

Peachpit Press
Berkeley, California

TypeStyle: How to Choose and Use Type on a Personal Computer

We gratefully wish to acknowledge Allen Haley and International Typeface Corporation for granting permission to reprint "Parts of a Character," © 1990 by International Typeface Corporation.

Peachpit Press, Inc., 1085 Keith Avenue, Berkeley, CA 94708
415/527-8555

Notice of Liability
The information in this book is distributed on an "As Is" basis, without warranty. While every precaution has been taken in the preparation of this book, neither the author nor Peachpit Press, Inc. shall have any liability to any person or entity with respect to any liability, loss or damage caused or alleged to be caused directly or indirectly by the instructions contained in this book or by the computer software and hardware products described herein.

Trademarks
Throughout this book trademarked names are used. Rather than put a trademark symbol in every occurrence of a trademarked name, we state that we are using the names only in an editorial fashion and to the benefit of the trademark owner with no intention of infringement of the trademark.

All illustrations for Chapters 1 through 14 by Daniel Will-Harris.
Copy editing by Elizabeth Swoope Johnston.

Portions of this book have appeared in *Compute!, Publish, Personal Publishing, Desktop Communications*, and *Ventura Professional* magazines.

Library of Congress Cataloging-in-Publication Data

Will-Harris, Daniel.
TypeStyle : how to choose and use type on a personal computer : featuring bitstream fonts / Daniel Will-Harris.
p. cm.
Includes bibliographical references and index.
ISBN: 0-938151-23-1
1. Desktop publishing—Style manuals. 2. Printing, Practical-Layout—Data processing. 3. Type and type-founding—Data processing. I. Title.
Z286.D47W535 1990 90-14213
686.2'2'0285416—dc20 CIP

9 8 7 6 5 4 3 2 1
Printed and bound in the United States of America

Dedication

To Toni, of course. For her beauty, intelligence, wit, charm, perseverance, ingenuity, integrity—and the fact that she's wise beyond her years.

Her name really should be on the cover of this book because it couldn't have been done without her.

Table of Contents

?

Preface

The who,
what,
when,
where,
why &
how
of this book

What are the keys to working with type?

The who, what, when, where, why & how of this book

What are the keys to working with type?

Asking the right questions and good old common sense. Who, what, when, where, why, and how are not only the most basic (and often most important) questions in the world, they're also the questions this book will have you asking about type, so it makes sense for you to ask them about this book, too.

Who is this book for?

This book is for anyone who puts words on paper. It doesn't matter what software you use; it doesn't matter if you use a word processor or a desktop publishing program—all that matters is that somewhere along the line you print characters on a page. If that description applies to you, then you need this book.

Type is nothing more than a group of letters (usually about 26 of them) in a variety of different shapes and styles. But while you may have been putting characters on paper for years, you may never have noticed the letters themselves. This book brings them into focus and helps you to notice them.

Why do you need this book?

Otherwise known as
"What's in it for me?"

While you may have been able to communicate with simple typewritten messages in the past, type (and typesetting) can now help you to communicate more effectively.

The simple truth is that the better a page looks, the better chance there is that someone will read it. People don't often go out of their way to read something unless they *have* to or *want* to, so the more inviting and easier-to-read you make your documents, the more likely someone will *want* to read them. Even when people *have* to read, good typography can make your message more appealing, easier to follow, and therefore more useful.

All the most sophisticated and expensive hardware and software in the world won't produce a truly effective (much less professional) document *unless* you have a solid understanding of the basics of type.

While all of this may seem like alien territory, don't be intimidated. If you're not the artistic type, that's OK. You don't have to be able to draw to be able to work with type.

What's in it for you?

The answer is: *plenty.* Success, fame, wealth, happiness. You think of it, you can express it—using type.

What will this book do for you?

This book takes a somewhat different approach than other books about type. Yes, you'll learn the essential "rules" of using type effectively. Yes, you'll also learn how to use type beautifully. And you'll learn how to use type to your advantage.

But rules can only take you so far. You'll learn how to *think* about type. It won't be hard or painful, I promise. If you know how to make your own decisions about type, you'll never encounter a situation that stumps you.

Swiss Compressed
Goudy Old Style Italic

You'll also learn how to better achieve your goals by communicating more effectively. This book is about type. Type is about communication. Communication means relaying information about our logic and emotions to others. You may even learn something about yourself because logic and emotion, along with 98% water, are what people are made of.

You'll learn the *logic* of type: the right questions to ask so you can choose the best typeface and use it the most effective way possible.

You'll learn the *emotion* of type: How something that few people ever consciously notice can have a powerful subliminal effect that can work for or against you.

As well as a solid understanding of how to use type, you'll also gain (as my free bonus gift) a new understanding and appreciation of type itself. You may even be able to amaze and impress your friends by naming the typefaces on menus while they're puzzling over the cholesterol differences between chicken and fish.

If nothing else, this book will make you *think* about type. Just to *notice* it is a good first step. It's the same as any situation in life: just being aware that it exists is half the battle.

When should you use this book?

Well, preferably now, but basically any time you put words on paper, a computer or TV screen, a presentation slide, a T-shirt, a shopping bag, the side of a van, the side of a building, or whenever you indulge in skywriting.

All you will need in order to use this book are your eyes and light to read it by. No one has yet to perfect a book that glows in the dark (and if someone does, 25 years later someone else will probably discover that it's hazardous to your health).

Where do you start?

Start at the very beginning. A very good place to start. But while you start at the beginning, you don't have to read everything in order. (You can if you want to, though.)

Often the best way to learn is to jump around, reading the sections that you find most interesting first, or even those you find most boring but most relevant to what you do.

How does this book work?

Well, first you open the cover, then you turn the pages. It's amazing, it requires no electricity or video tape. What a great invention books are.

No, all joking aside, this book was designed so that it's easy to find what you're looking for. Leaf through and you'll notice there are many subheads so you don't have to read every word to locate the topics that interest you.

This book is organized into two sections: *Choosing* type and *Using* type. You *could* read the book from the back to the front—but unless you're already fluent in fonts, I don't recommend it.

Choosing type

This part of the book covers all the bases, from basic to advanced. You'll learn what type terms mean, how to *think* about type, which faces to use for which projects, which faces work together, and how to build your own library of type.

Using type

This part of the book helps you *set* type. The *Basic Training* chapter covers what you absolutely need to know. These fundamentals have been culled from years of experience—both mine and hundreds of other people's. The basics are all here, in one place. This chapter alone will take you from apprentice to artisan in only 35 pages. Best of all, it's high in fiber (if you eat it) and contains absolutely no cholesterol.

The book provides numerous illustrations of specific type do's and don'ts, as well as charts and forms to organize your pages, and it *shows* you interesting variations on standard type elements such as headlines, subheads, drop caps, pull quotes, and many more.

I had a lot of fun writing, creating, and producing all the examples and illustations for the first 14 chapters of this book, and I think you'll find them illuminating. They are all actual samples of what you can do with desktop publishing on a PC if you put your mind to it.

In the final section you'll see over 50 full-page examples of type in action. Good typography and good design add up to a wealth of inspiration.

What's the point?

The purpose of this book is to get you to the point where you no longer need this book. Read it. Think about it. Let it percolate in the back of your head. And when you sit down to work with type, *think* about it, but don't worry about it.

What this book isn't

This book isn't for people interested in the detailed history of type or the technicalities of how type is classified or designed. Once you start using type you may want to learn those things, but few people make decisions about using typefaces according to their classification or history. Just as you don't have to know how a transmission works to drive a car, you don't have to know where a typeface came from in order to use it well. This book offers a bibliography highlighting other sources of information about the history and creation of typography for those interested in that kind of detail.

Why Bitstream type?

Why an "a"
isn't an "a"
isn't an **"a"**

Did you know that two fonts with the same name can be completely different? They can. Not all fonts are alike because not all font makers are alike. Quality standards differ from one font company to another. And that difference in quality can spell the difference between a professional, good-looking, readable page, and an awkward, unattractive, hard-to-read page.

Quality

My decision to use Bitstream type in this book was simple. I use type from all the major foundries and I consistently find Bitstream's to be of the very highest quality.

By

Bitstream never changes the original font design based on purely technical considerations. Bitstream researches and restores typeface characteristics that might have been removed because of old technological limitations. Whenever possible it consults with the original type designer to create the most authentic version of the typeface. Some other major foundries provide only a few kerning pairs, but Bitstream fonts average 350 kerning pairs. This makes your typesetting more professional and easier to read.

Design

There's an old saying about buying diamonds: "If you don't know jewelry, know your jeweler." Because the little letters in a typeface are not unlike so many gems, the saying applies here as well: "If you don't know type, know your type foundry."

If you *do* know type, you'll certainly choose Bitstream. It was founded by typographers. At Bitstream they know type, and they care about type.

Matthew Carter, one of Bitstream's founders and Vice President of Design, has been designing type for decades, from the old hot metal to the latest digital formats. He knows type. Type is a friend of his. His classic designs range from the glamorous ITC Galliard and Snell Roundhand to the modern Charter and the striking Helvetica Compressed. Your name probably has been set in one of his typefaces—the ubiquitous Bell Centennial, designed specifically for phone books.

For some other foundries, type is a sideline to selling typesetting machines or computer languages. Bitstream's only business is type and it supplies type to more companies than anyone else. Much of the type you see in magazines and on TV comes from Bitstream.

Bitstream not only offers more fonts than any other digital type foundry, its fonts work on more printers, typesetters, slide makers, and TV production equipment than anyone else's. This gives Bitstream a unique perspective and unmatched experience in developing typographic products.

You can be sure that when you buy a Bitstream typeface it will be of the highest quality. On the economic front, Bitstream fonts have always protected your investment because they have kept pace with changing font formats and provided users with an upgrade path.

What's in a name?

or, A Times Roman by any other name

When you begin working with type it's hard enough to tell one typeface from another, and then there's the added confusion when the *same* typeface has different names.

For example, why is Bitstream's version of Times Roman called "Dutch" and its version of Optima called "Zapf Humanist?"

The reason might interest you. Then again it might not. But interesting or not, it is important. In most countries of the world (including the US) typeface designs can't be copyrighted. Typefaces require a huge amount of time and effort to design, but unlike other artistic pursuits, such as drawings, paintings, or sculpture, they can't be protected by a copyright. Typeface names, on the other hand, can be protected by trademark. The names "Helvetica" and "Times Roman," for example, are trademarked and can only be used by their owners and licensees. Hence "Swiss" and "Dutch."

While foundries *do* license typefaces from each other (and many of Bitstream's typefaces are licensed), sometimes the owner of the face refuses to license it. That's what happened in the case of Palatino, Optima, and Melior, three typefaces indispensable to a modern type library. Bitstream consulted closely with Hermann Zapf, the eminent designer of these typefaces, and he publicly endorsed the results as the best currently available. In this case, the names are different, but according to the original designer (who should know), the type itself is the most authentic you can get.

Another reason for name changes is that a foundry sometimes redesigns a face to improve it. Just as you don't judge a book by it's cover, you can't judge a font by its name.

A licensed name is almost always a guarantee of *authenticity*, but that doesn't mean it's a guarantee of *quality*. I've seen some licensed typefaces that were awful and some nonlicensed versions that were excellent.

A number of typeface names have the acronym ITC in front of them. ITC stands for International Typeface Corporation, the first company devoted solely to type design, not manufacturing. Other originators of type designs, Bitstream among them, add their foundry names to their face names.

1

What is type?

or
They don't call them *characters* for nothing

While you can do without graphics, you can't do without type, and yet type remains one of the most mysterious and misused elements in desktop publishing.

What is type?

or They don't call them characters for nothing

Every piece of printed material you read in your entire lifetime is made up of three basic elements: *Text*—the written content of a page; *Typeface*—the type style or styles in which the text is set; and *Graphics*—the non-text art on the page, in the form of illustrations or photographs. While you can do without graphics, *you can't do without type*, and yet type remains one of the most mysterious and misused elements in desktop publishing.

Type is your personality on paper

While you may never have thought about type before, perhaps never even noticed it, you have seen so many zillions of letters, billions of words, millions of pages, that if you stop and *think* about it, all the seemingly complicated details in this book will seem more familiar.

Considering how important type is, it's strange that it has been so neglected. The typeset word is one of the few ways to communicate precisely—and for posterity.

While most people recognize the TV newscasters who read the news, few recognize or can name the typefaces they read in the newspaper.

Type and typography (the art/craft of using type) are taken for granted—except when they're poorly executed. When that happens, the reader complains because something is difficult to read, or the publisher complains because no one is reading the publication.

Type is powerful

Like anything powerful, type can be good or bad, and work for you or against you. The right typeface can help make your message more attractive, readable, understandable, authoritative, persuasive, and effective.

The right typeface can compel people to read your message.

The wrong typeface or bad typography can make your message go unread, or just make it difficult to read.

Presented with two documents side by side, one well written but ugly, and the other rambling but attractive, which do you think people will read first? They'll read the one that looks more professional and appealing. The amateurish ugly one gets put at the bottom of the pile—unread.

I know that may be difficult to believe. You probably think that no one consciously notices what typeface they are reading. And you're right, we don't *consciously* notice. But type and typography do affect the way we *feel* about the words we are reading.

If the words in your document are complicated and difficult, good type can help make them easier to understand. If they are only mediocre, good type can help make them look brilliant. If the words in your document *are* brilliant and profound, unskilled typography can make them *seem* mediocre, and undermine your credibility.

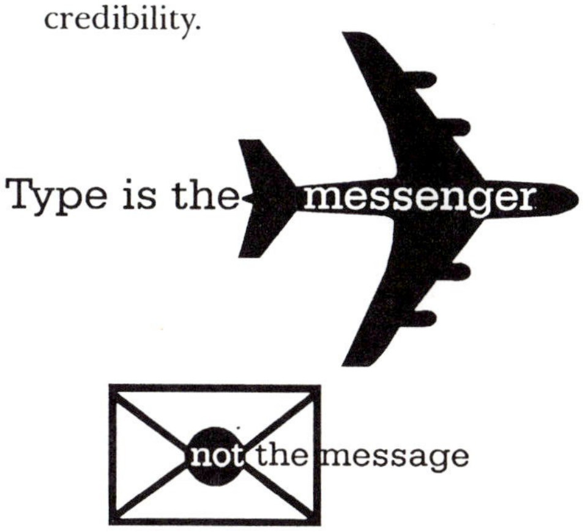
Type is the messenger
not the message

Serifa with ITC Zapf Dingbats (airplane and envelope).

So, you may not have noticed what typeface you're reading right now—and that's good. But you *are* reading it, and that's even better. (The typeface is Baskerville.)

The true purpose of type is to enhance the message, not merely carry it. Type can be an art, but its most important job is to serve the text, not to decorate the page and distract the reader.

Type is not just some shallow surface ornament used to get attention. If used carefully, type can help to visually organize your message so people get the point more easily.

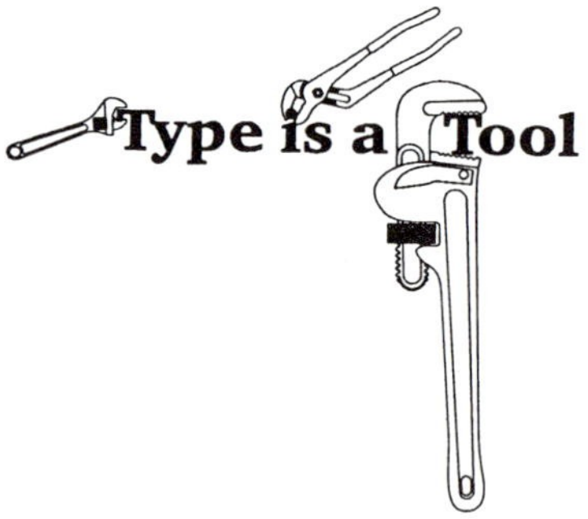

Bitstream Charter

Type is a tool, like a hammer or a set of oil paints

Type isn't the end result. Even with the best tools or type, if you don't use them properly, the end result won't be good.

B a d   t y p o g r a p h y   i s   r u d e   a n d   d i s t r a c t - i n g .

Type is subliminal

Good typography seems invisible but is really subliminal

Good typography doesn't make you stop and wonder what it is. Instead, it conveys the message of the text, and equally important, it conveys a *feeling. ITC Galliard has a very different* feeling from Swiss.

Type is full of subconscious associations and connotations. Sometimes these refer to specific events and places, sometimes these are just general feelings.

- **What does this typeface remind you of?**

When I see Century Schoolbook I'm reminded of those "See Jane run. Run, Jane, run," books that were foisted on me when I really just wanted to read the funnies.

- **What does this typeface remind you of?**

When I see Swiss (Helvetica) I'm reminded of brain-numbingly boring high school geometry books.

- **What does this typeface remind you of?**

When I see Zapf Humanist (Optima) the words "modern," "cool," and "elegant" come to mind.

- What does this typeface remind you of?

University Roman says the Roaring Twenties. The "Gatsby" era. Green grass and white tennis outfits.

Chances are these typefaces said different things to you, but if you listened closely to that little voice in the back of your head (the one you try so hard to ignore when it says things like "Don't eat that second piece of cake") you probably heard or felt *something*.

The idea is to tap into that *something* and use it. It's tricky, because while *you* might think that

Galliard Italic is elegant and Tiffany isn't

other people might think that

Tiffany is elegant and Galliard isn't.

The trick is to find the typeface that strikes the proper balance between its "connotations" or feelings, and its ability to serve the words on the page. A typeface may convey the right mood but may not work in the size or length you need:

Cloister seems formal, serious, reminiscent of a traditional wedding, law office, or the New York Times. But it's too hard to read in paragraph form.

Bad typography sends a message to the reader that says "ignore me." People don't stop and think that, but when something is sloppy, messy, inconsistent, or just plain ugly, it gives them an excellent excuse to avoid reading it.

Type is emotional

Type is an emotional matter. It's the "body language" of your text. You can say the same words, but different typefaces make them *sound* different. Some typefaces, such as Goudy Old Style, are elegant and refined. Others, such as Century Schoolbook, are basic and no-nonsense. Benguiat is eccentric and lively, while Zurich is simple and modern. If you send a "how come you said my check is in the mail but I haven't received it yet" letter set in ITC Souvenir it's not going to seem as serious or official as the same letter set in Swiss or Zurich.

Type is like...

A musical instrument

Just as the same melody sounds different played on a flute and played on a banjo, the same words seem different when set in Zapf Humanist (Optima) and set in Korinna.

Just as the same melody sounds different played on a flute and played on a banjo, the same words seem different when set in Zapf Humanist (Optima) and set in Korinna.

Just as the same melody sounds different played on a flute and played on a banjo, the same words seem different when set in Zapf Humanist (Optima) and set in Korinna.

Type is like the background music in a movie

If it's good, you probably don't even notice it. If it's bad, it's distracting. If it's good, it makes you *feel* differently about the action on-screen. Turn off the sound next time you're watching a movie and see how it loses excitement. Without music, a chase scene isn't as exciting. A love scene isn't as lovely. Imagine the *wrong* music. Picture *Psycho* with *The Sound of Music*'s soundtrack. Think of *The Sound of Music* with *Psycho's* soundtrack.

A good typeface can not only make people read your message, but also "like" your message. It can make people take your message more seriously. Or less seriously.

Type is like clothing

The typeface you use is to the printed page as the different colors and textures of fabrics are to clothes. A suit made of gray flannel would make a completely different impression than the same suit made of blue jean denim.

To take the clothes/type analogy a step further (or a step too far, you could say), the design of a suit equals the design of the document; the fabric and color equal the typeface; the accessories, such as a tie or jewelry, equal graphics; and finally, the person inside the suit parallels the contents of the document. Clearly the most important part is the person/contents. All the other elements are there to present the personality and meaning of the person/contents to the best possible advantage.

Type is image

If you're part of a company, a typeface is your corporate *image* on paper. The right type can make a small company look like IBM. The wrong type can make a big company look like it's being run out of someone's garage.

Typography *is* inflection

The way you *set* type can change the very meaning of a sentence. Italicizing a single word emphasizes it, and can change the entire meaning.

The sentence: "I said I liked it" could have five meanings:

"*I* said I liked it."
"I *said* I liked it."
"I said *I* liked it."
"I said I *liked* it."
or "I said I liked *it*."

Punctuation is another important element of typesetting. Change the punctuation and your statement's entirely different again:

"*I* said I liked it?"
"I *said* I liked it?"
"I said *I* liked it?"
"I said I *liked* it?"
or "I said I liked *it?*"

Type is fun

I know, every how-to book you've ever read has said that its subject is fun. But type really *is* fun.

You can be a type-spotter (someone who finds it challenging to figure out what typeface you're looking at) or a typesetter (some-one who actually gets down and dirty, rolling around in all those letters).

When you start to use and notice type, it's kind of like being a kid again. You perceive things you have seen for years but never really *noticed.* It opens a whole new world to explore.

Type helps you impress, express, stress, address, digress, suppress, caress, access, redress—even oppress (though only under duress).

Type helps you: communicate,

accentuate, activate, alleviate, animate, appreciate, appropriate, articulate, capitulate, *celebrate*, compensate, complicate, conciliate, congregate, consecrate, consummate, cooperate, coordinate, correlate, culminate, cultivate, delegate, *demonstrate*, denigrate, depreciate, devastate, deviate, dissipate, domesticate, dominate, duplicate, elaborate, elevate, *emancipate,* enunciate, equate, estimate, exaggerate, *exhilarate,* extrapolate, extricate, fabricate, facilitate, fluctuate, formulate, generate, hallucinate, homogenate, *illuminate*, imitate, impersonate, incorporate, incriminate, incubate, infiltrate, insulate, inflate, ingratiate, initiate, *innovate*, insinuate, instigate, insulate, interpolate, *interrogate*, intoxicate, invalidate, *investigate,* irritate, isolate, levitate, *liberate*, liquidate, litigate, locate, lubricate, luxuriate, machinate, manipulate, marinate, matriculate, migrate, mitigate, moderate, modulate, *motivate*, mutate, narrate, nauseate, navigate, necessitate, negotiate, nominate, obfuscate, obliterate, orate, perpetrate, perpetuate, pirate, pontificate, postulate, precipitate, predicate, prefabricate, *prestidigitate,* promulgate, proliferate, propagate, pulsate, punctuate, radiate, reciprocate, reconciliate, recuperate, redecorate, regenerate, regulate, regurgitate, rehabilitate, *reiterate,* relegate, relocate, remonstrate, remunerate, replicate, resonate, resuscitate, *retaliate,* salivate, satiate, sedate, separate, skate, speculate, state, strangulate, sublimate, subrogate, *substantiate,* suffocate, summate, supplicate, syndicate, terminate, *titillate*, *translate*, update, vacillate, validate, venerate, vibrate, vindicate, violate, and vociferate. (You can't say it in a single breath, but you can say it in a single sentence.)

Type can help you get
what you want and
avoid what you don't want,
help you improve yourself, and
help you improve the world.

Type is...

Type is never having to say you're sorry when you could say you're *sorry.*

Type is never having to admit you're illegible.

Type is a warm puppy.

Type is your Final Notice.

Type is an "I Love Lucy" Marathon.

Type is a Black Tie Gala.

Type is Not to be Missed.

Type makes annuals report.

Type makes a memo memorable.

Type makes a note noteworthy.

Type puts character into your characters.

Type makes a statement stately.

Type makes an election electric.

Type gives your contentions conviction.

Type puts the "official" into your office.

Type makes a Sale sell.

Type makes a bear of a job bearable.

Type makes schoolbooks scholarly instead of schlocky.

Type makes a trip trippy.

Type puts the "good" in goodwill.

Type makes a happening happy.

Type gives your work a workout.

Type puts some fun into fundamentals.

Type can even put some *con* into a *con*cept.

Type makes your facsimiles feasible.

Type makes the volume volcanic.

Most importantly

Type can make the difference between ***acceptable*** *and* ***exceptional***

Acceptable
Axceptable
Exceptable
Exceptional

Swiss Light
Zurich Light
Futura Light
Hammersmith Italic

2

Say What?

Type terms

Before you talk about type, you need to know what the words mean.

Say What?

Type terms

Before you talk about type, you need to know what the words mean. There's a complete glossary in the back of this book, but the terms discussed in this chapter will give you a better understanding of type in general.

Font

A font is a single style, weight, and size of a typeface, such as Baskerville Bold 12-point. Baskerville Bold 10-point is a different font. Both are in the same Baskerville family.

This terminology refers to a time when a typesetter needed a different font for each size of type. When you use *scalable fonts,* such as those available in PostScript, LaserMaster, and LaserJet III printers, a single font can be scaled to any size, so a font now refers to a particular weight or width of a typeface, but not its size.

Legibility

Legible
Legible

Zurich Black
ITC Garamond

Legibility refers to how readily identifiable each individual character is. Legibility is most important in cases like classified ads, phone numbers, and highway signs where characters are not part of a continuous text and have to be deciphered one at a time. Most common text faces have about the same inherent legibility. Some fancy display types are less legible, and only good at large sizes.

Certain influences also come into play here. Although Europeans have a long tradition of using sans serif faces for body text, Americans find sans serifs to be more legible/identifiable in short blocks, such as headlines or signs.

Posture

Posture
Posture
Posture
Posture

Zurich Light, Light Italic
Goudy Old Style, Italic

Most types come in pairs: an upright version and a slanted companion. These are called roman and italic. In many sans serifs, the italic letterforms are basically the same as the roman, but slanted. In many serif types, the italic letterforms are both slanted and distinctive in shape, particularly in the lowercase.

Readability

Readability refers to ease of reading in continuous text, and is often more a function of the arrangement of type than of the typeface itself. Normally we read by recognizing word shapes, not individual letterforms. Making it easy for the eye to scan a line and go to the next line is the key to readability. Lines that are too short, too long, too close together, or otherwise cockeyed make scanning difficult and tiring. This slows down the flow of information from page to brain, leading to mistakes and bad temper.

Sans serif

A typeface without serifs. What's a serif?

Sans Serif

Sans is French for "without"

Futura Light

Serif

A serif is the small cross-bar (or finishing stroke) that ends the main stroke of letters. A serif typeface is a typeface that has serifs.

Baskerville

Typeface

A typeface is a specific design of a set of letters, numbers, and symbols, such as Dutch, Baskerville, Goudy, Garamond, Swiss, or Zurich.

Typeface family

The various weights and styles of a typeface make up a typeface family. Baskerville medium, italic, bold, and bold italic together make up a typeface family. Some families include only two styles, others contain 12 or more variations. (Happy, Sleepy, Grumpy, Doc, Dopey, Sneezy, and Bashful would make up a typeface family if they weren't already dwarves. Can you remember all the reindeer names?)

Roman Style

Italic *Style*

Bold **Style**

Bold Italic ***Style***

Baskerville

Typestyle

A typestyle is a variation of weight or width within a typeface family. Standard typestyles include roman, italic, bold, condensed, or extended but there are many different weights and widths, each of which is a typestyle.

Weight

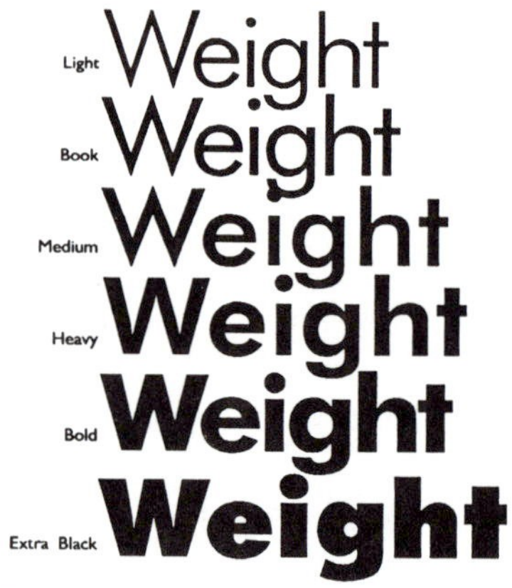

Futura

Many typefaces come in four weights: Medium, italic, bold, and bold italic. While some typefaces come in only two weights, some come in a large variety including thin, extra light, light, book, medium, demi, bold, extra bold, heavy, black, extra black, and ultra black, with italic versions of some or all of these.

The same weights can have different names: Medium is also often called roman, or sometimes has no special designation beyond the typeface name. "Book" doesn't mean you can automatically use the typeface in a book; it's a weight between light and medium.

Width

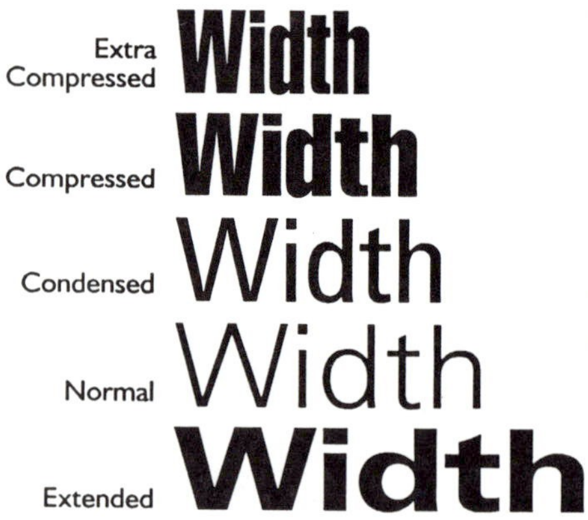

Swiss Extra Compressed, & Compressed
Zurich Condensed, Light, Extended

This refers to the relative width of a typeface. A typeface can be Condensed or Expanded. Condensed (also known as Compact) is a narrow version of a typeface. Expanded (also known as Extended) is a wide version of a typeface. Swiss Condensed is a narrow version of Swiss. Zurich Extended is a wide version of Zurich. Other widths include Compressed, which is narrower than Condensed, and Extra Compressed which is, no surprise here, compressed even more.

X-height

This sounds like something to do with NASA, but all it really means is the height of the lowercase letter "x." One of the archaic things about type is that the point size is really relative. Avant Garde at 10-point appears to be bigger than Bodoni at 10-point. Avant Garde has a very large x-height; the lowercase letters are almost as tall as the uppercase letters. Bodoni has a very small x-height, so that 12-point Bodoni still doesn't look as big as 10-point Avant Garde.

In the case of Avant Garde, the x-height is *so* large that it actually makes it somewhat more difficult to read. It's fine for headlines, but not good for body text. Futura, a similar sans serif with an average x-height, is much better for body text. A large x-height also means that the individual letters take up more space on a line. This reduces the number of characters that fit on a line and makes the typeface less suitable for narrow columns.

Specific type terms

As you will recall, if you read the Preface, a number of typeface names have the acronym ITC in front of them. ITC stands for International Typeface Corporation, the first company devoted solely to type design, not manufacturing. ITC has kindly given me permission to reprint an excellent example they prepared about typeface terms, and you can see it for yourself if you turn the page.

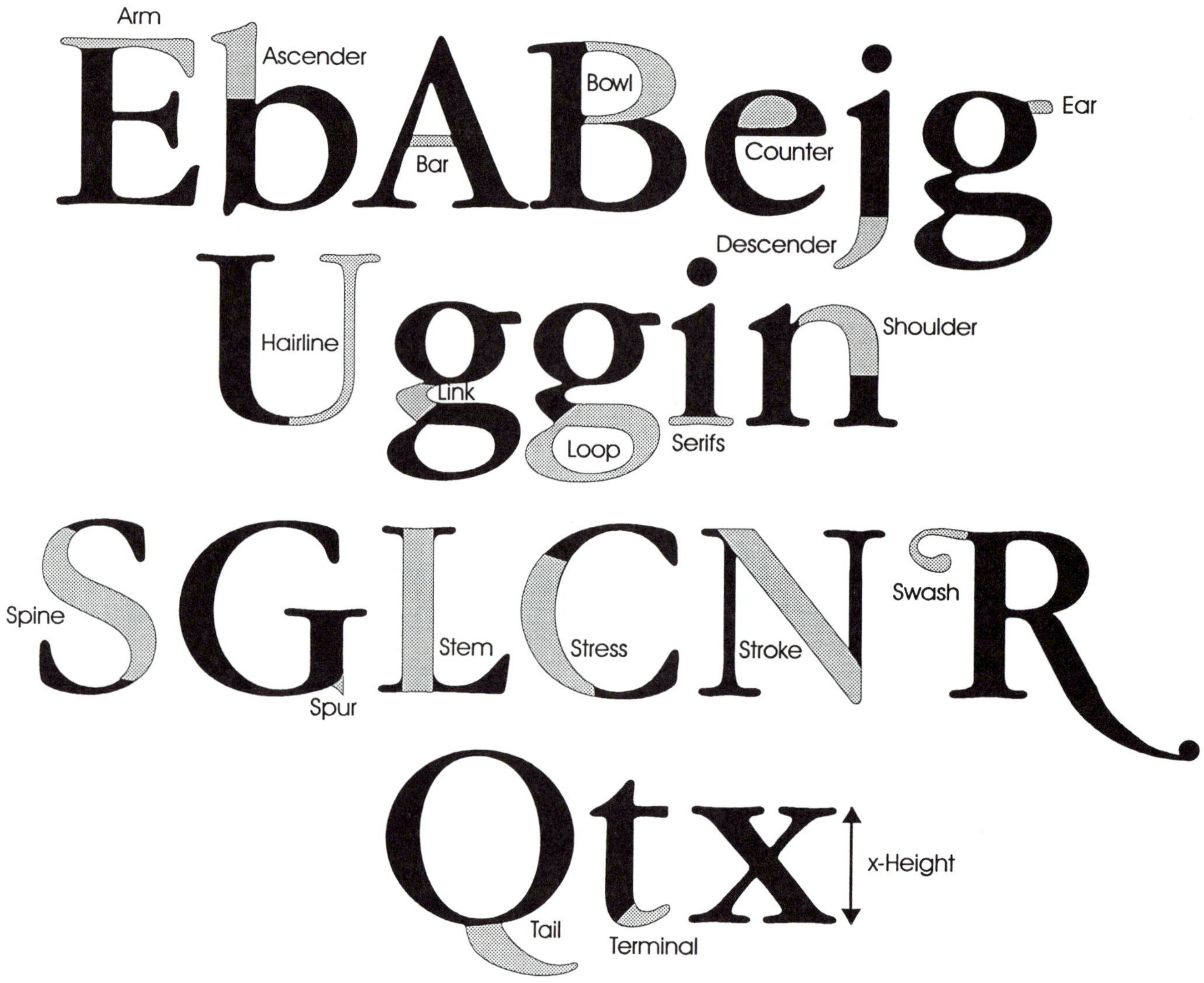
Arm
Ascender
Bowl
Ear
Bar
Counter
Descender
Hairline
Link
Shoulder
Loop
Serifs
Spine
Stem
Stress
Stroke
Swash
Spur
x-Height
Tail
Terminal

Parts of a Character

Arm: A horizontal stroke that is free on one end.

Ascender: The part of the lowercase letters b, d, f, h, k, l, and that extends above the height of the lowercase x.

Bar: The horizontal stroke in the A, H, e, t, and similar letters.

Bowl: A curved stroke which makes an enclosed space within a character. The bump on a P is a bowl.

Counter: The full or partially enclosed space within a character.

Descender: The part of the letters g, j, p, q, y, and sometimes J, that extends below the baseline.

Ear: The small stroke projecting from the top of the lowercase g.

Hairline: A thin stroke usually common to serif typestyles.

Link: The stroke connecting the top and the bottom of a lowercase g.

Loop: The lower portion of the lowercase roman g.

Serif: A line crossing the main strokes of a character. There are many varieties.

Shoulder: The curved stroke of the h, m, and n.

Spine: The main curved stroke of a lowercase or capital S.

Spur: A small projection of a main stroke; found on many capital G's *(but amusingly enough, not really on ITC Garamond, the typeface illustrated on the opposite page).*

Stem: A straight vertical stroke, or main straight diagonal stroke in a letter which has no vertical strokes.

Stress: The direction of thickening in a curved stroke.

Swash: A fancy flourish replacing a terminal or serif.

Tail: The descender of Q or short diagonal stroke of the R.

Terminal: The end of a stroke not terminated with a serif.

x-Height: The height of the lowercase letters excluding ascenders and descenders.

3

Body and soul

Body text treatments

Body type is the staple of typography. Sure, headlines grab your attention, but it's the body text that contains those all-important details.

Body and soul

You're having a typographical nightmare. You've been kidnapped by a nefarious gang of big bad Art Directors and forced at dangerously sharp and frighteningly expensive serif-point to choose among eight different body typefaces as if your life depended on it. What will you do? What *will* you do?

Will you make a decision? Will it be a good one? (There is no *right* one but there are *wrong* ones.) Will you read the rest of this chapter or have you been thoroughly bewildered by the first paragraph? Will the fog lift? Read on and find out.

Body type is the staple of typography. Sure, headlines grab your attention, but it's the body text that contains those all-important details. If headlines are the flash, body text is the pan (or the substance). Body text can be anything from a paragraph in an advertisement to the full text of a magazine or book.

In a world of art directors, designers, and type zealots like myself, you might have started to think that your choice of typefaces is a life or death decision. Let's get real—it isn't. As far as I know there are no terrorists groups bent on the eradication of Dutch (Times Roman) as we know it (Park Avenue maybe, but not Dutch).

Any good typographer will tell you that well-done body text (as opposed to medium rare) is invisible body text. You read right through it to the words. But that doesn't mean it's not important. The correct choice of body text is extremely important. However, you need to put it in perspective. If you set the same page in two different typefaces, many people couldn't tell the difference, even if it were pointed out to them. They *might* notice a difference between Dutch and Baskerville, but they probably wouldn't notice the difference between Baskerville and Garamond.

As a consultant, I've worked with countless people who have never thought about and don't understand the difference between Courier and Dutch. It's simply not something they've been taught to notice. It's never been *important* to them.

If you know about typefaces, you'll look at a page and see "New Century Schoolbook." If you don't, you'll see "See Jane run." So why bother with different typefaces? "Oh, Boy," you think, "I'm spending $100 on something no one will notice."

Associations

While display faces seem to elicit more associations than body text, body text is like the background music for your pages; the wall paper or paint color. Even when people don't notice the typeface, it *colors* the way they look at the page. Superficial? Perhaps. Important? You betcha.

Serif vs. sans

Goudy Old Style Italic, Roman
Swiss Compressed

Associations take a back seat to readability. We've all heard the one about serif typefaces being easier to read. The debate raged for years. Which is easier to read: serif or sans serif? And then someone finally figured out that whatever you grew up reading was easiest, and that makes sense. For Americans that means serifs, for Europeans it means sans serifs. The only exception I can think of would be books of fiction. I've never seen a novel set in Swiss (Helvetica) and I hope I never do. I've seen many magazines, both American and European, set in Swiss, Zurich (Univers), Zapf Humanist (Optima), Hammersmith (Gill Sans), and Futura, and I've seen "picture" books that also use sans serif faces. But a novel? It would be too hard to read.

Sans serifs can be difficult to read over long stretches because they are too monotone. Serifs give letters a more distinctive appearance and *shape*. And since we read as much by the shape of words as by the letters alone, shapes are an important ingredient in making serif typefaces easier to read. If you use sans serifs, shorten the line lengths and add more white space to the page.

What "color" is Bodoni?

You probably think you know what "color" means. But in typography, color doesn't mean red, yellow, blue, or anything in between; it means shades of black. Naturally, bold typefaces are darker than light typefaces, but even in the same weight, a page full of Zapf Calligraphic (Palatino, a dark typeface) will look darker than a page full of Goudy Old Style (a light typeface).

If you know your pages will be text-intensive, you may choose to use a lighter typeface so the pages won't look oppressively dark. You might also want a lighter typeface if your printing method tends to make the type appear heavier. If you're going to have less text, and want it to stand out, you may want to choose a darker typeface.

The final frontier—font efficiency

There's an added technical piece to this puzzle—efficiency. Each typeface takes up a different amount of space. For example, Dutch (Times Roman) is much more compact and space-efficient than Swiss (Helvetica).

But even versions of the same typeface from different manufacturers can be different widths. Adobe's Times Roman, for example, is about 5% narrower than Bitstream's Dutch.

Here's how the standard 35 typefaces built into PostScript printers stack up in terms of efficiency. I'll use Times Roman as the reference point, as it's the most efficient. Helvetica is 11% wider, Palatino is 7% wider, New Century Schoolbook is 13% wider, Bookman is 19% wider, Avant Garde is 20% wider. Helvetica Narrow, which is completely unsuitable for body text, is 10% narrower, while Zapf Chancery, good only for very specialized applications, is 13% narrower.

Bitstream's regular font packages of these typefaces do not have these same widths, but Bitstream "Postscript Width Compatible" (SWA) fonts, which are included with certain hardware and software products, do have widths identical to those found resident in PostScript printers.

Of course, if you want to use Helvetica and you need to pack the same amount of information on the page as when you use Times, you can make it 11% smaller. If you were using 11-point Times, you'd need to use 10-point Helvetica. It's never a good idea to reduce leading to fit more words on a page. Make the type a bit smaller but keep *at least* one point of extra leading (two points of leading is even better).

The specific typeface entries that follow include a "Character Per Pica" count (there are approximately six picas per inch). The CPP tells you, on average, how many characters will fit into a line one pica wide. Of course, you're never going to set a line only one pica wide, but if you multiply this number times the width of your column in picas, and then multiply that times the length of your columns in lines, you'll get an idea of how many characters will fit in any given space, using 10-point type. A complete CPP chart arranged by typeface name appears on page 3-31.

Even if you don't go through all that math (and no one will blame you if you don't), these numbers will give you an idea of which typefaces permit an abundance of words on a page, and which won't. The chart below is arranged by typeface efficiency.

Characters per pica at 10-point
Sorted from most space efficient to the least efficient.

Coronet	4.38	Futura Book	2.77
Swiss Extra Compressed	4.02	Bitstream Cooper	2.72
Dom Casual	3.84	ITC Avant Garde	2.72
Futura Condensed	3.78	Bitstream Charter	2.72
Park Ave	3.67	ITC Garamond Book	2.70
Cloister Black	3.55	Activa (Trump Medieval)	2.68
University Roman	3.53	Slate (Rockwell)	2.68
ITC Garamond Condensed	3.42	Swiss (Helvetica)	2.68
Brush Script	3.34	Futura Medium	2.67
P.T. Barnum	3.29	Zurich Light	2.66
Swiss Compressed	3.25	Baskerville	2.65
Zapf Chancery	3.25	Zapf Calligraphic (Palatino)	2.64
Exotic Demi	3.12	ITC Cheltenham	2.64
Zurich Condensed	3.07	Century Schoolbook	2.63
Swiss Condensed	3.07	Blippo Black	2.63
Kaufmann Bold	3.05	Zapf Elliptical (Melior)	2.61
Bodoni	3.01	ITC Benguiat	2.60
Bernhard Modern	3.00	Zurich (Univers)	2.60
Goudy Old Style	2.94	Serifa	2.59
Exotic Bold	2.93	ITC Bookman	2.53
Futura Light	2.90	ITC Tiffany	2.51
Hammersmith (Gill Sans)	2.90	Provence (Antique Olive)	2.46
ITC Clearface	2.88	Windsor	2.46
Bitstream Amerigo	2.85	Mermaid	2.45
News Gothic	2.83	Franklin Gothic	2.43
Zapf Humanist (Optima)	2.82	Handel Gothic	2.41
ITC Souvenir	2.82	Clarendon	2.38
ITC Korinna	2.82	ITC Lubalin Graph	2.35
Dutch (Times Roman)	2.81	Clarendon Bold	2.33
ITC Galliard	2.79	Futura Extra Black	2.26
Hobo	2.78	Bitstream Cooper Black	2.12
Swiss Light	2.77	ITC Bolt Bold	2.11
Futura Black	2.77	Broadway	2.01

Style patrol

Let's get back to *style,* that unconscious persuader. Like display faces, the choice of body text sets the style and tone of a document, colors how readers interpret the words, and defines the underlying feeling of the page.

The following typeface specimens will allow you to compare various typefaces to see how light/dark and efficient they are. All are printed at 10-point with 11.5-point leading (10/11.5).

Activa

This is a modern, angular face that some people claim is "neutral," but I find it very distinctive, sometimes almost too much so. Activa, Bitstream's version of Trump Medieval, often elicits a strong response; most people either love it or hate it. I like its chiseled look, especially in larger sizes. In smaller sizes it looks modern but can also look busy. If you like it, use it, and you'll get noticed.

10/11.5
2.68 CPP

"**To coin a phrase.** *Don't touch that dial.* ***The moment you've all been waiting for.*** The real thing. Today's the first day of the rest of your life. The long and short of it. Tell it like it is. Out of the mouths of babes. That's the way it was. Something for everyone. It's always darkest before the dawn. When it rains it pours. Every cloud has a silver lining. The light at the end of the tunnel. Good things come in small packages. Let's put on a show. All systems are go. It's a once in a lifetime opportunity."

Only yesterday. Time flies. What do you want to be when you grow up? You're only as old as you feel. You're not getting older you're getting better. It's just a phase. Another day older and deeper in debt. *Are we having fun yet?* Time is money. You've got to pay your dues. Do you take American Express? Nothing succeeds like success. Nothing exceeds like excess. Go for broke. Rags to riches. Concept by Al Masini. If they could see me now. That's when a million dollars was worth something. Value for money. The check is in the mail.

Collect 'em all. Nice guys finish last. I never met a man I didn't like. She speaks 14 different languages and she can't say "no" in any of them. Tell it to the Marines. When you've seen one, you've seen 'em all. How can I miss you if you won't go away? This will hurt you more than it hurts me. How can you believe me when I tell you that I love you when you know I've been a liar all my life?

Art imitates life. What you see is what you get. Look out for number one. With friends like that, who needs enemies. What are friends for? A friend in need is a friend indeed. A friend in need is indeed a pest. People in glass houses shouldn't throw stones. Speak softly and carry a big stick. What you don't know won't hurt you. Ignorance is bliss.

Pure as the driven snow. Once upon a time. Boy meets girl. To know him is to love him. One bad apple don't spoil the whole bunch, girl. He made me an offer I couldn't refuse. For better or for worse. Sign on the dotted line. A lifetime guarantee. Don't knock it till you've tried it. Man does not live by bread alone. Builds strong bodies 12 ways. Bring home the bacon. What's for dinner?

Soon to be made into a major motion picture. Nothin' says lovin' like somethin' from the oven. We reserve the right to serve refuse to anyone. Meanwhile, back at the ranch. Father knows best. I leave those decisions to my wife. The rules of the road. Don't chew with your mouth open. Do as I say, not as I do. Wait 'til your father gets

Bitstream Amerigo

This font always reminds me of futuristic calligraphy. Amerigo's serifs are flared, so instead of jutting out the way other serifs do, they seem to grow organically, like crystals. Amerigo, like Charter, is a new face, which adds to its novelty. If you want a sci-fi look, Amerigo is an excellent choice. Adjust your laser printer to print as light as possible, though, or Amerigo may look heavy.

10/11.5
2.85 CPP

"To coin a phrase. *Don't touch that dial.* ***The moment you've all been waiting for.*** The real thing. Today's the first day of the rest of your life. The long and short of it. Tell it like it is. Out of the mouths of babes. That's the way it was. Something for everyone. It's always darkest before the dawn. When it rains it pours. Every cloud has a silver lining. The light at the end of the tunnel. Good things come in small packages. Let's put on a show. All systems are go. It's a once in a lifetime opportunity."

Only yesterday. Time flies. What do you want to be when you grow up? You're only as old as you feel. You're not getting older you're getting better. It's just a phase. Another day older and deeper in debt. *Are we having fun yet?* Time is money. You've got to pay your dues. Do you take American Express? Nothing succeeds like success. Nothing exceeds like excess. Go for broke. Rags to riches. Concept by Al Masini. If they could see me now. That's when a million dollars was worth something. Value for money. The check is in the mail.

Collect 'em all. Nice guys finish last. I never met a man I didn't like. She speaks 14 different languages and she can't say "no" in any of them. Tell it to the Marines. When you've seen one, you've seen 'em all. How can I miss you if you won't go away? This will hurt you more than it hurts me. How can you believe me when I tell you that I love you when you know I've been a liar all my life?

Art imitates life. What you see is what you get. Look out for number one. With friends like that, who needs enemies. What are friends for? A friend in need is a friend indeed. A friend in need is indeed a pest. People in glass houses shouldn't throw stones. Speak softly and carry a big stick. What you don't know won't hurt you. Ignorance is bliss.

Pure as the driven snow. Once upon a time. Boy meets girl. To know him is to love him. One bad apple don't spoil the whole bunch, girl. He made me an offer I couldn't refuse. For better or for worse. Sign on the dotted line. A lifetime guarantee. Don't knock it till you've tried it. Man does not live by bread alone. Builds strong bodies 12 ways. Bring home the bacon. What's for dinner?

Soon to be made into a major motion picture. Nothin' says lovin' like somethin' from the oven. We reserve the right to serve refuse to anyone. Meanwhile, back at the ranch. Father knows best. I leave those decisions to my wife. The rules of the road. Don't chew with your mouth open. Do as I say, not as I do. Wait 'til your father gets home. It's 10 p.m., do you know

Bernhard Modern

Bernhard Modern may be used for body text in very short blocks; a few paragraphs at most. It's a lovely face, but too decorative for long stretches. Its tall ascenders require extra leading.

10/11.5 3.00 CPP

"To coin a phrase. *Don't touch that dial. The moment you've all been waiting for.* The real thing. Today's the first day of the rest of your life. The long and short of it. Tell it like it is. Out of the mouths of babes. That's the way it was. Something for everyone. It's always darkest before the dawn. When it rains it pours. Every cloud has a silver lining. The light at the end of the tunnel. Good things come in small packages. Let's put on a show. All systems are go. It's a once in a lifetime opportunity."

Only yesterday. Time flies. What do you want to be when you grow up? You're only as old as you feel. You're not getting older you're getting better. It's just a phase. Another day older and deeper in debt. *Are we having fun yet?* Time is money. You've got to pay your dues. Do you take American Express? Nothing succeeds like success. Nothing exceeds like excess. Go for broke. Rags to riches. Concept by Al Masini. If they could see me now. That's when a million dollars was worth something. Value for money. The check is in the mail.

Collect 'em all. Nice guys finish last. I never met a man I didn't like. She speaks 14 different languages and she can't say "no" in any of them. Tell it to the Marines. When you've seen one, you've seen 'em all. How can I miss you if you won't go away? This will hurt you more than it hurts me. How can you believe me when I tell you that I love you when you know I've been a liar all my life?

Art imitates life. What you see is what you get. Look out for number one. With friends like that, who needs enemies. What are friends for? A friend in need is a friend indeed. A friend in need is indeed a pest. People in glass houses shouldn't throw stones. Speak softly and carry a big stick. What you don't know won't hurt you. Ignorance is bliss.

Pure as the driven snow. Once upon a time. Boy meets girl. To know him is to love him. One bad apple don't spoil the whole bunch, girl. He made me an offer I couldn't refuse. For better or for worse. Sign on the dotted line. A lifetime guarantee. Don't knock it till you've tried it. Man does not live by bread alone. Builds strong bodies 12 ways. Bring home the bacon. What's for dinner?

Soon to be made into a major motion picture. Nothin' says lovin' like somethin' from the oven. We reserve the right to serve refuse to anyone. Meanwhile, back at the ranch. Father knows best. I leave those decisions to my wife. The rules of the road. Don't chew with your mouth open. Do as I say, not as I do. Wait 'til your father gets home. It's 10 p.m., do you know where your children are? My, how you've grown.

Bodoni

This face is *different.* It's sharp, formal, and extremely elegant. And because of this, it poses special challenges. Because each letter has great contrasts between thick and thin, it requires extra leading and white space, even though you may be tempted to give it less. Bodoni is frequently used in high fashion magazines and ads, and I've even seen it used in a novel with excellent results. Bodoni has a very small x-height, which means that 12-point Bodoni will look like 10-point something else, yet Bodoni still needs more leading than most. If you're high style, Bodoni will suit you.

10/11.5
3.01 CPP

"To coin a phrase. *Don't touch that dial.* ***The moment you've all been waiting for.*** The real thing. Today's the first day of the rest of your life. The long and short of it. Tell it like it is. Out of the mouths of babes. That's the way it was. Something for everyone. It's always darkest before the dawn. When it rains it pours. Every cloud has a silver lining. The light at the end of the tunnel. Good things come in small packages. Let's put on a show. All systems are go. It's a once in a lifetime opportunity."

Only yesterday. Time flies. What do you want to be when you grow up? You're only as old as you feel. You're not getting older you're getting better. It's just a phase. Another day older and deeper in debt. *Are we having fun yet?* Time is money. You've got to pay your dues. Do you take American Express? Nothing succeeds like success. Nothing exceeds like excess. Go for broke. Rags to riches. Concept by Al Masini. If they could see me now. That's when a million dollars was worth something. Value for money. The check is in the mail.

Collect 'em all. Nice guys finish last. I never met a man I didn't like. She speaks 14 different languages and she can't say "no" in any of them. Tell it to the Marines. When you've seen one, you've seen 'em all. How can I miss you if you won't go away? This will hurt you more than it hurts me. How can you believe me when I tell you that I love you when you know I've been a liar all my life?

Art imitates life. What you see is what you get. Look out for number one. With friends like that, who needs enemies. What are friends for? A friend in need is a friend indeed. A friend in need is indeed a pest. People in glass houses shouldn't throw stones. Speak softly and carry a big stick. What you don't know won't hurt you. Ignorance is bliss.

Pure as the driven snow. Once upon a time. Boy meets girl. To know him is to love him. One bad apple don't spoil the whole bunch, girl. He made me an offer I couldn't refuse. For better or for worse. Sign on the dotted line. A lifetime guarantee. Don't knock it till you've tried it. Man does not live by bread alone. Builds strong bodies 12 ways. Bring home the bacon. What's for dinner?

Soon to be made into a major motion picture. Nothin' says lovin' like somethin' from the oven. We reserve the right to serve refuse to anyone. Meanwhile, back at the ranch. Father knows best. I leave those decisions to my wife. The rules of the road. Don't chew with your mouth open. Do as I say, not as I do. Wait 'til your father gets home. It's 10 p.m., do you know where your children are? My, how you've grown.

ITC Bookman

Old fashioned and almost funny looking, Bookman is popular for body text. Personally, I find it a little too odd, but art directors at *TV Guide* and sections of the *New York Times* (not the news sections) seem to disagree with me. Bookman is not elegant, sophisticated, or business-like. It is eccentric, funny, casual, and certainly not boring. It's also somewhat heavy, so take care to leave plenty of white space.

10/11.5
2.53 CPP

"To coin a phrase. *Don't touch that dial.* ***The moment you've all been waiting for.*** The real thing. Today's the first day of the rest of your life. The long and short of it. Tell it like it is. Out of the mouths of babes. That's the way it was. Something for everyone. It's always darkest before the dawn. When it rains it pours. Every cloud has a silver lining. The light at the end of the tunnel. Good things come in small packages. Let's put on a show. All systems are go. It's a once in a lifetime opportunity."

Only yesterday. Time flies. What do you want to be when you grow up? You're only as old as you feel. You're not getting older you're getting better. It's just a phase. Another day older and deeper in debt. *Are we having fun yet?* Time is money. You've got to pay your dues. Do you take American Express? Nothing succeeds like success. Nothing exceeds like excess. Go for broke. Rags to riches. Concept by Al Masini. If they could see me now. That's when a million dollars was worth something. Value for money. The check is in the mail.

Collect 'em all. Nice guys finish last. I never met a man I didn't like. She speaks 14 different languages and she can't say "no" in any of them. Tell it to the Marines. When you've seen one, you've seen 'em all. How can I miss you if you won't go away? This will hurt you more than it hurts me. How can you believe me when I tell you that I love you when you know I've been a liar all my life?

Art imitates life. What you see is what you get. Look out for number one. With friends like that, who needs enemies. What are friends for? A friend in need is a friend indeed. A friend in need is indeed a pest. People in glass houses shouldn't throw stones. Speak softly and carry a big stick. What you don't know won't hurt you. Ignorance is bliss.

Pure as the driven snow. Once upon a time. Boy meets girl. To know him is to love him. One bad apple don't spoil the whole bunch, girl. He made me an offer I couldn't refuse. For better or for worse. Sign on the dotted line. A lifetime guarantee. Don't knock it till you've tried it. Man does not live by bread alone. Builds strong bodies 12 ways. Bring home the bacon. What's for dinner?

Century Schoolbook

This is a face I used to *hate*. Of course, I thought Dick and Jane were little more than spoiled brats, so that may color my view. I now tolerate Century Schoolbook because it's a very readable typeface. Not elegant, formal, or charming, it approximates the Velveeta of the typeface world—not as good as some other cheeses, but then again, it doesn't require refrigeration.

10/11.5
2.63 CPP

"To coin a phrase. *Don't touch that dial.* ***The moment you've all been waiting for.*** The real thing. Today's the first day of the rest of your life. The long and short of it. Tell it like it is. Out of the mouths of babes. That's the way it was. Something for everyone. It's always darkest before the dawn. When it rains it pours. Every cloud has a silver lining. The light at the end of the tunnel. Good things come in small packages. Let's put on a show. All systems are go. It's a once in a lifetime opportunity."

Only yesterday. Time flies. What do you want to be when you grow up? You're only as old as you feel. You're not getting older you're getting better. It's just a phase. Another day older and deeper in debt. *Are we having fun yet?* Time is money. You've got to pay your dues. Do you take American Express? Nothing succeeds like success. Nothing exceeds like excess. Go for broke. Rags to riches. Concept by Al Masini. If they could see me now. That's when a million dollars was worth something. Value for money. The check is in the mail.

Collect 'em all. Nice guys finish last. I never met a man I didn't like. She speaks 14 different languages and she can't say "no" in any of them. Tell it to the Marines. When you've seen one, you've seen 'em all. How can I miss you if you won't go away? This will hurt you more than it hurts me. How can you believe me when I tell you that I love you when you know I've been a liar all my life?

Art imitates life. What you see is what you get. Look out for number one. With friends like that, who needs enemies. What are friends for? A friend in need is a friend indeed. A friend in need is indeed a pest. People in glass houses shouldn't throw stones. Speak softly and carry a big stick. What you don't know won't hurt you. Ignorance is bliss.

Pure as the driven snow. Once upon a time. Boy meets girl. To know him is to love him. One bad apple don't spoil the whole bunch, girl. He made me an offer I couldn't refuse. For better or for worse. Sign on the dotted line. A lifetime guarantee. Don't knock it till you've tried it. Man does not live by bread alone. Builds strong bodies 12 ways. Bring home the bacon. What's for dinner?

Soon to be made into a major motion picture. Nothin' says lovin'

Bitstream Charter

This was not a favorite at first sight. My tastes tend toward more elegant typefaces such as Galliard, Baskerville, and Goudy Old Style. But then I had to design and produce a newsletter to look official, not too "pretty," but at the same time "friendly." After I tried everything else I finally gave in and tried Charter. It was perfect. Its modern, almost mechanical look makes it good for business, and its black and black italic weights have beautiful details, which make them perfect for headlines. Because Charter is a new typeface, it's distinctive and carries with it a feeling of energy.

10/11.5
2.72 CPP

"To coin a phrase. *Don't touch that dial.* ***The moment you've all been waiting for.*** The real thing. Today's the first day of the rest of your life. The long and short of it. Tell it like it is. Out of the mouths of babes. That's the way it was. Something for everyone. It's always darkest before the dawn. When it rains it pours. Every cloud has a silver lining. The light at the end of the tunnel. Good things come in small packages. Let's put on a show. All systems are go. It's a once in a lifetime opportunity."

Only yesterday. Time flies. What do you want to be when you grow up? You're only as old as you feel. You're not getting older you're getting better. It's just a phase. Another day older and deeper in debt. *Are we having fun yet?* Time is money. You've got to pay your dues. Do you take American Express? Nothing succeeds like success. Nothing exceeds like excess. Go for broke. Rags to riches. Concept by Al Masini. If they could see me now. That's when a million dollars was worth something. Value for money. The check is in the mail.

Collect 'em all. Nice guys finish last. I never met a man I didn't like. She speaks 14 different languages and she can't say "no" in any of them. Tell it to the Marines. When you've seen one, you've seen 'em all. How can I miss you if you won't go away? This will hurt you more than it hurts me. How can you believe me when I tell you that I love you when you know I've been a liar all my life?

Art imitates life. What you see is what you get. Look out for number one. With friends like that, who needs enemies. What are friends for? A friend in need is a friend indeed. A friend in need is indeed a pest. People in glass houses shouldn't throw stones. Speak softly and carry a big stick. What you don't know won't hurt you. Ignorance is bliss.

Pure as the driven snow. Once upon a time. Boy meets girl. To know him is to love him. One bad apple don't spoil the whole bunch, girl. He made me an offer I couldn't refuse. For better or for worse. Sign on the dotted line. A lifetime guarantee. Don't knock it till you've tried it. Man does not live by bread alone. Builds strong bodies 12 ways. Bring home the bacon. What's for dinner?

Soon to be made into a major motion picture. Nothin' says lovin' like somethin' from the oven. We reserve the right to serve refuse to anyone. Meanwhile, back at the ranch. Father knows best. I leave those

ITC Cheltenham

This is an interesting face because it has some of the roundness of ITC Souvenir without the feeling that you're going to be hugged and slobbered over. Cheltenham can be business-like and traditional, yet not really formal. It is a good choice for those times when you want to be serious but not intimidating. Its italics have a unique shape—unusual without being obtrusive.

10/11.5
2.64 CPP

"To coin a phrase. *Don't touch that dial.* ***The moment you've all been waiting for.*** The real thing. Today's the first day of the rest of your life. The long and short of it. Tell it like it is. Out of the mouths of babes. That's the way it was. Something for everyone. It's always darkest before the dawn. When it rains it pours. Every cloud has a silver lining. The light at the end of the tunnel. Good things come in small packages. Let's put on a show. All systems are go. It's a once in a lifetime opportunity."

Only yesterday. Time flies. What do you want to be when you grow up? You're only as old as you feel. You're not getting older you're getting better. It's just a phase. Another day older and deeper in debt. *Are we having fun yet?* Time is money. You've got to pay your dues. Do you take American Express? Nothing succeeds like success. Nothing exceeds like excess. Go for broke. Rags to riches. Concept by Al Masini. If they could see me now. That's when a million dollars was worth something. Value for money. The check is in the mail.

Collect 'em all. Nice guys finish last. I never met a man I didn't like. She speaks 14 different languages and she can't say "no" in any of them. Tell it to the Marines. When you've seen one, you've seen 'em all. How can I miss you if you won't go away? This will hurt you more than it hurts me. How can you believe me when I tell you that I love you when you know I've been a liar all my life?

Art imitates life. What you see is what you get. Look out for number one. With friends like that, who needs enemies. What are friends for? A friend in need is a friend indeed. A friend in need is indeed a pest. People in glass houses shouldn't throw stones. Speak softly and carry a big stick. What you don't know won't hurt you. Ignorance is bliss.

Pure as the driven snow. Once upon a time. Boy meets girl. To know him is to love him. One bad apple don't spoil the whole bunch, girl. He made me an offer I couldn't refuse. For better or for worse. Sign on the dotted line. A lifetime guarantee. Don't knock it till you've tried it. Man does not live by bread alone. Builds strong bodies 12 ways. Bring home the bacon. What's for dinner?

Soon to be made into a major motion picture. Nothin' says lovin' like somethin' from the oven. We reserve the right to serve refuse to

ITC Clearface

Like ITC Garamond Condensed, ITC Clearface is a narrow typeface, good when you need to load more text on a page. It's upright, honest, thrifty, and somewhat old-fashioned looking, if not glamorous or exciting. Its plainness is a virtue and, true to its name, it's clear and easy to read. It does have somewhat prominent serifs, though, which some people find distracting.

10/11.5
2.88 CPP

"To coin a phrase. *Don't touch that dial.* ***The moment you've all been waiting for.*** The real thing. Today's the first day of the rest of your life. The long and short of it. Tell it like it is. Out of the mouths of babes. That's the way it was. Something for everyone. It's always darkest before the dawn. When it rains it pours. Every cloud has a silver lining. The light at the end of the tunnel. Good things come in small packages. Let's put on a show. All systems are go. It's a once in a lifetime opportunity."

Only yesterday. Time flies. What do you want to be when you grow up? You're only as old as you feel. You're not getting older you're getting better. It's just a phase. Another day older and deeper in debt. *Are we having fun yet?* Time is money. You've got to pay your dues. Do you take American Express? Nothing succeeds like success. Nothing exceeds like excess. Go for broke. Rags to riches. Concept by Al Masini. If they could see me now. That's when a million dollars was worth something. Value for money. The check is in the mail.

Collect 'em all. Nice guys finish last. I never met a man I didn't like. She speaks 14 different languages and she can't say "no" in any of them. Tell it to the Marines. When you've seen one, you've seen 'em all. How can I miss you if you won't go away? This will hurt you more than it hurts me. How can you believe me when I tell you that I love you when you know I've been a liar all my life?

Art imitates life. What you see is what you get. Look out for number one. With friends like that, who needs enemies. What are friends for? A friend in need is a friend indeed. A friend in need is indeed a pest. People in glass houses shouldn't throw stones. Speak softly and carry a big stick. What you don't know won't hurt you. Ignorance is bliss.

Pure as the driven snow. Once upon a time. Boy meets girl. To know him is to love him. One bad apple don't spoil the whole bunch, girl. He made me an offer I couldn't refuse. For better or for worse. Sign on the dotted line. A lifetime guarantee. Don't knock it till you've tried it. Man does not live by bread alone. Builds strong bodies 12 ways. Bring home the bacon. What's for dinner?

Soon to be made into a major motion picture. Nothin' says lovin' like somethin' from the oven. We reserve the right to serve refuse to anyone. Meanwhile, back at the ranch. Father knows best. I leave those decisions to my wife. The rules of the road. Don't chew with your mouth open. Do as I

Dutch

An excellent body text face. It's easy to read, even in small sizes, good for long stretches of text, and it's attractive, if ubiquitous. However, Dutch (Times Roman) has become almost completely neutral. It's the beige of the typeface world. People almost never notice the type at all when it's Dutch. This doesn't mean Dutch is boring, it just means that it's so universal that it's become almost invisible. That makes it a safe choice for occasions where you don't want the type to be an issue, and an unsuitable one when you *do* want to project an image.

10/11.5
2.81 CPP

"To coin a phrase. *Don't touch that dial. The moment you've all been waiting for.* The real thing. Today's the first day of the rest of your life. The long and short of it. Tell it like it is. Out of the mouths of babes. That's the way it was. Something for everyone. It's always darkest before the dawn. When it rains it pours. Every cloud has a silver lining. The light at the end of the tunnel. Good things come in small packages. Let's put on a show. All systems are go. It's a once in a lifetime opportunity."

Only yesterday. Time flies. What do you want to be when you grow up? You're only as old as you feel. You're not getting older you're getting better. It's just a phase. Another day older and deeper in debt. *Are we having fun yet?* Time is money. You've got to pay your dues. Do you take American Express? Nothing succeeds like success. Nothing exceeds like excess. Go for broke. Rags to riches. Concept by Al Masini. If they could see me now. That's when a million dollars was worth something. Value for money. The check is in the mail.

Collect 'em all. Nice guys finish last. I never met a man I didn't like. She speaks 14 different languages and she can't say "no" in any of them. Tell it to the Marines. When you've seen one, you've seen 'em all. How can I miss you if you won't go away? This will hurt you more than it hurts me. How can you believe me when I tell you that I love you when you know I've been a liar all my life?

Art imitates life. What you see is what you get. Look out for number one. With friends like that, who needs enemies. What are friends for? A friend in need is a friend indeed. A friend in need is indeed a pest. People in glass houses shouldn't throw stones. Speak softly and carry a big stick. What you don't know won't hurt you. Ignorance is bliss.

Pure as the driven snow. Once upon a time. Boy meets girl. To know him is to love him. One bad apple don't spoil the whole bunch, girl. He made me an offer I couldn't refuse. For better or for worse. Sign on the dotted line. A lifetime guarantee. Don't knock it till you've tried it. Man does not live by bread alone. Builds strong bodies 12 ways. Bring home the bacon. What's for dinner?

Soon to be made into a major motion picture. Nothin' says lovin' like somethin' from the oven. We reserve the right to serve refuse to anyone. Meanwhile, back at the ranch. Father knows best. I leave those decisions to

Futura

A highly geometric sans serif, Futura is often used for body text. Unlike Avant Garde, which can be painfully difficult to read in long stretches, Futura's simplicity (and smaller x-height) works in its favor. It appears to be more modern than Helvetica, even though it was designed 30 years earlier, and it's a classic face that is always in style. Futura is available in many weights, from light to extra black, so it offers a good deal of variety. One warning: not everyone likes to read body text in Futura because it's somewhat monotone. Futura Light is shown here:

10/11.5
2.90 CPP

"To coin a phrase. *Don't touch that dial. The moment you've all been waiting for.* The real thing. Today's the first day of the rest of your life. The long and short of it. Tell it like it is. Out of the mouths of babes. That's the way it was. Something for everyone. It's always darkest before the dawn. When it rains it pours. Every cloud has a silver lining. The light at the end of the tunnel. Good things come in small packages. Let's put on a show. All systems are go. It's a once in a lifetime opportunity."

Only yesterday. Time flies. What do you want to be when you grow up? You're only as old as you feel. You're not getting older you're getting better. It's just a phase. Another day older and deeper in debt. *Are we having fun yet?* Time is money. You've got to pay your dues. Do you take American Express? Nothing succeeds like success. Nothing exceeds like excess. Go for broke. Rags to riches. Concept by Al Masini. If they could see me now. That's when a million dollars was worth something. Value for money. The check is in the mail.

Collect 'em all. Nice guys finish last. I never met a man I didn't like. She speaks 14 different languages and she can't say "no" in any of them. Tell it to the Marines. When you've seen one, you've seen 'em all. How can I miss you if you won't go away? This will hurt you more than it hurts me. How can you believe me when I tell you that I love you when you know I've been a liar all my life?

Art imitates life. What you see is what you get. Look out for number one. With friends like that, who needs enemies. What are friends for? A friend in need is a friend indeed. A friend in need is indeed a pest. People in glass houses shouldn't throw stones. Speak softly and carry a big stick. What you don't know won't hurt you. Ignorance is bliss.

Pure as the driven snow. Once upon a time. Boy meets girl. To know him is to love him. One bad apple don't spoil the whole bunch, girl. He made me an offer I couldn't refuse. For better or for worse. Sign on the dotted line. A lifetime guarantee. Don't knock it till you've tried it. Man does not live by bread alone. Builds strong bodies 12 ways. Bring home the bacon. What's for dinner?

Soon to be made into a major motion picture. Nothin' says lovin' like somethin' from the oven. We reserve the right to serve refuse to anyone. Meanwhile, back at the ranch. Father knows best. I leave those decisions to

ITC Galliard

An exquisite face—the italics are perhaps the most gorgeous and glamorous of any typeface. Galliard has many details and might be too fussy for some applications, but it's still extremely versatile. From body text to poster size, Galliard does it with style. Galliard is not overused, like Zapf Calligraphic (Palatino), so it retains its individuality. The italics resemble calligraphy and are more sophisticated and luxurious than Zapf Chancery.

10/11.5
2.79 CPP

"To coin a phrase. ***Don't touch that dial. The moment you've all been waiting for.*** The real thing. Today's the first day of the rest of your life. The long and short of it. Tell it like it is. Out of the mouths of babes. That's the way it was. Something for everyone. It's always darkest before the dawn. When it rains it pours. Every cloud has a silver lining. The light at the end of the tunnel. Good things come in small packages. Let's put on a show. All systems are go. It's a once in a lifetime opportunity."

Only yesterday. Time flies. What do you want to be when you grow up? You're only as old as you feel. You're not getting older you're getting better. It's just a phase. Another day older and deeper in debt. *Are we having fun yet?* Time is money. You've got to pay your dues. Do you take American Express? Nothing succeeds like success. Nothing exceeds like excess. Go for broke. Rags to riches. Concept by Al Masini. If they could see me now. That's when a million dollars was worth something. Value for money. The check is in the mail.

Collect 'em all. Nice guys finish last. I never met a man I didn't like. She speaks 14 different languages and she can't say "no" in any of them. Tell it to the Marines. When you've seen one, you've seen 'em all. How can I miss you if you won't go away? This will hurt you more than it hurts me. How can you believe me when I tell you that I love you when you know I've been a liar all my life?

Art imitates life. What you see is what you get. Look out for number one. With friends like that, who needs enemies. What are friends for? A friend in need is a friend indeed. A friend in need is indeed a pest. People in glass houses shouldn't throw stones. Speak softly and carry a big stick. What you don't know won't hurt you. Ignorance is bliss.

Pure as the driven snow. Once upon a time. Boy meets girl. To know him is to love him. One bad apple don't spoil the whole bunch, girl. He made me an offer I couldn't refuse. For better or for worse. Sign on the dotted line. A lifetime guarantee. Don't knock it till you've tried it. Man does not live by bread alone. Builds strong bodies 12 ways. Bring home the bacon. What's for dinner?

Soon to be made into a major motion picture. Nothin' says lovin' like somethin' from the oven. We reserve the right to serve refuse to anyone. Meanwhile, back at the ranch. Father knows best. I leave those decisions

ITC Garamond

This is an all-around useful face. Like most ITC typefaces, the big x-height makes Garamond reproduce especially well on laser printers and also makes it easy to read. It has a classic appearance without being stuffy. Garamond is one of the essentials of any type library, and ITC Garamond is only one of many beautiful and versatile versions. Bitstream's book-weight package is somewhat dark, however, so print it as light as possible.

10/11.5
2.70 CPP

"To coin a phrase. *Don't touch that dial. The moment you've all been waiting for.* The real thing. Today's the first day of the rest of your life. The long and short of it. Tell it like it is. Out of the mouths of babes. That's the way it was. Something for everyone. It's always darkest before the dawn. When it rains it pours. Every cloud has a silver lining. The light at the end of the tunnel. Good things come in small packages. Let's put on a show. All systems are go. It's a once in a lifetime opportunity."

Only yesterday. Time flies. What do you want to be when you grow up? You're only as old as you feel. You're not getting older you're getting better. It's just a phase. Another day older and deeper in debt. *Are we having fun yet?* Time is money. You've got to pay your dues. Do you take American Express? Nothing succeeds like success. Nothing exceeds like excess. Go for broke. Rags to riches. Concept by Al Masini. If they could see me now. That's when a million dollars was worth something. Value for money. The check is in the mail.

Collect 'em all. Nice guys finish last. I never met a man I didn't like. She speaks 14 different languages and she can't say "no" in any of them. Tell it to the Marines. When you've seen one, you've seen 'em all. How can I miss you if you won't go away? This will hurt you more than it hurts me. How can you believe me when I tell you that I love you when you know I've been a liar all my life?

Art imitates life. What you see is what you get. Look out for number one. With friends like that, who needs enemies. What are friends for? A friend in need is a friend indeed. A friend in need is indeed a pest. People in glass houses shouldn't throw stones. Speak softly and carry a big stick. What you don't know won't hurt you. Ignorance is bliss.

Pure as the driven snow. Once upon a time. Boy meets girl. To know him is to love him. One bad apple don't spoil the whole bunch, girl. He made me an offer I couldn't refuse. For better or for worse. Sign on the dotted line. A lifetime guarantee. Don't knock it till you've tried it. Man does not live by bread alone. Builds strong bodies 12 ways. Bring home the bacon. What's for dinner?

Soon to be made into a major motion picture. Nothin' says lovin' like somethin' from the oven. We reserve the right to serve refuse to

ITC Garamond Condensed

This is an excellent serif face for tight places. It's attractive and easy to read, but narrow, so you can get more text on a page than you can using standard ITC Garamond. As you can see from this example, you shouldn't use this typeface in long stretches or when there's too much text on the page.

10/11.5
3.42 CPP

To coin a phrase. *Don't touch that dial.* ***The moment you've all been waiting for.*** The real thing. Today's the first day of the rest of your life. The long and short of it. Tell it like it is. Out of the mouths of babes. That's the way it was. Something for everyone. It's always darkest before the dawn. When it rains it pours. Every cloud has a silver lining. The light at the end of the tunnel. Good things come in small packages. Let's put on a show. All systems are go. It's a once in a lifetime opportunity."

Only yesterday. Time flies. What do you want to be when you grow up? You're only as old as you feel. You're not getting older you're getting better. It's just a phase. Another day older and deeper in debt. *Are we having fun yet?* Time is money. You've got to pay your dues. Do you take American Express? Nothing succeeds like success. Nothing exceeds like excess. Go for broke. Rags to riches. Concept by Al Masini. If they could see me now. That's when a million dollars was worth something. Value for money. The check is in the mail.

Collect 'em all. Nice guys finish last. I never met a man I didn't like. She speaks 14 different languages and she can't say "no" in any of them. Tell it to the Marines. When you've seen one, you've seen 'em all. How can I miss you if you won't go away? This will hurt you more than it hurts me. How can you believe me when I tell you that I love you when you know I've been a liar all my life?

Art imitates life. What you see is what you get. Look out for number one. With friends like that, who needs enemies. What are friends for? A friend in need is a friend indeed. A friend in need is indeed a pest. People in glass houses shouldn't throw stones. Speak softly and carry a big stick. What you don't know won't hurt you. Ignorance is bliss.

Pure as the driven snow. Once upon a time. Boy meets girl. To know him is to love him. One bad apple don't spoil the whole bunch, girl. He made me an offer I couldn't refuse. For better or for worse. Sign on the dotted line. A lifetime guarantee. Don't knock it till you've tried it. Man does not live by bread alone. Builds strong bodies 12 ways. Bring home the bacon. What's for dinner?

Soon to be made into a major motion picture. Nothin' says lovin' like somethin' from the oven. We reserve the right to serve refuse to anyone. Meanwhile, back at the ranch. Father knows best. I leave those decisions to my wife. The rules of the road. Don't chew with your mouth open. Do as I say, not as I do. Wait 'til your father gets home. It's 10 p.m., do you know where your children are? My, how you've grown.

Trip down memory lane. Having a wonderful time, wish you were here. If you can't stand the heat, get out of the kitchen. A nice place to visit but I wouldn't want to live there. Keep those cards and letter coming. To make a long story short. That's life. From all of us to all of

Goudy Old Style

A very delicate face, but surprisingly hardy at the same time. If you like your type light, then Goudy Old Style is for you. It's easy to read, even in long books (I should know, I set my last 664-page book in Goudy Old Style.) Its diamond-capped i's and periods give it a grace which has made it one of the most popular display faces in advertising. The italics are lovely and readable. Because it's so light, it fares well even when pages are terribly over-inked and printed too dark.

10/11.5
2.94 CPP

"To coin a phrase. *Don't touch that dial.* **The moment you've all been waiting for.** The real thing. Today's the first day of the rest of your life. The long and short of it. Tell it like it is. Out of the mouths of babes. That's the way it was. Something for everyone. It's always darkest before the dawn. When it rains it pours. Every cloud has a silver lining. The light at the end of the tunnel. Good things come in small packages. Let's put on a show. All systems are go. It's a once in a lifetime opportunity."

Only yesterday. Time flies. What do you want to be when you grow up? You're only as old as you feel. You're not getting older you're getting better. It's just a phase. Another day older and deeper in debt. *Are we having fun yet?* Time is money. You've got to pay your dues. Do you take American Express? Nothing succeeds like success. Nothing exceeds like excess. Go for broke. Rags to riches. Concept by Al Masini. If they could see me now. That's when a million dollars was worth something. Value for money. The check is in the mail.

Collect 'em all. Nice guys finish last. I never met a man I didn't like. She speaks 14 different languages and she can't say "no" in any of them. Tell it to the Marines. When you've seen one, you've seen 'em all. How can I miss you if you won't go away? This will hurt you more than it hurts me. How can you believe me when I tell you that I love you when you know I've been a liar all my life?

Art imitates life. What you see is what you get. Look out for number one. With friends like that, who needs enemies. What are friends for? A friend in need is a friend indeed. A friend in need is indeed a pest. People in glass houses shouldn't throw stones. Speak softly and carry a big stick. What you don't know won't hurt you. Ignorance is bliss.

Pure as the driven snow. Once upon a time. Boy meets girl. To know him is to love him. One bad apple don't spoil the whole bunch, girl. He made me an offer I couldn't refuse. For better or for worse. Sign on the dotted line. A lifetime guarantee. Don't knock it till you've tried it. Man does not live by bread alone. Builds strong bodies 12 ways. Bring home the bacon. What's for dinner?

Soon to be made into a major motion picture. Nothin' says lovin' like somethin' from the oven. We reserve the right to serve refuse to anyone. Meanwhile, back at the ranch. Father knows best. I leave those decisions to my wife. The rules of the road. Don't chew with your mouth open. Do as I say,

Hammersmith
(Gill Sans)

One of the few sans serifs I'd recommend for body text, Hammersmith is widely used in England because it has a less rigid form than faces such as Helvetica. Hammersmith is also a favorite of designers, even the most trendy. It's old fashioned looking but not antiquated, and it manages to seem warm without being informal. Not everyone likes it for body text, though; some people find it too heavy, but it's one of my favorites.

10/11.5
2.90 CPP

"To coin a phrase. *Don't touch that dial.* ***The moment you've all been waiting for.*** The real thing. Today's the first day of the rest of your life. The long and short of it. Tell it like it is. Out of the mouths of babes. That's the way it was. Something for everyone. It's always darkest before the dawn. When it rains it pours. Every cloud has a silver lining. The light at the end of the tunnel. Good things come in small packages. Let's put on a show. All systems are go. It's a once in a lifetime opportunity."

Only yesterday. Time flies. What do you want to be when you grow up? You're only as old as you feel. You're not getting older you're getting better. It's just a phase. Another day older and deeper in debt. *Are we having fun yet?* Time is money. You've got to pay your dues. Do you take American Express? Nothing succeeds like success. Nothing exceeds like excess. Go for broke. Rags to riches. Concept by Al Masini. If they could see me now. That's when a million dollars was worth something. Value for money. The check is in the mail.

Collect 'em all. Nice guys finish last. I never met a man I didn't like. She speaks 14 different languages and she can't say "no" in any of them. Tell it to the Marines. When you've seen one, you've seen 'em all. How can I miss you if you won't go away? This will hurt you more than it hurts me. How can you believe me when I tell you that I love you when you know I've been a liar all my life?

Art imitates life. What you see is what you get. Look out for number one. With friends like that, who needs enemies. What are friends for? A friend in need is a friend indeed. A friend in need is indeed a pest. People in glass houses shouldn't throw stones. Speak softly and carry a big stick. What you don't know won't hurt you. Ignorance is bliss.

Pure as the driven snow. Once upon a time. Boy meets girl. To know him is to love him. One bad apple don't spoil the whole bunch, girl. He made me an offer I couldn't refuse. For better or for worse. Sign on the dotted line. A lifetime guarantee. Don't knock it till you've tried it. Man does not live by bread alone. Builds strong bodies 12 ways. Bring home the bacon. What's for dinner?

Soon to be made into a major motion picture. Nothin' says lovin' like somethin' from the oven. We reserve the right to serve refuse to anyone. Meanwhile, back at the ranch. Father knows best. I leave those decisions to

ITC Korinna

It's lovely in short doses—but don't set a book in it. Korinna reproduces incredibly well at 300 dpi and it's loaded with personality. Despite its unusual shapes, it's extremely easy to read. Still, an entire book would be too busy set in Korinna. Friendly, informal, very warm, and personable, Korinna is great in all sizes. Suitable for personal correspondence, ads, and flyers, I wouldn't use it for anything too serious, but then again, we tend to take things much too seriously.

10/11.5
2.82 CPP

"To coin a phrase. *Don't touch that dial.* ***The moment you've all been waiting for.*** The real thing. Today's the first day of the rest of your life. The long and short of it. Tell it like it is. Out of the mouths of babes. That's the way it was. Something for everyone. It's always darkest before the dawn. When it rains it pours. Every cloud has a silver lining. The light at the end of the tunnel. Good things come in small packages. Let's put on a show. All systems are go. It's a once in a lifetime opportunity."

Only yesterday. Time flies. What do you want to be when you grow up? You're only as old as you feel. You're not getting older you're getting better. It's just a phase. Another day older and deeper in debt. *Are we having fun yet?* Time is money. You've got to pay your dues. Do you take American Express? Nothing succeeds like success. Nothing exceeds like excess. Go for broke. Rags to riches. Concept by Al Masini. If they could see me now. That's when a million dollars was worth something. Value for money. The check is in the mail.

Collect 'em all. Nice guys finish last. I never met a man I didn't like. She speaks 14 different languages and she can't say "no" in any of them. Tell it to the Marines. When you've seen one, you've seen 'em all. How can I miss you if you won't go away? This will hurt you more than it hurts me. How can you believe me when I tell you that I love you when you know I've been a liar all my life?

Art imitates life. What you see is what you get. Look out for number one. With friends like that, who needs enemies. What are friends for? A friend in need is a friend indeed. A friend in need is indeed a pest. People in glass houses shouldn't throw stones. Speak softly and carry a big stick. What you don't know won't hurt you. Ignorance is bliss.

Pure as the driven snow. Once upon a time. Boy meets girl. To know him is to love him. One bad apple don't spoil the whole bunch, girl. He made me an offer I couldn't refuse. For better or for worse. Sign on the dotted line. A lifetime guarantee. Don't knock it till you've tried it. Man does not live by bread alone. Builds strong bodies 12 ways. Bring home the bacon. What's for dinner?

Soon to be made into a major motion picture. Nothin' says lovin' like somethin' from the oven. We reserve the right to serve refuse to anyone. Meanwhile, back at the ranch. Father knows best. I leave those decisions

Serifa

Yes, this face has serifs, but they're *slab* serifs. Many people confuse Serifa with typewriter type, so while pages set in Serifa look modern, they don't have the same traditionally "typeset" feeling as pages set in Baskerville, Dutch, Garamond, or Goudy Old Style. Still, Serifa's contemporary look is effective when you want a high-tech or "Euro" look. Despite this, it's somehow kind of cute. Since this typeface was designed using Univers as its source, it works well with Univers or Bitstream's Zurich.

10/11.5
2.59 CPP

"To coin a phrase. *Don't touch that dial. The moment you've all been waiting for.* The real thing. Today's the first day of the rest of your life. The long and short of it. Tell it like it is. Out of the mouths of babes. That's the way it was. Something for everyone. It's always darkest before the dawn. When it rains it pours. Every cloud has a silver lining. The light at the end of the tunnel. Good things come in small packages. Let's put on a show. All systems are go. It's a once in a lifetime opportunity."

Only yesterday. Time flies. What do you want to be when you grow up? You're only as old as you feel. You're not getting older you're getting better. It's just a phase. Another day older and deeper in debt. *Are we having fun yet?* Time is money. You've got to pay your dues. Do you take American Express? Nothing succeeds like success. Nothing exceeds like excess. Go for broke. Rags to riches. Concept by Al Masini. If they could see me now. That's when a million dollars was worth something. Value for money. The check is in the mail.

Collect 'em all. Nice guys finish last. I never met a man I didn't like. She speaks 14 different languages and she can't say "no" in any of them. Tell it to the Marines. When you've seen one, you've seen 'em all. How can I miss you if you won't go away? This will hurt you more than it hurts me. How can you believe me when I tell you that I love you when you know I've been a liar all my life?

Art imitates life. What you see is what you get. Look out for number one. With friends like that, who needs enemies. What are friends for? A friend in need is a friend indeed. A friend in need is indeed a pest. People in glass houses shouldn't throw stones. Speak softly and carry a big stick. What you don't know won't hurt you. Ignorance is bliss.

Pure as the driven snow. Once upon a time. Boy meets girl. To know him is to love him. One bad apple don't spoil the whole bunch, girl. He made me an offer I couldn't refuse. For better or for worse. Sign on the dotted line. A lifetime guarantee. Don't knock it till you've tried it. Man does not live by bread alone. Builds strong bodies 12 ways. Bring home the bacon. What's for dinner?

Soon to be made into a major motion picture. Nothin' says lovin' like

ITC Souvenir

Looking for a friendly face? Something informal and non-threatening? I think Souvenir has this reputation because it's so rounded, with no sharp edges on which to bruise yourself. Souvenir is the right choice for something that should seem familiar and comfortable, not slick and glamorous. I often find Souvenir too cute, but it's very popular, and it's a fact that people get all mushy for "cute."

10/11.5 2.82 CPP

"To coin a phrase. *Don't touch that dial.* ***The moment you've all been waiting for.*** The real thing. Today's the first day of the rest of your life. The long and short of it. Tell it like it is. Out of the mouths of babes. That's the way it was. Something for everyone. It's always darkest before the dawn. When it rains it pours. Every cloud has a silver lining. The light at the end of the tunnel. Good things come in small packages. Let's put on a show. All systems are go. It's a once in a lifetime opportunity."

Only yesterday. Time flies. What do you want to be when you grow up? You're only as old as you feel. You're not getting older you're getting better. It's just a phase. Another day older and deeper in debt. *Are we having fun yet?* Time is money. You've got to pay your dues. Do you take American Express? Nothing succeeds like success. Nothing exceeds like excess. Go for broke. Rags to riches. Concept by Al Masini. If they could see me now. That's when a million dollars was worth something. Value for money. The check is in the mail.

Collect 'em all. Nice guys finish last. I never met a man I didn't like. She speaks 14 different languages and she can't say "no" in any of them. Tell it to the Marines. When you've seen one, you've seen 'em all. How can I miss you if you won't go away? This will hurt you more than it hurts me. How can you believe me when I tell you that I love you when you know I've been a liar all my life?

Art imitates life. What you see is what you get. Look out for number one. With friends like that, who needs enemies. What are friends for? A friend in need is a friend indeed. A friend in need is indeed a pest. People in glass houses shouldn't throw stones. Speak softly and carry a big stick. What you don't know won't hurt you. Ignorance is bliss.

Pure as the driven snow. Once upon a time. Boy meets girl. To know him is to love him. One bad apple don't spoil the whole bunch, girl. He made me an offer I couldn't refuse. For better or for worse. Sign on the dotted line. A lifetime guarantee. Don't knock it till you've tried it. Man does not live by bread alone. Builds strong bodies 12 ways. Bring home the bacon. What's for dinner?

Soon to be made into a major motion picture. Nothin' says lovin' like somethin' from the oven. We reserve the right to serve refuse to anyone. Meanwhile, back at the ranch. Father knows best. I leave those decisions

Swiss
(Helvetica)

This provides a clean, modern, professional, impersonal look, but I find it so impersonal that it's boring. I don't recommend it for lengthy text settings, but many people use it that way and no one has gone blind reading it—yet. Still, it's not attractive, it doesn't have personality, and there are many more interesting and readable choices out there. If you're thinking about using Swiss, consider using Zurich (Univers) instead.

10/11.5
2.68 CPP

"To coin a phrase. *Don't touch that dial.* ***The moment you've all been waiting for.*** The real thing. Today's the first day of the rest of your life. The long and short of it. Tell it like it is. Out of the mouths of babes. That's the way it was. Something for everyone. It's always darkest before the dawn. When it rains it pours. Every cloud has a silver lining. The light at the end of the tunnel. Good things come in small packages. Let's put on a show. All systems are go. It's a once in a lifetime opportunity."

Only yesterday. Time flies. What do you want to be when you grow up? You're only as old as you feel. You're not getting older you're getting better. It's just a phase. Another day older and deeper in debt. *Are we having fun yet?* Time is money. You've got to pay your dues. Do you take American Express? Nothing succeeds like success. Nothing exceeds like excess. Go for broke. Rags to riches. Concept by Al Masini. If they could see me now. That's when a million dollars was worth something. Value for money. The check is in the mail.

Collect 'em all. Nice guys finish last. I never met a man I didn't like. She speaks 14 different languages and she can't say "no" in any of them. Tell it to the Marines. When you've seen one, you've seen 'em all. How can I miss you if you won't go away? This will hurt you more than it hurts me. How can you believe me when I tell you that I love you when you know I've been a liar all my life?

Art imitates life. What you see is what you get. Look out for number one. With friends like that, who needs enemies. What are friends for? A friend in need is a friend indeed. A friend in need is indeed a pest. People in glass houses shouldn't throw stones. Speak softly and carry a big stick. What you don't know won't hurt you. Ignorance is bliss.

Pure as the driven snow. Once upon a time. Boy meets girl. To know him is to love him. One bad apple don't spoil the whole bunch, girl. He made me an offer I couldn't refuse. For better or for worse. Sign on the dotted line. A lifetime guarantee. Don't knock it till you've tried it. Man does not live by bread alone. Builds strong bodies 12 ways. Bring home the bacon. What's for dinner?

Soon to be made into a major motion picture. Nothin' says lovin' like somethin' from the oven. We reserve the right to serve refuse to

ITC Tiffany

ITC Tiffany is not really a body text face because it's too ornate. And yet, if the body text is large enough, say 12-point, and you use plenty of white space, Tiffany works for short blocks of text in ads, flyers, and even a very carefully designed newsletter or other not-too-long publication. It's on the busy side, and not traditional, but if you want an unusual look, try it. As body text for books—no way.

10/11.5 2.51 CPP

"**To coin a phrase.** *Don't touch that dial.* ***The moment you've all been waiting for.*** The real thing. Today's the first day of the rest of your life. The long and short of it. Tell it like it is. Out of the mouths of babes. That's the way it was. Something for everyone. It's always darkest before the dawn. When it rains it pours. Every cloud has a silver lining. The light at the end of the tunnel. Good things come in small packages. Let's put on a show. All systems are go. It's a once in a lifetime opportunity."

Only yesterday. Time flies. What do you want to be when you grow up? You're only as old as you feel. You're not getting older you're getting better. It's just a phase. Another day older and deeper in debt. *Are we having fun yet?* Time is money. You've got to pay your dues. Do you take American Express? Nothing succeeds like success. Nothing exceeds like excess. Go for broke. Rags to riches. Concept by Al Masini. If they could see me now. That's when a million dollars was worth something. Value for money. The check is in the mail.

Collect 'em all. Nice guys finish last. I never met a man I didn't like. She speaks 14 different languages and she can't say "no" in any of them. Tell it to the Marines. When you've seen one, you've seen 'em all. How can I miss you if you won't go away? This will hurt you more than it hurts me. How can you believe me when I tell you that I love you when you know I've been a liar all my life?

Art imitates life. What you see is what you get. Look out for number one. With friends like that, who needs enemies. What are friends for? A friend in need is a friend indeed. A friend in need is indeed a pest. People in glass houses shouldn't throw stones. Speak softly and carry a big stick. What you don't know won't hurt you. Ignorance is bliss.

Pure as the driven snow. Once upon a time. Boy meets girl. To know him is to love him. One bad apple don't spoil the whole bunch, girl. He made me an offer I couldn't refuse. For better or for worse. Sign on the dotted line. A lifetime guarantee. Don't knock it till you've tried it. Man does not live by bread alone. Builds strong bodies 12 ways. Bring home the bacon. What's for dinner?

Zapf Calligraphic
(Palatino)

No doubt about it, Zapf Calligraphic, Bitstream's version of Palatino, is probably used more by desktop publishers than any face other than Times/Dutch and Swiss/Helvetica. The reason is simple: Zapf Calligraphic is a beautiful typeface, efficient at all sizes from body text to gigantic. It's classic and elegant, reminiscent of Roman letters carved in stone. The italics are perfect for invitations and other events benefitting from calligraphy. Zapf Calligraphic is so popular that it doesn't have the same feel of distinction that Galliard has. Still, if you love it (and it's hard not to), don't let that stop you from using Zapf Calligraphic.

10/11.5
2.64 CPP

"To coin a phrase. *Don't touch that dial.* ***The moment you've all been waiting for.*** The real thing. Today's the first day of the rest of your life. The long and short of it. Tell it like it is. Out of the mouths of babes. That's the way it was. Something for everyone. It's always darkest before the dawn. When it rains it pours. Every cloud has a silver lining. The light at the end of the tunnel. Good things come in small packages. Let's put on a show. All systems are go. It's a once in a lifetime opportunity."

Only yesterday. Time flies. What do you want to be when you grow up? You're only as old as you feel. You're not getting older you're getting better. It's just a phase. Another day older and deeper in debt. *Are we having fun yet?* Time is money. You've got to pay your dues. Do you take American Express? Nothing succeeds like success. Nothing exceeds like excess. Go for broke. Rags to riches. Concept by Al Masini. If they could see me now. That's when a million dollars was worth something. Value for money. The check is in the mail.

Collect 'em all. Nice guys finish last. I never met a man I didn't like. She speaks 14 different languages and she can't say "no" in any of them. Tell it to the Marines. When you've seen one, you've seen 'em all. How can I miss you if you won't go away? This will hurt you more than it hurts me. How can you believe me when I tell you that I love you when you know I've been a liar all my life?

Art imitates life. What you see is what you get. Look out for number one. With friends like that, who needs enemies. What are friends for? A friend in need is a friend indeed. A friend in need is indeed a pest. People in glass houses shouldn't throw stones. Speak softly and carry a big stick. What you don't know won't hurt you. Ignorance is bliss.

Pure as the driven snow. Once upon a time. Boy meets girl. To know him is to love him. One bad apple don't spoil the whole bunch, girl. He made me an offer I couldn't refuse. For better or for worse. Sign on the dotted line. A lifetime guarantee. Don't knock it till you've tried it. Man does not live by bread alone. Builds strong bodies 12 ways. Bring home the bacon. What's for dinner?

Soon to be made into a major motion picture. Nothin' says lovin' like somethin' from the oven. We reserve the right to serve refuse to

Zapf Elliptical
(Melior)

Zapf Elliptical is Bitstream's version of Melior, a highly readable face originally developed for newspaper text. But Zapf Elliptical is more than that; it's an unusual body text face because the characters are somewhat squared. Zapf Elliptical isn't "pretty" in the traditional sense, but it has a spare, cool, modern look that makes it perfect for all types of business.

10/11.5
2.61 CPP

"**To coin a phrase.** *Don't touch that dial.* ***The moment you've all been waiting for.*** The real thing. Today's the first day of the rest of your life. The long and short of it. Tell it like it is. Out of the mouths of babes. That's the way it was. Something for everyone. It's always darkest before the dawn. When it rains it pours. Every cloud has a silver lining. The light at the end of the tunnel. Good things come in small packages. Let's put on a show. All systems are go. It's a once in a lifetime opportunity."

Only yesterday. Time flies. What do you want to be when you grow up? You're only as old as you feel. You're not getting older you're getting better. It's just a phase. Another day older and deeper in debt. *Are we having fun yet?* Time is money. You've got to pay your dues. Do you take American Express? Nothing succeeds like success. Nothing exceeds like excess. Go for broke. Rags to riches. Concept by Al Masini. If they could see me now. That's when a million dollars was worth something. Value for money. The check is in the mail.

Collect 'em all. Nice guys finish last. I never met a man I didn't like. She speaks 14 different languages and she can't say "no" in any of them. Tell it to the Marines. When you've seen one, you've seen 'em all. How can I miss you if you won't go away? This will hurt you more than it hurts me. How can you believe me when I tell you that I love you when you know I've been a liar all my life?

Art imitates life. What you see is what you get. Look out for number one. With friends like that, who needs enemies. What are friends for? A friend in need is a friend indeed. A friend in need is indeed a pest. People in glass houses shouldn't throw stones. Speak softly and carry a big stick. What you don't know won't hurt you. Ignorance is bliss.

Pure as the driven snow. Once upon a time. Boy meets girl. To know him is to love him. One bad apple don't spoil the whole bunch, girl. He made me an offer I couldn't refuse. For better or for worse. Sign on the dotted line. A lifetime guarantee. Don't knock it till you've tried it. Man does not live by bread alone. Builds strong bodies 12 ways. Bring home the bacon. What's for dinner?

Soon to be made into a major motion picture. Nothin' says lovin' like somethin' from the oven. We reserve the right to serve refuse to

Zapf Humanist
(Optima)

Perhaps the most readable sans serif typeface, Zapf Humanist is almost a sans serif with serifs. Its wonderful sculptured shape makes it less severe than other sans serifs, as well as more beautiful. If you want elegance and a sans serif face, look no farther. Zapf Humanist is both classic and modern and works at all sizes. In smaller sizes the subtle contours may not be obvious (especially on a 300 dpi laser printer) but in large sizes this deceptively simple design is full of detail. Some people say you shouldn't use Zapf Humanist on a laser printer, but I disagree. Some of the detail may be obscured, but it still works.

10/11.5
2.82 CPP

"To coin a phrase. *Don't touch that dial.* ***The moment you've all been waiting for.*** The real thing. Today's the first day of the rest of your life. The long and short of it. Tell it like it is. Out of the mouths of babes. That's the way it was. Something for everyone. It's always darkest before the dawn. When it rains it pours. Every cloud has a silver lining. The light at the end of the tunnel. Good things come in small packages. Let's put on a show. All systems are go. It's a once in a lifetime opportunity."

Only yesterday. Time flies. What do you want to be when you grow up? You're only as old as you feel. You're not getting older you're getting better. It's just a phase. Another day older and deeper in debt. *Are we having fun yet?* Time is money. You've got to pay your dues. Do you take American Express? Nothing succeeds like success. Nothing exceeds like excess. Go for broke. Rags to riches. Concept by Al Masini. If they could see me now. That's when a million dollars was worth something. Value for money. The check is in the mail.

Collect 'em all. Nice guys finish last. I never met a man I didn't like. She speaks 14 different languages and she can't say "no" in any of them. Tell it to the Marines. When you've seen one, you've seen 'em all. How can I miss you if you won't go away? This will hurt you more than it hurts me. How can you believe me when I tell you that I love you when you know I've been a liar all my life?

Art imitates life. What you see is what you get. Look out for number one. With friends like that, who needs enemies. What are friends for? A friend in need is a friend indeed. A friend in need is indeed a pest. People in glass houses shouldn't throw stones. Speak softly and carry a big stick. What you don't know won't hurt you. Ignorance is bliss.

Pure as the driven snow. Once upon a time. Boy meets girl. To know him is to love him. One bad apple don't spoil the whole bunch, girl. He made me an offer I couldn't refuse. For better or for worse. Sign on the dotted line. A lifetime guarantee. Don't knock it till you've tried it. Man does not live by bread alone. Builds strong bodies 12 ways. Bring home the bacon. What's for dinner?

Soon to be made into a major motion picture. Nothin' says lovin' like somethin' from the oven. We reserve the right to serve refuse to anyone. Meanwhile, back at the ranch. Father knows best. I leave those decisions

Zurich

(Univers)

While Zurich (Univers) may look a lot like Swiss, it's more graceful and easier to read. I don't recommend it for body text, but if you're thinking about using Helvetica, try Univers instead. The Condensed version of the typeface is good for squeezing long words into short spaces, and for short paragraphs, but not for long pages of text.

10/11.5
2.60 CPP

"To coin a phrase. *Don't touch that dial.* ***The moment you've all been waiting for.*** The real thing. Today's the first day of the rest of your life. The long and short of it. Tell it like it is. Out of the mouths of babes. That's the way it was. Something for everyone. It's always darkest before the dawn. When it rains it pours. Every cloud has a silver lining. The light at the end of the tunnel. Good things come in small packages. Let's put on a show. All systems are go. It's a once in a lifetime opportunity."

Only yesterday. Time flies. What do you want to be when you grow up? You're only as old as you feel. You're not getting older you're getting better. It's just a phase. Another day older and deeper in debt. *Are we having fun yet?* Time is money. You've got to pay your dues. Do you take American Express? Nothing succeeds like success. Nothing exceeds like excess. Go for broke. Rags to riches. Concept by Al Masini. If they could see me now. That's when a million dollars was worth something. Value for money. The check is in the mail.

Collect 'em all. Nice guys finish last. I never met a man I didn't like. She speaks 14 different languages and she can't say "no" in any of them. Tell it to the Marines. When you've seen one, you've seen 'em all. How can I miss you if you won't go away? This will hurt you more than it hurts me. How can you believe me when I tell you that I love you when you know I've been a liar all my life?

Art imitates life. What you see is what you get. Look out for number one. With friends like that, who needs enemies. What are friends for? A friend in need is a friend indeed. A friend in need is indeed a pest. People in glass houses shouldn't throw stones. Speak softly and carry a big stick. What you don't know won't hurt you. Ignorance is bliss.

Pure as the driven snow. Once upon a time. Boy meets girl. To know him is to love him. One bad apple don't spoil the whole bunch, girl. He made me an offer I couldn't refuse. For better or for worse. Sign on the dotted line. A lifetime guarantee. Don't knock it till you've tried it. Man does not live by bread alone. Builds strong bodies 12 ways. Bring home the bacon. What's for dinner?

Characters Per Pica by Font Name

Font name	12pt	11pt	10pt
Activa (Trump Medieval)	2.24	2.44	2.68
Bitstream Amerigo	2.37	2.59	2.85
ITC Avant Garde	2.26	2.47	2.72
Baskerville	2.21	2.41	2.65
ITC Benguiat	2.16	2.36	2.60
Bernhard Modern	2.50	2.73	3.00
Blippo Black	2.19	2.39	2.63
Bodoni	2.51	2.74	3.01
ITC Bolt Bold	1.76	1.92	2.11
ITC Bookman	2.11	2.30	2.53
Broadway	1.68	1.83	2.01
Brush Script	2.79	3.04	3.34
Century Schoolbook	2.19	2.39	2.63
Bitstream Charter	2.26	2.47	2.72
ITC Cheltenham	2.20	2.40	2.64
Clarendon	1.98	2.16	2.38
Clarendon Bold	1.94	2.12	2.33
ITC Clearface	2.40	2.62	2.88
Cloister Black	2.96	3.23	3.55
Bitstream Cooper	2.26	2.47	2.72
Bitstream Cooper Black	1.77	1.93	2.12
Coronet	3.65	3.98	4.38
Dom Casual	3.20	3.49	3.84
Dutch (Times Roman)	2.34	2.55	2.81
Exotic Bold	2.44	2.66	2.93
Exotic Demi	2.60	2.84	3.12
Franklin Gothic	2.03	2.21	2.43
Futura Light	2.42	2.64	2.90
Futura Book	2.31	2.52	2.77
Futura Medium	2.23	2.43	2.67
Futura Condensed	3.15	3.44	3.78
Futura Extra Black	1.88	2.05	2.26
Futura Black	2.31	2.52	2.77

Font name	12pt	11pt	10pt
ITC Galliard	2.33	2.54	2.79
ITC Garamond Book	2.25	2.45	2.70
ITC Garamond Cond.	2.85	3.11	3.42
Goudy Old Style	2.45	2.67	2.94
Hammersmith (Gill Sans)	2.42	2.64	2.90
Handel Gothic	2.01	2.19	2.41
Hobo	2.32	2.53	2.78
Kaufmann Bold	2.54	2.77	3.05
ITC Korinna	2.35	2.56	2.82
ITC Lubalin Graph	1.96	2.14	2.35
News Gothic	2.36	2.57	2.83
Mermaid	2.04	2.23	2.45
Park Ave	3.06	3.34	3.67
Provence (Antique Olive)	2.05	2.24	2.46
P.T. Barnum	2.74	2.99	3.29
Serifa	2.15	2.35	2.59
Slate (Rockwell)	2.24	2.44	2.68
ITC Souvenir	2.35	2.56	2.82
Swiss (Helvetica)	2.24	2.44	2.68
Swiss Condensed	2.56	2.79	3.07
Swiss Compressed	2.70	2.95	3.25
Swiss Extra Compressed	3.35	3.65	4.02
Swiss Light	2.31	2.52	2.77
ITC Tiffany	2.09	2.28	2.51
University Roman	2.94	3.21	3.53
Windsor	2.05	2.24	2.46
Zapf Calligraphic (Palatino)	2.20	2.40	2.64
Zapf Chancery	2.70	2.95	3.25
Zapf Elliptical (Melior)	2.17	2.37	2.61
Zapf Humanist (Optima)	2.35	2.56	2.82
Zurich (Univers)	2.16	2.36	2.60
Zurich Condensed	2.56	2.79	3.07
Zurich Light	2.22	2.42	2.66

ITC Avant Garde

This is not a very good face for body text. Its x-height is so large that it is often hard to tell the capitals from the lower case letters. You can use it for short blocks, but if you want something with a similar feeling that works better as body text, use Futura.

Baskerville

This is the body text face of this book, and supposedly the most popular serif typeface in the world (yes, even more popular than Dutch/Times). Baskerville is very traditional without looking stuffy. It's clear and easy to read, yet doesn't suffer from Times' stiff and somewhat sterile feeling. Baskerville's italics are delicate and full of details so they can be used for graceful invitations or other special text. Baskerville is also excellent in large sizes.

ITC Benguiat

This is not a good body text font, even though its normal weight is called "book." This lively face is wonderful for display work but terrible for body copy because it's too busy. I see Benguiat on menus and invitations all the time, and there it looks good.

ITC Lubalin Graph

This is ITC Avant Garde with slab serifs. Designed by ITC co-founder Herb Lubalin, it can be used as a modern, geometric alternative to American Typewriter. Do not use it for body text unless you're setting something you don't want to be read easily.

Swiss Condensed

This is not just an electronically narrowed version of Swiss, the way "Helvetica Narrow" (found in most PostScript printers) is a narrowed version of Helvetica. It's designed to be narrow, so it's actually an attractive face—far more attractive than plain Swiss. Its narrowness is good in short bursts, but an entire letter-size page of this typeface could make you cry. Bitstream itself uses it quite successfully for some of its Fontware manuals by placing it on a small page (5½" tall by 8" wide), devoting almost half the page to white space, using block paragraphs and three points of leading instead of the normal two, and giving the most text-intensive page just five paragraphs.

Subliminal messages

The implication behind the face

So far, all this has been logical. You find out who's reading and why, and you try to plan accordingly. But human beings are remarkably illogical (just ask Mr. Spock). They'll tell you they like one thing when they really like another. They'll tell you what they think you want to hear. Or, they'll say they like one typeface, but in reality what they really like is the design of the page. Or perhaps what they really like is that the typeface reminds them of the ice cream bars they got when they were good as a kid. It's hard to tell.

Why do you like what you do? We often fail to notice exactly what catches our eye. But subliminal mental associations are very powerful persuaders. They can help you to snare your audience or they can hurt you by turning people off before they've even read your copy.

As human beings, everything reminds us of something else. Even something as simple as a blank piece of paper can stir memories from way back. Was it a paper cut you remembered? Origami? Paper airplanes? Fresh snow? Snow White in a snowstorm? Shadow puppets on backlit paper? Passing notes in school? Paper-thin slices of Provolone? You name it.

Dry Cleaner

Park Avenue (Yuk).

Type is the same way. To me, certain typefaces have *terrible* associations. Park Avenue always reminds me of a hot, dusty, dry cleaning store that was once the height of fashion but hasn't been refurbished or even painted in 20 years. The "D" of Coronet reminds me of the "D" in "Desilu" at the end of every *I Love Lucy* episode (and I've seen every episode at least six times).

D

Coronet. (Desilu—yeah!)

As you can see, display faces tend to have the most baggage attached because they are the most distinctive. Most body text faces are relatively free from this kind of deep-seated emotion because they are almost transparent on the page. But there are exceptions—Century Schoolbook really does remind me of schoolbooks so I never have liked it. Bodoni seems to speak to the type of person who likes high fashion magazines, precisely because so many high fashion magazines use it.

Mixed messages

You don't want to send mixed messages or schizophrenic signals

It's important for your typeface to complement the text. Yes, that's right, it's "appropriate" time (not unlike cherry blossom time, only less pink). Don't say one thing with your text and another with your typeface.

Garden Party **Garden Party**

Brake Pads *Brake Pads*

I've stressed how much type can do for you, but this is the time to remind you that type can also work *against* you. While the positive impacts of type are sometimes subtle, the negative ones are usually unmistakable. People may like your publication a little more because of a typeface. They not only read it, but feel favorably about it—they *trust* it. But a poor choice of typefaces or unattractive typography just plain means they will never read your message. End of story.

Why not Times, Dutch, Helvetica, or Swiss?

First, that's a trick question. We all know that Times and Dutch are similar type designs, as are Helvetica and Swiss. Trick questions aside, the answer is simple: While Dutch and Swiss are serviceable typefaces, there's no one single typeface or even two typefaces that will fit every job.

Remember, Times Roman was designed for *The Times* of London, a daily newspaper. Its main job was to be very readable and pack a lot of words on a page. A newspaper face is *designed* to have no personality, just as news articles are written so they don't have personality that might editorialize the story.

Dutch is the "undecided" of the typeface world. It is now as common as typewriter type, and just about as effective.

Dutch and Swiss are *practical.* That's it. They are rather sterile typefaces with very little personality and very few connotations. You could use all your typographical prowess and do everything perfectly, and yet if you use Times or Helvetica, your results will be functional, but that's all. You won't be embarrassed, but you won't be all that excited, either. There's nothing wrong with that, but that's not taking advantage of type's inherent power. With all the typographic richness available, it's a shame to just use those two simply because "they're there."

The point of typography is to enhance the message, not merely carry it, and a better quality typeface makes your message *look* better and adds personality.

Of course, if you *want* your body text to have no personality, if you want something completely ubiquitous, something that doesn't stand out from the pages virtually everyone else is producing, go right ahead. Your message may get lost or confused with other people's messages, but then again, there are times when you may want that, such as when you have bad news you want to downplay or hide.

Swiss has a few more strikes against it—it's a pretty unattractive typeface. There are a few people who would fight to the death to defend it, but face it: it's faceless. The shapes themselves are not particularly appealing, and once set, it just kind of sits there.

Other variants of Swiss, such as Light, Black, and Condensed don't seem to suffer from the antiseptic lifelessness that seems to characterize Swiss roman.

If you want a face with the advantages of Swiss, but without it's clunkiness, I strongly recommend Zurich (Univers). When you first start looking at type, you can see the two and think, "Geez, aren't these exactly the same?" They *are* similar, but when you add up all the subtle differences between them, Zurich is just as clean and modern as Swiss, but less ugly and more graceful.

Zurich comes in as many weights and styles as Swiss, but unlike Swiss, it won't bore people. You can also stretch it and squeeze it (within reason) and it doesn't look deformed.

Think of it this way. Dutch and Swiss are *acceptable* but not exceptional.

In the end, acceptable will do, but excellent is always better.

Type as a weapon

I've been concentrating on the "positive side of the force," the powers of good typography. But there is also a way to use bad typography for your own devices.

A very sneaky friend of mine (whose name has been changed to protect the guilty) told me how he uses bad typography to gain the upper hand against his rivals. It's not very nice, but he's a firm believer in "all's fair in love and war," and "business is war."

John says that if you use the worst possible body text face, people won't read what you send them. This is invaluable when you are duty-bound to send them something, but don't really want them to read it.

He gave me the following example. John had a meeting where his team was working with another team on a project. The two teams had different approaches, and while they were supposed to be working together, each wanted its own approach to be adopted. John was required to create a report that everyone would read.

He wanted his own team to read the report, so he set it in Zapf Elliptical (Melior), which he says looks so official and businesslike that people can't help but read it, and is very easy to read. *The result:* his team read the report.

He *didn't* want the opposing team to read the information, so that they would be unprepared for the meeting. So, he set the same report in Futura Bold, a typeface much too heavy for body text, with little leading. (Swiss Bold would have been just as bad.) The resulting page was horribly dark, unappealing, hard to read, and unprofessional looking. *The result:* no one on the opposing team read the report.

At the meeting, John's team was prepared while the opposing team wasn't. He had given them the information, but in a form that insured they wouldn't read it. *The result:* his team had the upper hand and won approval, the other team lost.

The moral of the story: Well actually, this wasn't a very moral story. But it does teach an important lesson—the right body face and good typography will get people to read your pages while the wrong ones will keep them from reading your material.

4

Display some style

A display typeface
is worth a thousand words

You can say almost as much with your choice of typeface as you do with your choice of words.

Display some style

A display typeface is worth a thousand words, or so my new cliche goes

You can say almost as much with your choice of typeface as you do with your choice of words. The typeface you choose sets the style and tone of a document, colors how readers interpret the words, and defines the underlying feeling of the page.

So how do you choose? Like any art, type is emotional, and emotion is subjective. So while there are no hard and fast rules, there is, common sense, rearing its tedious little head. As always, you have to think about who your audience is. Once you've answered that first question, you decide next how you want them to feel about your publication.

Letter by letter

Unlike body text faces, where you must look at the typeface set in paragraphs, display faces require you to look at the typeface letter by letter.

When you are trying to decide on a face to use, write down the actual words you are going to use, then look at those particular letters in various typefaces. Sometimes you'll find, as I do, that faces you would never have considered using are perfect, because the individual letters you'll use are particularly interesting in that typeface, or the general feeling is right. It can surprise you.

Trial and error

In fact, sometimes the *obvious* choices don't work, and the surprising ones do. Desktop publishing is useful because it allows you to quickly try out all your various typefaces in context—which would have been virtually impossible (if not prohibitively expensive) in the past.

If you don't have a large library of typefaces, and don't want to buy ones you may not use, see if a friendly dealer will help you out by setting the words you need in the typefaces you *think* you'll buy (if they work out).

Service bureaus tend to have every typeface imaginable, so if you create a single page containing a slew of typefaces, printing it at a service bureau will only cost you a few dollars per page and you'll be able to see many faces in action.

Failing that, try making a photocopy of a type catalog, then piece the letters together. This may sound tedious, but it isn't meant to be perfect, it's only meant to quickly show you whether or not a typeface will work for your purposes, and it's practically free.

Rorschach type test

Let's try one of those psychological tests where you rattle off the first things that come into your mind. For this Rorschach typeface test we'll design an advertisement for an expensive product, Aqua Rodeo (as in Ro-day-o Drive in Beverly Hills, not a western ro-dee-o), one of those new "designer waters" that turns simple H_2O into $H_{\$}O$.

We want the product to appear elegant and appeal to *Lifestyles of the Rich and Gullible* crowd. We want luxury, class, and perhaps something exotic, unusual, and unexpected to attract attention.

The first step is deceptively simple. Since different typefaces elicit distinct feelings, you need to sit down and look at a variety of typefaces and see how they make you feel. What do they remind you of? Go for the immediate reaction. Don't think about it too much, just choose the fonts that "speak" to you.

Aqua
Rodeo

Freeze Dried H_2O
Just Add Water

Cooper Black

What we're looking for here is a true "display" face—something with enough personality to enhance just a few words. Most display faces, such as the exotic Mermaid, are designed especially for larger sizes. This means that you shouldn't set more than a word or two in them. Others, such as Bernhard Modern with it's art deco top hat and cane look, could be used for a few paragraphs of text, but not much more.

Aqua
Rodeo

Freeze Dried H_2O
Just Add Water

Dom Casual

Display faces have big, flashy features that convey their message in a moment. For this job we could select from many, each appealing to a slightly different type of elegance, from whimsical to sophisticated.

When I try to find a face, I don't just sit and try to think of font names. I look through font catalogs and try to picture text set in each face being used. Try it with me...

Let's see, how about—Cooper. All wrong. It looks like it has water weight buildup. Cooper is nice enough on its own: short, dark, and cuddly, but not this time. Dom Casual. All wrong. Too

Aqua
Rodeo
Freeze Dried H_2O
Just Add Water

Cloister Black

Aqua
Rodeo
Freeze Dried H_2O
Just Add Water

Blippo Black

Aqua
Rodeo
Freeze Dried H_2O
Just Add Water

Swiss Compressed

Aqua
Rodeo
Freeze Dried H_2O
Just Add Water

Broadway

Aqua
Rodeo
Freeze Dried H_2O
Just Add Water

Mermaid

Aqua
Rodeo
Freeze Dried H_2O
Just Add Water

University Roman

AQUA
RODEO
Freeze Dried H_2O
Just Add Water

University Roman uppercase.

informal, not elegant. Cloister Black. Wrong, wrong, wrong. Dark, antique, the antithesis of sun splashing on water. No.

Blippo? The unknown Marx brother? Ha! I don't think so. Definitely not light, and too funny looking. For some reason it reminds me of pool equipment. What possessed me? Never mind, let's try... Swiss Compressed? Well, it's not light, but there's something so modern about it that it looks upscale. Hmmm, no, too dark.

Broadway? I love art deco and this reminds me of an ocean liner—but much too heavy. Water is a light drink so we want a typeface that suggests that.

Mermaid? Yes, that's unusual. It's fluid. That's the word I'm looking for. Sometimes it's easier to tell what you don't like than what you do, and what we need here is fluidity. Unfortunately, when Mermaid is used here it looks Arabian—too much like the desert.

University? Yes, I like that. A delicate typeface like University Roman is charming and old fashioned, eccentric with a touch of jazz. It suggests 1920's picnics by a lake, so I feel a connection with water. One thing to remember is that typefaces look different if you set them U&lc (upper and lowercase), all caps (not too often), or in bold or italics. In this case, I know University has a wonderful long tail on the uppercase "Q," so I try it. Unfortunately, the bar across the A is so high that it makes AQUA (with two "A"s) very hard to read.

I could stop at University, but I think I can do better. If not, I can always come back to this. I'll see if something else doesn't surprise me.

Bernhard Modern? Well, it's *very* elegant; I love those big serifs. The caps of Bernhard Modern are striking, but I think this needs something less stiff. Let's try U&lc. It's a possibility, though quite upright, and I think of water as having more movement. Let's try it in italics. Yup, that does look better. Let's try some more italics.

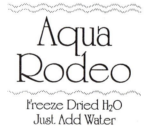

AQUA
RODEO
FREEZE DRIED H_2O
JUST ADD WATER

Bernhard Modern Uppercase

Aqua
Rodeo
Freeze Dried H_2O
Just Add Water

Bernhard Modern Italic

Aqua
Rodeo
Freeze Dried H_2O
Just Add Water

Bodoni

Aqua
Rodeo
Freeze Dried H_2O
Just Add Water

Bodoni Italic

AQUA
RODEO
FREEZE DRIED H_2O
JUST ADD WATER

Bodoni Uppercase

Most people just think of italics as *slanting* to the right; they don't realize that the italics of serif faces are *very* different from their roman weights. Serif italics are more script-like than roman weights, and often can be used instead of a formal script. Italics in headlines look *completely* different, and give a casual, more personal impression than roman or bold weights.

Often you can use text faces for display purposes as well. Bodoni is a text face that is often used for display work and lends an air of formality to a page. It doesn't do anything for me in U&lc. The italics are clean and simple, but not quite it. Small caps? I like Bodoni better in small caps, but it still lacks fluidity.

Let's go back to italics. No one has flashier italics than Galliard. Well, it's light; it says splash. These fancy italics are sophisticated and elegant and would make mere water seem like champagne. Possible, though it's slightly difficult to read in this setting.

Goudy Old Style has lovely italics. But not distinctive enough. Zapf Calligraphic's italics are also wonderful, but not fancy enough. Benguiat is full of interesting shapes, but it just doesn't look right for this.

Aqua
Rodeo
Freeze Dried H_2O
Just Add Water

ITC Galliard Italic

Aqua
Rodeo
Freeze Dried H_2O
Just Add Water

Goudy Old Style Italic

Aqua
Rodeo
Freeze Dried H_2O
Just Add Water

Zapf Calligraphic (Palatino)

Aqua
Rodeo
Freeze Dried H_2O
Just Add Water

ITC Benguiat

Aqua
Rodeo

Freeze Dried H_2O
Just Add Water

Zapf Humanist (Optima)

Aqua
Rodeo

Freeze Dried H_2O
Just Add Water

Futura Light

A Q U A

RODEO

FREEZE DRIED H20

JUST ADD WATER

Futura Extra Black, Light, Condensed

Let's try some sans serifs. I know, I wanted something more traditional, but I think I'll just try anyway. Zapf Humanist? Hmmm. Elegant and modern, but too subtle. It doesn't jump out from the competing clutter on a typical magazine or newspaper page unless you set it apart with ample amounts of white space.

Futura? Well, it's clean, modern, light, and graphic. It wouldn't block one's view of the water itself. For some reason it seems maritime to me. Portholes, that's it. I could use several weights (extra black, light, condensed) and come up with something easy and fashionable. Interesting.

Still, while elegant in a very simple way, we want something more fluid, something that says "beach, splash, sun, surf." Nothing's more fluid than script typefaces.

Aqua
Rodeo

Freeze Dried H_2O
Just Add Water

ITC Zapf Chancery

Let's give Zapf Chancery a chance. It has never seemed truly elegant to me. Some people absolutely love it and think it's the most beautiful typeface on the face of the earth. I think these are people who have not seen a wide variety of fonts. Me, I think it's nice but casual, like simple hand-drawn calligraphy. Actually, the word that springs to my mind is "funky." Not what I'm looking for.

Aqua
Rodeo

Freeze Dried H_2O
Just Add Water

Brush Script

Brush Script is a common script that I don't much like, but I'll try it because it's handy. No, I still don't care for it. It's too heavy, too informal. It doesn't say anything to me, it doesn't make me think of another era or anything specific. I don't hate it but I don't like it either.

I do dislike Park Avenue. Despise everything about it. But in the interest of good sportsmanship (which I was never very good at) I'll give it a try.

Aqua
Rodeo

Freeze Dried H_2O
Just Add Water

Park Avenue (Yuk)

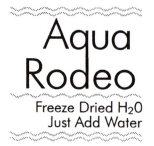

Ugly. I still hate it. The "A" is appalling, the "R" is repulsive, the lowercase "d" looks deformed, and the lowercase "e" is enormously awful. Whenever someone threatens to use Park Avenue, I beg them to use Coronet instead, so I'll try that.

Coronet

Kaufmann

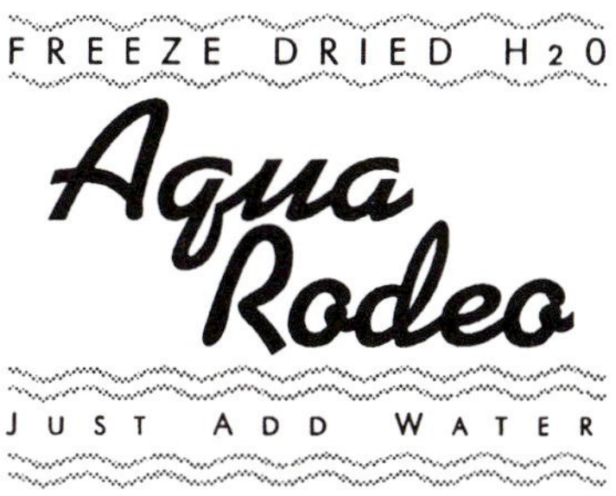

Kaufmann & Futura

Coronet? Normally I wouldn't dream of using it because it's too Fifties, but I actually like it in this setting. The "A" and "R" are decorative, and the lower case letters are fluid. Yet it has such a small x-height that it's not easy to read, and the bottom two lines are almost impossible.

One script with a larger x-height is Kaufmann. Kaufmann reminds me more of neon than water, but I'll try it anyway. Hey. I like that. I wouldn't have thought of it, but I like it. Very Miami. Big. Easy to read. Not too light. Not too dark. I think I've found it.

That's my opinion. Would you have chosen one of the other faces? If so, why?

Different places for different faces

Notice that the settings are slightly different for the different faces. Some are flush left, some centered, some flush right. You must use your eye and decide which alignment looks best with a particular font. Each typeface has its own idiosyncracies, and you should improvise with them until you find the most pleasing arrangement. Page composition and draw programs make it easy to move the type around and see how it looks, so take advantage of it rather than just settling for a standard treatment.

As I worked with these faces, I found that I liked the alignment either flush left or flush right better than centered, because centering ate up the white space. Flush right turned out to be my favorite, because it used the white space to separate the type from any other clutter. It gave the type breathing room and made it lighter.

Just to prove a point, I also set this in Dutch Italic and Swiss. Swiss is clearly wrong. It just sits there. Dutch Italic fares better; it isn't ugly, but it's too plain and *uninspiring*.

If you have the standard 35 typefaces built into many PostScript printers, then Palatino italic probably would be the best choice, but it still doesn't have the punch a real display face would. What about the other 34? Helvetica? It's downright inappropriate. ITC Avant Garde? Too modern. Bookman? Too pedestrian. Century Schoolbook? Don't make me laugh.

One final note: One of the ugliest things you can do with type is to set script faces in all caps. It looks horrible and is the sure sign of a rank amateur. See what I mean:

NEVER SET ITC ZAPF CHANCERY OR OTHER SCRIPT FACES IN ALL CAPS. NEVER!

Aqua Rodeo

Freeze Dried H_2O
Just Add Water

Dutch (Times Roman)

Aqua Rodeo

Freeze Dried H_2O
Just Add Water

Swiss (Helvetica)

Aqua Rodeo

Freeze Dried H_2O
Just Add Water

ITC Avant Garde

Aqua Rodeo

Freeze Dried H_2O
Just Add Water

Hammersmith (Gill Sans)

Aqua Rodeo

Freeze Dried H_2O
Just Add Water

Bitstream Amerigo

Aqua Rodeo

Freeze Dried H_2O
Just Add Water

ITC Tiffany Italic

5

Building a type library

A few classic novels,
a few trashy paperbacks,
and a few Calvin and Hobbes collections

Type is addictive. Once you start to appreciate it, it's hard to keep from buying more.

Building a type library

A few classic novels, a few trashy paperbacks, and a few Calvin and Hobbes collections

Type is addictive. Once you start to appreciate it, it's hard to keep from buying more. Unfortunately, type isn't free, so we all have to decide which faces we'll succumb to and which we'll resist.

The very first thing you should buy is a good, all-around, serif body text face that can double as a display face. Luckily, most good text faces both are readable in small sizes and have interesting details in larger sizes.

Next, add a contrasting sans serif face. There are many from which you can choose, so think carefully about how it will work with your body text face.

Finally, add some interesting display faces. Bitstream's Headline packages are good because they give you a wide mix of faces. Headlines 1 is generally a good place to start because it includes four very different typefaces.

Type isn't cheap, but it can be a good value if you choose your faces wisely. Whenever you buy a typeface, try to find one you can use often, in a variety of contexts. The more you use it, the less expensive the type becomes.

Body or display?

Only your typographer knows for sure

Typefaces can be classified in several different ways. One of the most basic points to know about a typeface is which category it belongs in.

1. Body type. Type that can be used for body copy, in sizes from 9- to 12-point, is called body type. Set in paragraphs, this is the bulk of the type found on most pages. Body type's main job is readability, but it still has a huge impact on the personality of a page. Set the same page in Dutch (Times Roman) and again in Goudy Old Style and you'll see—the pages *feel* different. Most body type can also be used in large display sizes as well. (Condensed versions should not be set in long blocks as body type).

II. Display type. Type that should only be used in larger sizes, from 14-point (at the very lowest end) to infinity, is called display type. Often exciting to look at, one of its jobs is to attract attention. Because of its eccentricity, display type is not always the easiest to read.

Specialty. Faces that are actually display type that can be used for body text in some situations, such as *short* blocks of text at 12-point and above. In the list below, they are indicated with the ¶ symbol.

To make them easier to find, fonts are listed both under their Bitstream name and their industry name. Names in parenthesis are industry names.

Body text

Activa (Trump Mediæval)
Avant Garde, ITC¶
Baskerville
Amerigo, Bitstream
Benguiat, ITC¶
Bernhard Modern¶
Bodoni
Bookman
Century Schoolbook
Charter, Bitstream
Cheltenham, ITC
Clarendon¶
Clearface, ITC
Cooper, Bitstream
Dutch (Times Roman)
Futura
Futura Light
Futura Condensed
Galliard, ITC
Garamond, ITC
Garamond Condensed, ITC
Goudy Old Style
Hammersmith (Gill Sans)
Korinna, ITC¶
Provence¶ (Antique Olive)
Rockwell (Slate)
Serifa
Slate (Rockwell)
Souvenir, ITC
Swiss (Helvetica)
Swiss Condensed (Helvetica Condensed)
Swiss Light (Helvetica Light)
Tiffany, ITC¶
Univers (Zurich)
Univers Light (Zurich Light)
Zapf Calligraphic (Palatino)
Zapf Elliptical (Melior)
Zapf Humanist (Optima)
Zurich (Univers)
Zurich Light (Univers Light)

Display

American Typewriter, ITC
Avant Garde, ITC
Benguiat, ITC
Bernhard Modern
Blippo
Bolt Bold, ITC
Broadway
Brush Script
Cloister Black
Cooper Black
Coronet
Dom Casual
Exotic (Peignot)
Franklin Gothic, ITC
Futura Black
Futura Extra Black
Handel Gothic
Hobo
Kaufmann
Korinna, ITC
Lubalin Graph, ITC
Mermaid
News Gothic
P.T. Barnum
Park Avenue
Provence (Antique Olive)
Provence Black (Antique Olive Black)
Provence Compact (Antique Olive Compact)
Rockwell Extra Bold (Slate Ex Bold)
Script
Serifa Black
Slate Ex Bold (Rockwell Extra Bold)
Swiss Black (Helvetica Black)
Swiss Black Condensed (Helvetica Black Condensed)
Swiss Compressed (Helvetica Compressed)
Swiss Extra Compressed (Helvetica Extra Compressed)
Tiffany Heavy, ITC
Tiffany, ITC
University Roman
Windsor
Zapf Chancery, ITC
Zurich Black (Univers Black)
Zurich Black Extended (Univers Black Extended)

Suggested groups

If you don't yet have any fonts besides Dutch and Swiss and want to start building your library, or if you do have some other fonts purchased at random and are ready to get back to the basics, here are some suggestions for initial purchases, using the guidelines I explained at the beginning of this chapter.

The Basics #1

Baskerville

Futura Light/**Extra Black**

Headlines 1 (Broadway, Cloister Black, Cooper Black, Coronet)

The Basics #2

Goudy Old Style

Hammersmith (Gill Sans)

Bernhard Modern

The Basics #3

Zapf Calligraphic (Palatino)

Zapf Humanist (Optima)

ITC Benguiat

The Basics #4

Bitstream Charter

Zurich Condensed/**Expanded**

ITC Korinna or Headlines 1

The Basics #5

ITC Garamond

ITC Garamond Condensed

Zurich Light/**Black**

Choose your own

First Choice

Column A - Serifs	Column B - Sans Serifs	Column C - Display
Baskerville	Futura Light/Black	Benguiat
Bitstream Charter	Hammersmith	Bernhard Modern
ITC Cheltenham	Swiss Condensed	Headlines 1
ITC Galliard	Swiss Light	Headlines 6
Goudy Old Style	Zapf Humanist	ITC Korinna
Zapf Calligraphic	Zurich Black/Light	ITC Tiffany
Zapf Elliptical	Zurich Condensed/Expanded	

Second Choice

Column A	Column B	Column C
Activa	ITC Avant Garde	ITC American Typewriter
Bitstream Amerigo	ITC Franklin Gothic	Headlines 2
Cooper	Futura Book/Heavy	Headlines 4
Bodoni	News Gothic	Headlines 3
Century Schoolbook	Provence	Slate
ITC Clearface	Zurich	
ITC Garamond	Zurich Light	
ITC Garamond Condensed		
ITC Korinna		
Serifa		
ITC Souvenir		

What to look for in a font

Looking at the individual letters is not the best way to determine the quality of a typeface. That's because even if the individual letters are exquisite, the way they work together is just as important, if not more important.

While catalogs may be a good place to find display faces, you need to see more than just a line or paragraph of a body face to know whether it's appropriate for your particular application. It's like trying to choose wallpaper from little bitty scraps. When you see a whole page set in a specific typeface it can look different than a small sample.

Look at books, magazines, and newspapers and find a typeface that interests you. Then comes the fun part: trying to figure out what typeface it is. The trick to identifying typefaces is to look for distinctive characteristics. Find the features that look "different" to you, such as the shape of the bowl of the lowercase "g," and then compare them to samples in typeface catalogs.

If you're interested in *type spotting* (figuring out what typeface you're looking at), I particularly recommend *Rookledge's Type Finder*, a wonderful resource for anyone interested in type. The book uses clever methods to help you classify the typeface you're looking at. It highlights the common earmarks of each typeface so that they are easier to recognize.

Look at words, not just letters: Type is rarely used one letter at a time. Ordinarily it's used in groups of letters to form words. When you see type set in real words and paragraphs, you see how it looks on the page.

Letter shapes: Do all the letters go together, or do some stand out and call attention to themselves? Is the overall appearance even? Are the characters smooth or are they jagged? Is the baseline straight, or do certain letters print higher on the line than others, like on a bad typewriter?

Evenness: Examine how letters work together. They should all be the same weight or color. Notice if the normal weight looks bold, or if it's too light, so that parts of the characters disappear. Beware of fonts where certain characters stand out because they're lighter or darker.

Spacing Spacing can make or break a typeface. Even the most beautiful typeface can be destroyed if the spacing is not good. The letters should be spaced so they are close enough that words form easily recognized groups. If they're too close together they'll bunch up and become hard to read. If they're too far apart you'll have a hard time telling where the words begin and end. Look to see if certain pairs of letters are too close together or far apart. A good font will contain a large number of "kerning pairs" that will move specific pairs of letters closer or farther apart to improve their appearance and readability.

Overall appearance Don't look at the type under a magnifying glass. Normal readers don't look at type that closely. Look at the type as a reader would, at the same distance and in the same lighting conditions.

Resolution: Look at real type from a real printer with the same resolution as your own. Most type samples you receive from foundries are not laser-printed, but typeset on expensive, high-resolution typesetting machines. The result looks very different from what you'll get from a 300 dpi laser printer.

Because most type is now "outline" type, the same outlines can be used at many resolutions. While Bitstream's type looks good at all resolutions, some other companies' outlines look acceptable at 2450 dpi and terrible at 300 dpi.

One trick that font companies use to make their type look better in catalogs is to print their type on a 300-dpi laser printer, then photographically reduce it so it appears sharper. They can advertise it as "actual laser output," though what *you* get on your printer will look quite different. In other words, your mileage may vary.

The only solution is to look at what actually comes out of the kind of printer you have. That's not always easy to do. Even Bitstream's brochures feature type that is set on high-resolution machines. If possible, find a friendly/smart dealer who will print samples for you on a laser printer similar to yours.

6

Style vs. fashion

Styles change
but style never does

Styles of type, like clothing styles, go in and out of fashion, but what's hot at the moment isn't automatically what's right for you.

Style vs. fashion

Styles change but style never does

Styles of type, like clothing styles, go in and out of fashion, but what's *hot* at the moment isn't automatically what's right for you. One year Futura Extra Black is *all* the rage, the next year the pendulum swings, it's passé, and Swiss Compressed (Headlines 3) is *in*. What's best is *always* what's most appropriate for the job at hand.

This is one of the things art directors get paid to think about, but for the typical desktop publisher, font fashions may be a revelation. As Bill Blass says about clothing, certain typestyles "just look right now."

Here's an example: Century Schoolbook is about as *out* as a typeface can get. And yet, if you're typesetting a book, especially one for children where readability is critical, you could use it without hesitation. Why? Because just as you wouldn't dream of going to a hockey game wearing white chiffon (all that spattered blood), white chiffon is appropriate for certain occasions, such as a wedding or a Marilyn Monroe look-alike contest.

Why fashion changes

The key to this constant need for change is two-fold: First, while people tend to "like what they know," they also get bored with it eventually, and look to new designs for novelty and freshness. Second, there are the designers who get paid to redesign things, be it clothes, fonts or pages. Naturally it's in their best interest to change what's in style so they have more work.

Historically, the last decade of a century tends to be the wildest. The phrase "the Gay Nineties" refers to the frenzied, party attitude of the 1890s. So it's not surprising that this decade's trend in popular type is toward the extreme.

Trends in type

Display type is even more affected by trends than is body type. This is because for body type to remain readable, it can't be too extreme, while display faces can and do push the limits of good taste. Still, even body text is subject to the ebbs and flows of the tides of time.

During the 1970s and 1980s, body type with large x-height was popular because it looked big and modern. ITC was instrumental in redrawing classic faces with new proportions including larger x-heights, and for a while, small x-height faces seemed to almost disappear. Once people became used to type with large x-heights, then suddenly small x-heights seemed new again. Beginning in the late 80s a more *retro* look became popular, and faces with smaller x-heights now are enjoying a resurgence of popularity.

That doesn't mean ITC's large x-heights are out; they're still immensely popular and readable. It just means that older faces such as Bodoni, Goudy Old Style, and older versions of Garamond, have achieved renewed popularity.

Displaying around

Swiss Compressed
Swiss Extra Compressed
Baskerville
Bodoni
Bernhard Modern
ITC Galliard
Goudy Old Style
ITC Garamond
Zapf Calligraphic
(Palatino)

As this book is written, the two hottest typefaces are very sans serif and very serif. In the sans serif corner, for display faces it's *in* to be heavy and thin at the same time. That may sound like a contradiction in terms, but it's not. The hot fonts are narrow, yet dense. Compact and thick. Typographers call this "condensed" or "compressed."

Compressed sans serifs are cropping up in headlines and logos everywhere: Bitstream has Swiss Compressed and Extra Compressed in a package called Headlines 3, which includes the very *out* Exotic typeface (remember the credits on the Mary Tyler Moore show—they're about as up-to-date as those little outfits she wore).

In the serif corner, small x-heights, distinctive serifs and formality are in. Baskerville, Bodoni, Bernhard Modern, ITC Galliard, and Goudy Old Style are all in—but then they're almost always in, as are ITC Garamond and Palatino.

No good, no bad, just *appropriate*

Now that you know the in's and out's—forget them.

Good taste is a matter of opinion; good design isn't.

"Good taste" doesn't have rules, good design does. "Good taste" was invented to sell products every couple of years, when what *was* considered good becomes *bad*, requiring you to buy something new. Good design was invented to make pages easier to read. "Good taste" is often bad design.

Good design is always in good taste. Bad design is always bad news, bad taste, and bad for business.

Futura Extra Black with Bernhard Modern.

The first question you should always ask yourself is, "What would be appropriate?" You'd be surprised how many people never even think about whether their typeface is appropriate to their content. They happily use some dainty typeface in a brochure for heavy equipment, or something clunky like Helvetica in a lingerie catalog. A brochure for heavy equipment doesn't necessarily call for heavy type, just as one about lingerie doesn't necessarily have to be light—but chances are they *will* have different readers, and so will probably end up set in different typefaces, each appropriate to its subject.

"Good taste" and "in style" are like anything else that can be preceded by the word "good" or "in"; they are always in the eye of the beholder. Don't let anyone tell you otherwise.

Good taste changes from year to year. It's like that episode of *I Love Lucy* when they went to Paris. Remember? Ricky and Fred have these ridiculous outfits made of burlap and feed bags put together for Lucy and Ethel. The men tell the women that the dresses are designer originals and the women are thrilled. But when Lucy and Ethel find out the truth they are horrified. Then a real Paris designer copies the clothes and suddenly they're really in style. The actual outfits didn't change, just people's view of them.

The difference here is between following a fad and doing the appropriate thing. It may be unfashionable to someone else, but if it's appropriate, don't hesitate to use it. Don't be afraid of a typeface just because *I* tell you it's ugly. It may be ugly to me, it may be ugly to others with my socioeconomic or educational background, but it may be right for you and your audience. You shouldn't care if I like it or not, as long as your readers like it.

So "good taste" or not, you always should select typefaces based on the likes and dislikes of your readers. You may find it helpful to know what is "in" at the moment, what other popular publications are using, to know what will appeal to your audience.

If you're a very secure and independent person, a "trend-setter," you can base your type selection on your own likes and dislikes and hope people catch up to you. People *do* get used to typefaces, even ones they may dislike initially.

You probably have pictures of yourself from not all that long ago wearing clothes and hair styles that would now be considered either embarrassing or just plain silly. Yet at the time, you were in style: "groovy," "hip," "now," and "happening." It's the same with type; just because something's "in" now doesn't mean it's good, and it most certainly doesn't mean it will always be in "good taste." Cooper Black is the typeface equivalent of Woodstock. That doesn't mean you can't use it now, and it doesn't mean that it might not be the perfect typeface for your particular application. It just means it doesn't say "now." Not everything has to look like it came out of a Fortune 500 ad—hip and slick. Nor does it have to be classy, chic, elegant, or sophisticated.

Woodstock

Cooper Black

While many "designers" design for other "designers," *good* designers design for their audience. Don't feel inferior if you don't aspire to pages that look like they came out of trendy magazines such as *Emigré*. You can consider yourself a success if your *readers* are happy with the results.

If your readers want what's trendy that's fine; if they want old-fashioned, cute, casual, funky, bizarre, or even tacky, that's fine, too. Those styles are not *bad*. They're are all valid, if not fashionable, styles. They may not be "in" at the moment, but then, bell-bottoms were once the height of fashion.

The classics, always in style

If you are not sure what your audience likes, or are concerned that your taste isn't "good enough," you should aim for classic design. This means using tried and true serif typefaces such as Baskerville, Bodoni, ITC Cheltenham, ITC Clearface, Dutch, ITC Galliard, ITC Garamond, Goudy Old Style, Zapf Calligraphic, and Zapf Elliptical, along with traditional graphic design.

Remember the Greek motto: everything in moderation, nothing in excess.

Nothing too big, nothing too small, nothing too heavy, nothing too light. This doesn't mean you should aim for mediocrity or the middle of the road; it just means you don't want to do anything too extreme. Nothing too modern, nothing too ancient. Aim for a balance. As in fashion, even the trendiest types (I'm talking people here, not typefaces) respond to the classics.

If you want classic, but you also want to be slightly more modern, you can introduce some sans serif faces into your design. Futura is probably the most classic of all sans serif faces because it was one of the first. It still looks more "modern" than Swiss (Helvetica), which was designed 30 years later. Swiss is classic, but nondescript. Zapf Humanist (Optima) is perhaps the most beautiful and elegant sans serif, as well as one of the easiest to read. Hammersmith (Gill Sans) is classic and distinctive, as are newer faces such as Univers and ITC Avant Garde.

Re: Design

The other advantage of classic design is that it lasts longer. You won't have to redesign as often. Redesigns are drastic, and you've probably seen magazines or newspapers that make a big deal about their "new look." They do that for a couple of reasons. First and foremost, when a publication changes its look, it's shocking to readers. You wonder if the content hasn't changed as well. Then there's also the fear that you might not even notice the redesign, and that next time you go looking for the publication you might not recognize it.

There's nothing wrong with taking the classic tried-and-true route. And don't let anyone tell you that it's boring. Classic design, executed properly, is unobtrusive but not boring.

Subtlety requires sophisticated readers

One thing designers complain about is that desktop publishers aren't subtle enough. "They all use Times Roman and Helvetica." The designers are right in complaining that many people have settled for the most convenient faces without exploring the possibilities of more varied typefaces, but they are wrong about subtlety.

The unsophisticated observer can't consciously tell the difference between Times Roman and Garamond. Even the sophisticated reader who gets a dozen different high-style magazines a month may not notice the difference. What they *do* notice are the more dramatic typefaces. They feel that Bodoni is more elegant than Times. Why? Not because there's a typeface gene that tells them this, but because they've seen enough elegant magazines set in Bodoni to associate it with high style.

Don't believe designers who tell you that using Cheltenham instead of Clearface is going to make all the difference in the world. It's not. Even other designers may fail to notice the difference. But using Galliard instead of Swiss *is* going to make a difference to even the most naive reader, because the two faces are so clearly different.

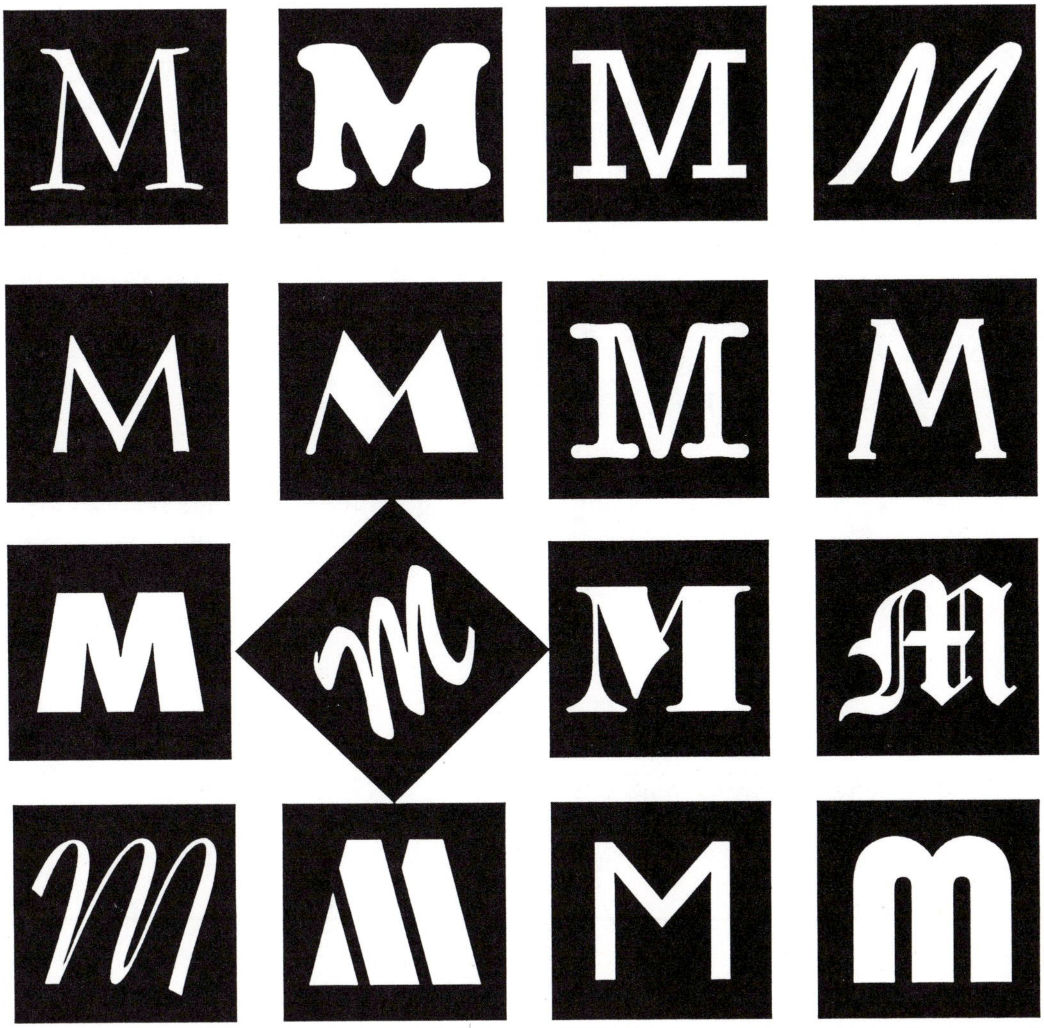

Getting a second opinion

How do you find out what typefaces your readers respond to? Do some research. Look at magazines, newsletters, and publications aimed at a similar audience. See what typefaces they use, what typefaces they don't use.

And don't be afraid to ask. If you have several typefaces available, print sample pages in all of them. Most DTP programs use style sheets that allow you to change the typeface of your entire document quickly. As long as you don't use a zillion different styles it's easy to change all the typefaces in your chapter. You can print the same page, set in Dutch, ITC Garamond Condensed, Bitstream Charter, or Zapf Elliptical, and they will create very different impressions.

Show the different pages to other people and ask which they like best. If you hand the pages to them one at a time, without letting them see them side by side, they may not notice any difference. Then again, they may prefer one in particular without knowing why. If you let them compare, side-by-side, they may notice the typeface— then again, they may not. Don't explain the differences. Find out which one people *like* best—not which ones they think other people will like, but which ones they personally prefer.

Choose a face and stick with it

Once you decide on a typeface (or typeface*s*), stick with it (or them). It's not a good idea to change typefaces from issue to issue, letter to letter, flyer to flyer, or menu to menu, unless you are doing a complete redesign.

Whatever you do, *look* at typefaces. Find one or more you like and want to use regularly. I can't stress enough how big a difference a typeface can make.

Charting the right course

The chart on the opposite page will give you an idea of fonts to use for specific applications.

Suggested Usage Chart

① = All Point Sizes

❷ = 14-point & Up

	Signage	Presentation Materials	Office Correspondence	Catalogs	Books	Flyers/Advertisements	Financial Reports	Proposals	Invitations	Instruction Manuals	Newsletters	Labels	Forms	Product Spec Sheets	Directories	
Activa *(Trump Medieval)*	②	②		❶	②	❶	②	❶	②		❶			❶		Activa *(Trump Medieval)*
ITC American Typewriter	②					❶				②	❶			②		ITC American Typewriter
Bitstream Amergio	②	②	❶	❶	②	❶		❶		❶	❶			❶		Bitstream Amergio
ITC Avant Garde Gothic	②	❶		❶	②	❶			②		②	❶				ITC Avant Garde Gothic
Baskerville	②		❶	❶	❶	❶	❶	❶	❶	❶	❶			❶		Baskerville
ITC Benguiat				②	②	❶			②		②			②		ITC Benguiat
Bernhard Modern	②			❶	②	❶			❶		②			②		Bernhard Modern
Bodoni	②	②	❶	❶	❶	❶	❶	❶	❶		❶			❶		Bodoni
ITC Bookman				❶		❶		❶			❶					ITC Bookman
Century Schoolbook	②		❶		❶		❶	❶		❶	❶			❶		Century Schoolbook
Bitstream Charter	②		❶	❶	❶		❶	❶		❶	❶		❶	❶	❶	Bitstream Charter
ITC Cheltenham	②		❶	❶	❶	❶	❶	❶		❶	❶			❶		ITC Cheltenham
ITC Clearface				❶			❶	❶			❶			❶		ITC Clearface
Bitstream Cooper	②	❶		❶		❶			❶		❶			❶		Bitstream Cooper
Dutch (Times)		❶			❶		❶			❶		❶	❶	❶	❶	Dutch *(Times)*
Franklin Gothic	②	②			②	②		②		②	②	❶	❶	②		Franklin Gothic
Futura Light/Black	②	❶	❶	❶	②	❶	②	②		②	❶	❶	❶	❶	❶	Futura Light/Black
Futura Book/Heavy	②	❶		❶	②	❶	②	②		②	❶	❶	❶	❶		Futura Book/Heavy
Futura Medium/Bold	②	②		②	②	②	②	②		②	②			②		Futura Medium/Bold
ITC Galliard	②	❶		❶	❶	❶	❶	❶	❶	②	❶			❶		ITC Galliard
ITC Garamond	②	❶	❶	❶		❶	❶	❶		❶	❶			❶		ITC Garamond
ITC Garamond Condensed	②	❶		❶		❶	❶						❶	❶	❶	ITC Garamond Condensed
Goudy Old Style	②			❶	❶	❶	❶		❶		❶			❶		Goudy Old Style
Hammersmith *(Gill Sans)*	②	❶	❶	❶	②	❶	②	②		❶	❶		❶	❶	❶	Hammersmith *(Gill Sans)*
ITC Korinna	②			❶	②	❶		❶			❶			②		ITC Korinna
ITC Lubalin Graph	②	❶		②	②	②		②		②	②	❶		②		ITC Lubalin Graph
News Gothic		②		②			②			②	②		❶	②		News Gothic
Provence *(Antique Olive)*		②		②	②	②		②		②	②	❶		❶		Provence *(Antique Olive)*
Serifa	②	❶	❶		②	❶	②	②		❶	②		❶	❶	❶	Serifa
Slate		②				②				②	②			②		Slate
ITC Souvenir	②		❶	❶	❶	❶		❶		❶	❶			❶		ITC Souvenir
Swiss *(Helvetica)*	②	❶								②		❶	❶	❶		Swiss *(Helvetica)*
Swiss Condensed	②	❶		❶		❶	②	②		②	②	❶	❶	❶	❶	Swiss Condensed
Swiss Light/Black	②	❶		②	②	❶	②	②		❶	②		❶	❶	❶	Swiss Light/Black
ITC Tiffany	②	②		❶	②	❶			❶		②					ITC Tiffany
Zapf Calligraphic *(Palatino)*	②		❶	❶	❶	❶		❶	❶	❶	❶			❶		Zapf Calligraphic *(Palatino)*
Zapf Elliptical *(Melior)*	②	❶	❶	❶	❶		❶	❶		❶	❶	❶	❶	❶	❶	Zapf Elliptical *(Melior)*
Zapf Humanist *(Optima)*	②	❶		❶	❶	❶	②	②	❶	❶	❶		❶	❶	❶	Zapf Humanist *(Optima)*
Zurich *(Univers)*	②	❶		❶			②	②		②	②	❶	❶	❶	❶	Zurich *(Univers)*
Zurich Condensed	②	❶		❶		❶	②	②		②	②	❶		❶	❶	Zurich Condensed
Zurich Light	②	❶		②	②	❶	②	②		❶	②		❶	❶	❶	Zurich Light

7

Matchmaking

Choosing fonts that work together.
Will it be a match made in heaven?

When faced with a huge list of fonts from which to choose, the real question is, "Which ones are going to look good together?"

Matchmaking

Choosing fonts that work together. Will it be a match made in heaven or end in divorce?

When faced with a huge list of fonts from which to choose, the real question is, "Which ones are going to look good together?" Just as you wouldn't want to be seen wearing stripes, plaids, and polka dots at the same time (unless you're Madonna), you wouldn't want to use certain typefaces together either.

Unless you're a pro, you will usually need just two different typeface families per document: one serif and one sans serif. Add more and you could be inviting visual complications—many of which cause publications to die a premature death.

Because typefaces have personality, you have to match them up in much the same way you'd match up people. Just as in the real world, if the typefaces have nothing in common, they're going to clash. If they are too much alike they may hate each other. They need to be complimentary, with one accomplishing something the other can't. And now, for your dining and dancing pleasure, a few brief design guidelines for choosing and using type.

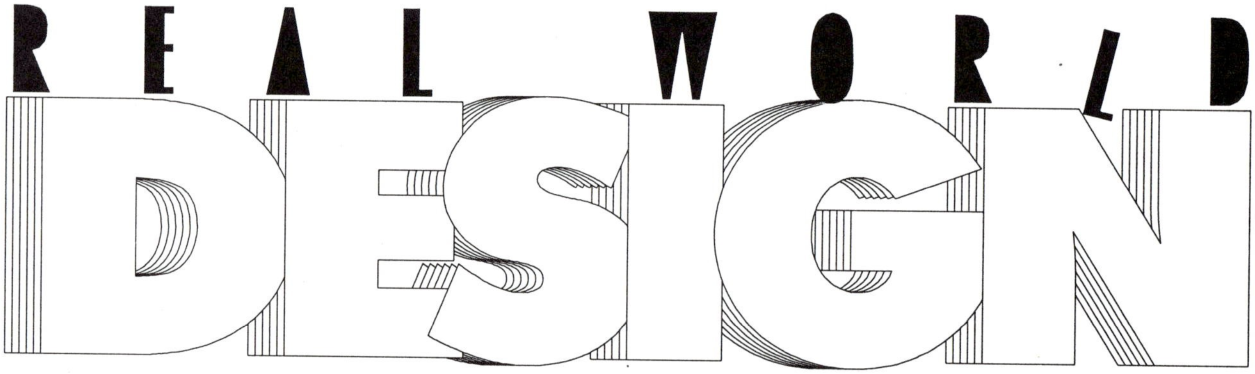

Futura Condensed and Futura Extra Black.

I. Serifs work with sans serifs

Mix and match

If you are going to mix, the most basic rule is that most serif typefaces work with most sans serif typefaces and vice versa.

But it can be dangerous to mix two serifs or two sans serifs. Here's an example. Dutch (Times Roman) and Swiss (Helvetica) are the most obvious serif and sans serif typefaces that work well together. But you wouldn't want to mix two serifs such as Dutch, for body text, and Zapf Calligraphic (Palatino), for headings. They share too many characteristics and instead of creating a contrast, they make a page look disorderly, as if you ran out of Dutch mid-project and had to use the next best thing.

Another example is mixing Swiss text with Avant Garde headings. Yuk. There's no contrast, and the results just look random. That's almost certainly not the look you want, so beware of it.

Also, and this is important, don't mix body typefaces. Don't use Baskerville for one article and Swiss for another. This doesn't apply to sidebars or a special piece of text, such as an "Inside" box. In general, though, it's important to be consistent in your use of a body face.

II. Never mix, never worry

If you hate matchmaking, or if people criticize you for wearing socks that don't match, this is the credo for you. If you can't decide what goes together, use a single typeface for the whole job. While this usually isn't as visually exciting as having contrasting typefaces, it's simple, it's safe, and it's economical.

For example, if you set the text of a magazine in Baskerville, you could also set the headlines in Baskerville. In small sizes it's easy to read; in large sizes it still relates to the body text, but its design details give it additional interest.

Often one family encompasses a wide range of "styles." Sans serif faces have bigger families than serif faces, so it's easier to mix within the family. Futura ranges from very light to extra-black, and all work well together. Zurich (Univers) is the same.

If you are going to stay within a single typeface family, avoid using pairs of styles that are too close in weight. In the ITC Garamond family, there is not enough contrast between the Book and Bold weights to combine them on a page. A better choice would be to use light and bold together, and book with ultra.

III. Use what's available

If you only use one typeface, take advantage of all its weights and styles (italics, bold, condensed, and expanded). You don't want to overuse variety, but you also don't want to set everything in roman. You'll use roman (medium, book, whatever) for the body text, so use bold or bold italics for headlines, bolds or italics for subheads, and italics for captions. If you don't, the texture may look sparse, gray, or just plain boring.

IV. Contrast is the key

Over 2,000 years ago the Greeks figured out the key to all drama—contrast, conflict, and tension. And that's also the key to a harmonious, commanding page. The contrast on a page is created by mixing typefaces or styles or sizes that are different enough from each other that the eye doesn't get bored. Commanding doesn't mean that your page should look like the cover of the *National Enquirer.* It just means that it should attract the reader's attention and keep it.

Of course, there's always the matter of appropriateness. If you're using an "elegant" typeface for body text, such as Goudy Old Style or ITC Galliard, you don't want something too high-tech or spare as a contrast, or it makes the elegant body face look out of place. In this case, other bad choices for headings would be Cooper, because it's decidedly informal, or Zapf Calligraphic, because it's another elegant serif that would not provide contrast. While Swiss would be tolerable, it's still uncomplimentary. A good choice would be Hammersmith (Gill Sans) or Futura, two more elegant and highly styled sans serif faces.

V. Moderation

Of course, you want to keep conflict and tension subtle, so they add interest to the page without making one element fight with another. Those clever ancient Greeks had another saying: "Everything in moderation, nothing to excess." In most cases, avoid the extremes in type mixing. You don't want to mix type that's *very* thick with type that's *very* thin.

If you use very light body text, then very dark headings would make it difficult to read the body text—your eye would keep jumping back to those dark headlines.

VI. Something in common

Even in contrast it's good to have some traits in common. Think simpatico. This may seem like a contradiction, but it's not. If the typefaces you choose are too different, too uncomplimentary, they will fight with each other for attention, and while one of them might win, your publication will lose.

In my previous book I used Goudy Old Style for the body text, and Hammersmith for the headings and subheadings. While these faces are a good contrast to each other, they also share some small, uncommon design features that make them look as if they go together. Most importantly, they're both "warm."

Compared with Dutch, Goudy is more elegant, but also more personal, and doesn't seem to convey just "the cold hard facts." Dutch can be somewhat impersonal, simply because, like Swiss, it is efficient but doesn't have a whole lot of personality. Hammersmith is certainly warmer than Swiss, partly because it is less severe. Sure, if your chosen body text is cold, you can warm up a page with your choice for a second typeface, but you don't want the two typefaces to suggest totally different messages.

VII. It's all subjective

But don't take my word for it; it's all subjective. Type is just like any other artistic pursuit: what's beautiful to one person may be nauseating to another. You have to be the judge. Not all experts agree, and you won't always agree with them. If you really like what you've come up with, even if other people turn green and look seasick, do it. Of course, if the seasick person is your boss, then you will probably be forced to think again. These are just suggestions for generally accepted norms of good typography.

If you want to use Zurich and Futura Extra Black together, there *are* publications that do. That doesn't mean it looks good; it doesn't make it right; it just makes it a possibility. The point is to have a good reason for what you do. If you're doing it just to be different, that may not be a good reason, but it is a reason.

VIII. The easy way out

If you still can't decide, buy a pre-packaged collection. Bitstream (and other type companies) offer collections of fonts, preassembled. It's like a ready-to-wear sportswear collection: you know all the pieces will work together. Here are some suggestions.

Spreadsheets: Zapf Elliptical (Melior), Monospaced, Zurich. Zapf Elliptical is elegant and business-like, Zurich is clean and modern, but not as overused as Swiss. Monospaced can be used for printing spreadsheets from programs that don't print well using proportional type, or when the spreadsheet is formatted using spaces instead of tabs. However, proportionally spaced fonts are always easier to read, even in columns of numbers.

Books & Manuals: Baskerville, Goudy Old Style, Zapf Calligraphic. Aha, you say, but these are all serif faces and they don't mix well together. And you're right. But these are three of the most popular and most versatile typefaces. They're excellent for body copy, and beautiful for headlines. They each have enough variety of weights and styles that they can stand on their own.

Reports & Proposals: Activa (Trump Mediæval), Bitstream Amerigo, Zapf Humanist (Optima). All three of these can be used for body text, and all three look smashing in large sizes. Zapf Humanist works with well with Activa, but is probably a little too similar to Amerigo to use them together.

Newsletters: Bitstream Charter, Headlines 1, Swiss Light. Charter is a hard-working body text face that never looks fussy, yet its Black and Black italic weights are wonderful in large sizes—very masculine-looking. Headlines 1 is a multifaceted package that contains Cooper Black, Cloister Black, University Roman, and Broadway. Broadway is art deco, stylish, and attention getting. University is Roaring Twenties, lighthearted, and yet not so silly that it can't be used for a charming wedding invitation. Cloister Black is the olde English style type, popular for newspaper names, certificates, or formal old-fashioned weddings. Cooper Black is big, round, cuddly, and impossible to miss. Swiss Light/Black rounds out the package with a sober sans serif style.

Flyers: Futura Light/Extra Black, Headlines 2, Headlines 4. Futura light is a wonderful sans serif. Its rounded geometry makes flyers look modern, not dull, as Helvetica (Swiss) could. Futura Extra Black is an indispensable typeface—very dark, yet clean and uncluttered. If you look at advertisements you'll see it used frequently. Also part of the package is Futura Medium Condensed, a space-saving face, great for working in tight places.

Presentations: Slate, Swiss Condensed, Headlines 5. Slate is a heavy, sturdy typeface that is graphic in large sizes. Swiss Condensed is an all-around useful typeface. It isn't monotonous like normal Helvetica, and it allows you to maneuver in crowded spots. Headlines 5 includes Park Avenue (about which I have nothing nice to say); Handel Gothic, a futuristic-looking sans serif; Futura Black, a wild stencil-like face; and Dom Casual, which has the feel of script hand-written with a brush or felt pen.

IX. Use this handy-dandy chart

Use the *Will-Harris Font-o-Matic* chart to see which typefaces work well with each other. Some typefaces mix beautifully (indicated by a circle), some should be handled with care (indicated by a triangle), and some don't work together at all (left blank). Specific faces have been chosen because of their availability for laser printers, and because of space considerations.

The *Font-o-Matic* was inspired by a chart created by ITC Vice President, Alan Haley, in his excellent book, *Phototypesetting* (although many of our recommendations differ). A chart containing every available face would not fit on the pages of this book, but the *Font-o-Matic* offers a wide enough range to give a good indication of what faces I feel mix well with others. While this chart is based on my experience with type, your actual mileage may vary.

X. Play with numbers

Always have at least ten points on any numbered list.

Will-Harris Font-o-matic

● Yes
▲ Maybe

	Activa	Bitstream Amerigo	ITC Avant Garde	Baskerville	ITC Benguiat	Bernhard Modern	Bodoni	ITC Bookman	Century Schbk	Bitstream Charter	ITC Cheltenham	ITC Clearface	Bitstream Cooper	Dutch	Franklin Gothic	Futura	ITC Galliard	ITC Garamond	Goudy Old Style	Hammersmith	ITC Korinna	Provence	ITC Souvenir	Swiss	ITC Tiffany	Zapf Calligraphic	Zapf Elliptical	Zapf Humanist	Zurich
Activa	●		●		▲								●		●	●				●		●		●				●	●
Bitstream Amerigo		●	●				●							▲	●	●	●	▲		●		▲		●				▲	●
ITC Avant Garde	●	●	●	●	●	●	●	●	●	●	●	●	●	●			▲	●	●		●		●		●	●	▲		
Baskerville			●	●		▲		▲							●	●				●		●		●				●	●
ITC Benguiat	▲		●		●					▲				▲	●	●				●	▲			●				▲	●
Bernhard Modern			●			●									●	●				●				▲				▲	●
Bodoni		●	●				●								●	●				●		▲		●				●	●
ITC Bookman			●	▲				●							●	●				●		●		●				▲	●
Century Schoolbk			●						●						●	●				●		●		●				●	●
Bitstream Charter			●							●					●	●				●		●		●				▲	●
ITC Cheltenham			●								●				●	●				●		●		●				▲	●
ITC Clearface			●									●			●	●				●		●		●				▲	●
Bitstream Cooper	●	▲	●										●	▲	●	●				●		●		●				●	●
Dutch		▲	●		▲								▲	●	●	●				●		●		●				●	●
Franklin Gothic	●	●		●	●	●	●	●	●	●	●	●	●	●	●		●	●	●		●		●		▲	▲	●		
Futura	●	●		●	●	●	●	●	●	●	●	●	●	●		●	●	●			▲		●			▲	▲		
ITC Galliard		●	▲												●	●	●			●		▲		●				●	●
ITC Garamond		▲	●			▲									●	●		●		●		●		●				●	●
Goudy Old Style			●			▲									●	●			●	●		●		▲				●	▲
Hammersmith	●	●		●	●	●	●	●	●	●	●	●	●	●			●	●	●	●	●		●			●	▲		
ITC Korinnna			●												●	▲				●	●	▲		●				▲	●
Provence	●	▲		●			▲	●	●	●	●	●	●	●			▲	●	●		▲	●	●		▲	▲	●		
ITC Souvenir			●												●	●				●		●	●	●			▲	▲	●
Swiss	●	●		●	●	▲	●	●	●	●	●	●	●	●			●	●	▲		●		●	●	●	▲	●		
ITC Tiffany			●												▲					●		▲		●	●			▲	●
Zapf Calligraphic			●												▲	▲				●		▲		▲		●		●	●
Zapf Elliptical			▲												●	▲		●		▲		●	▲	●			●	●	●
Zapf Humanist	●	▲		●	▲	▲	●	▲	●	▲	▲	▲	●	●			●	●	●		▲				▲	●	●	●	
Zurich	●	●		●	●	●	●	●	●	●	●	●	●	●			●	●	▲		●		●		●	●	●		●

8

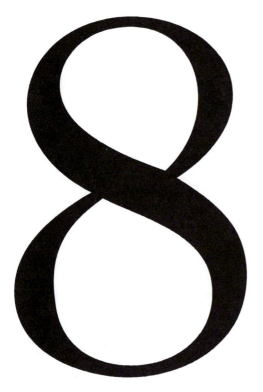

Basic training

If you don't have time to read anything else, read this

Whenever I start learning about a new field, I always wish the experts just would come right out and tell me its real secrets. Well, here they are.

Basic training

If you don't have time to read anything else, read this

Whenever I start learning about a new field, I always wish the experts just would come right out and tell me its real secrets. You know what I mean—the stuff you always seem to hit upon by accident after years of hard work. But no, they just want to assail me with all these do's and don'ts.

And the joke is, in many cases those do's and don'ts *are* the real secrets. They're the stuff people spend years learning. They're the stuff that *works.*

So if you read this chapter, you will save years of work, and you can spend all those saved years shopping, fishing, doing volunteer work, or whatever you really want to do.

The rules that follow are all based on common sense—and years of experience.

Sure, you can break any of these rules if you have a good reason to do so, but you shouldn't break them until you've given them a try. Once you have tried them, they'll start to make sense, and once they make sense, you won't feel so inclined to break them just for the heck of it.

But if you follow the rules and something just doesn't *look* right, bend the rule. It's more important that your type looks right than that it be technically correct.

So here are the rules. Just as it's easier to see that world is round by viewing it from space, as opposed to viewing it from inside a dense forest, this overview will likewise help you see the most important points all in one place. Remember:

Type should enhance a message, not merely carry it, and never obscure or overshadow it.

Body text

The root of all typography

Headlines attract attention, but the meat (or, if you're a vegetarian, the germ) of most messages is contained in the body text. Body text is really quite small, with each letter of normal body text being about one-third the size of the average ladybug. And yet, these tiny little letters can contain all the knowledge of humankind—thoughts, feelings, hopes, fears, warnings, discoveries, dreams.

Alignment

To traditional typesetters, alignment refers to the position of a character on a baseline. When used as a desktop publishing term, alignment refers to the ends of lines of type, such as flush right, flush left, justified, or centered.

Right Justified (also called "Full" or just plain "Justified") is more formal than unjustified text, and it fits more into less space. That's right—justified columns can hold more text. If not done carefully (with hyphenation), justified columns can be difficult to read because words or letters have extra space between them to fill out the line.

Flush Left (also called ragged right or unjustified) is less formal and easier to read, but uses more space. Unjustified type is becoming increasingly more accepted for all applications.

Centered type is only for short blocks of text in special uses
such as invitations or advertisements.

Flush Right (also called ragged left or right aligned) text is also only
appropriate for special occasions, such as continued lines,
captions, or a name at the end of a letter to the editor.

Do not set long blocks of text centered or flush right—it's much harder to read because it's difficult to find the beginning of each line. More importantly, too much type set flush right just plain looks strange.

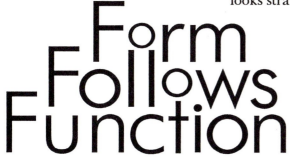

Form
Follows
Function

Aligned with spaces

Travel	999.94	22.45	333.19
Tips	27.88	19.00	45.00
Car	400.15	125.00	650.00

Aligned with tabs

Travel	999.94	22.45	333.19
Tips	27.88	19.00	45.00
Car	400.15	125.00	650.00

Zurich Light

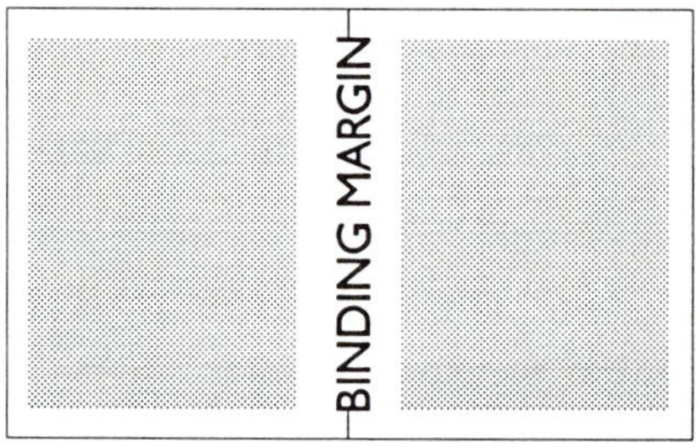

Aligning columns of numbers

Never use the space bar to align columns of numbers. Use *tabs* instead. When you use spaces, everything may appear to line up on-screen but it may not line up when printed.

Binding margins

The center of the book or magazine where the binding is located is called the "gutter." The way your project is bound will dictate how much room you need to leave there. Make sure to leave enough margin for the binding, or the type could get lost in the gutter. Gutters can also refer to the blank space between columns.

Block-style paragraphs

Block-style paragraphs don't begin with an indent, they simply have a blank space between paragraphs. These generally are easier to read, because the eye always starts along the left edge rather than having to scoot in at the start of each paragraph. They also look cleaner and add white space to the page.

No style, inexcusably bad

Always make sure there is blank space between block style paragraphs.
Never set paragraphs without either space between them (block style) or an indent at the start, or they will all look like one long paragraph.
This is one rule where there is no good reason to break it. Breaking this rule is a mortal sin and you don't want to know what will happen to you if you break it. Really.

Block-style, good

Always make sure there is blank space between block style paragraphs.

Never set paragraphs without either space between them (block style) or an indent at the start, or they will all look like one long paragraph.

This is one rule where there is *no* good reason to break it. Breaking this rule is a mortal sin and you don't want to know what will happen to you if you break it.

Indent style, good

  Always make sure there is blank space between block style paragraphs.
  Never set paragraphs without either space between them (block style) or an indent at the start, or they will all look like one long paragraph.
  This is one rule where there is *no* good reason to break it. Breaking this rule is a mortal sin and you don't want to know what will happen to you if you break it.

Bitstream Charter

While it seems natural to put an extra return between paragraphs by pressing the enter key, it's a better idea to allow your software to do the inter-paragraph spacing. If you press the enter key you are locked into your normal line spacing, whereas if your software does it you will have complete control over how much space you leave between paragraphs.

Boxed text

Make sure to leave a border of white space inside and outside of boxes. Don't let the text touch the border of the box. Text should never touch lines: it's ugly, it's disgusting, and it could lead to the downfall of civilization as we know it.

Bad

This box has no border of white space inside it.

Good

Make sure to leave a border of white space inside and outside.

Bullets

ITC Zapf Dingbats as bullets.

- Bullets normally are either flush left or indented slightly from the left margin. The text that follows should be indented further past the bullet.

Capitals

Don't set too much type in all capital letters. Whole sentences or paragraphs in all caps are especially difficult to read.

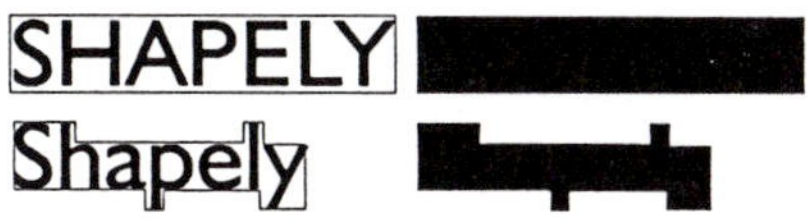

People recognize words by shapes as well as the letters themselves. Words made up of upper- and lowercase letters have distinctive shapes, but words set entirely in caps all have the same rectangular shape.

If you are so insecure about your copy that you feel the need to set it in all caps or all italics, then you may lack self-confidence. Just by setting type properly you can save on those expensive psychiatrist bills.

Never, *ever* use all caps if you are using a display face that has ornate capital letters, such as ITC Zapf Chancery, or script faces such as Brush Script, Coronet, Park Avenue, or Kaufmann. That is the sign of a rank amateur.

If the caption is below—it can be left, right, or centered, in two or more columns.

If the caption is on the right—use a flush right setting so that the straight edge aligns with the picture.

If the caption is on the left—use a flush right setting so that the straight edge aligns with the picture.

Captions

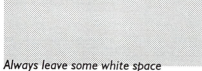

Always leave some white space between the picture and the caption.

Captions under pictures and other artwork usually should be a different font than your body text. Set them in italic or bold, or in the same typeface you're using for subheads and headlines.

Captions are one of the few places where italics are accepted for complete sentences or paragraphs—but you still need to take care. If your italics are too ornate then use your headline/subhead typeface instead.

Colored or patterned backgrounds

If you place text on a gray, colored, or patterned background, make sure it can be read easily. Making the type larger or darker will make it easier to read on a background. Common sense (and your vision) tells you that black text will be difficult to read on a dark gray background. If you use a dark background, then you may have to reverse the text, making it white so it stands out better.

Background too dark
Text too light

Background OK
Text could be darker

Background OK
Text OK

Colored backgrounds also can make type harder to read. Studies have shown that black text on a white background is up to 40% easier to read than white text on a black background.

Black type on a yellow background is much easier to read than black type on a red background or red type on a black background.

Remember, while these colorful backgrounds attract attention, you don't want them to compete with your message and make it harder to read.

Columns

Columns help you to organize your text, and keep lines from getting too long. On a standard 8½- by 11-inch page, the lines of text in one wide column are too long for comfortable reading. You can easily use two or three columns on a standard-size page. More than that may result in columns that are too narrow. Not all columns have to contain body text. Some can be reserved for white space or pull quotes.

This book may *look* like a one-column format, but it's really two. The left is used only for headings, illustrations, and white space. The right contains the body text.

Columns, space between

Make sure to leave enough white space between columns for the gutter. About .25 to .33 inch is the average size gutter for two- and three-column pages. The more space you leave, the more separation you create. If you leave too much, each column looks like a separate entity. (See also *Line length.*)

Consistency

Yes, foolish consistency is the hobgoblin of little minds, but when it comes to working with type, consistency isn't foolish—it works. Be consistent about the paragraph style, indents, margins, the amount of white space you use between paragraphs and above and below headlines and subheads.

Copy fitting

One of the most challenging tasks is always one of the most basic—getting the text to fit in the space available. It's not as easy as it sounds.

The most basic way to solve the problem is to shorten the text, by editing, if it's too long, or adding text if it's too short. But there are other, less drastic and more creative ways. Also, the person who sets the text may not have the authority to make editorial changes.

▪ **If it's too long**

Adjust Type Size: Most DTP programs that use "scalable" type can adjust type sizes in tiny increments, often as small as a tenth of a point. If you are creating an eight-page newsletter and you have 8½ pages of text, making the body text only ½ point smaller could make the text fit without creating a noticeable difference. This is fast and easy to do with desktop publishing programs, but use this tip with care. Don't change just a single page or article on the page, because then it will call attention to itself (it will wear tacky clothes and scream "Yoo hoo" at total strangers, causing no end of embarrassment).

Adjust Margins: You don't want to break the "rule of thumb" for margins, or get too close to your binding margins, but sometimes even a tenth of an inch difference can make your text fit better.

Adjust Leading: *Never* make your leading too small. But if you were using leading more than two points larger than the type size, you have some room to make the leading smaller.

▪ **If it's too short**

Add Subheads: Not only is this a good way to make your text longer, it makes the text easier to read and keeps pages from looking gray.

Adjust Type Size: Even a mere half-point increase in type size can make a substantial difference. On a standard size page try not to go over 12-point for normal body text or it can begin to look odd.

Adjust Leading: While two points extra leading is standard, you can use more if you want. Up to four points is OK; after that it starts to become noticeable.

One more point: Make sure to apply these adjustment to *all* your text, leading, and margins. Be consistent. You don't want the reader to notice the adjustments you've made.

Dashes

Most fonts include three lengths of dashes:

A hyphen (-) for connecting words or hyphenating the end of a line;

An em dash (—), so called because it's the width of the letter "m". This is what is typed on a typewriter as two hyphens in a row (- -). It's a form of punctuation that is good for indicating a pause because it's more visible than a comma—but don't overdo it;

An en dash (–), the width of the letter "n."

Sometimes in larger display text you might want to substitute an en dash for an em dash so it doesn't leave such a big gap.

Never use two hyphens in a row (- -) when you should use a real dash (—). Many programs will automatically convert two hyphens. Check and see if the one you use will.

Shortcuts:

- **Ventura Publisher**

To create an em dash (—), hold down **Ctrl** and press **]**
or place <197> in the text file

To create an en dash (–), hold down **Ctrl** and press **[**
or place <196> in the text file

- **PageMaker PC**

To create an em dash (—), hold down **Ctrl** and **Shift** and press **=**

To create an en dash (–), hold down **Ctrl** and press **=**

- **Mac**

To create an em dash (—), hold down **Option** and **Shift** and **-**

To create an en dash (–), hold down **Option** and **-**

Drop caps

Drop caps are an excellent way to start an article or chapter because they attract attention and add graphic interest to the page. But don't overuse drop caps. The bottom of the drop cap shouldn't "float" between the lines of the paragraph but should sit on the same baseline as one of the lines of text. Because drop caps are usually large (at least 24-point, but 72-point is not out of the question) you should use a typeface which is graphically interesting, not just big.

This is a called a *drop cap* because the first letter drops into the body of the paragraph.

This is called a *raised cap* because the first letter is raised above the body of the paragraph.

Zapf Calligraphic (Palatino)

Ellipsis...

Three little dots, which indicate that something has been removed. Perfect for when you want to quote someone but remove the bad parts. They're supposed to have a thin space between them, like. . . rather than ...

Some programs can access a true ellipsis character …

- **Ventura PC**

Hold down **Alt** and type **193** on the keypad (cursor pad), or place three consecutive periods in the text file.

- **WordPerfect**

Hold down **Ctrl** and press **V** then type **4,56**

- **Mac**

Hold down **Option** and press **;**

Fiction

One type of book that does not need subheads or substantial white space is a work of fiction, such as a novel or short story. These books flow naturally from page to page, with chapter titles being the only regular breaks. But because they have no breaks, special care must be taken with the margins, typeface, type size, leading, headers, footers, and page numbers.

Fine print

If you need to set any fine print (6 point) then it's a good idea to choose a typeface with a large x-height. This is so that the "counters" (the closed areas, such as the inside of an "e") won't clog with ink.

Fractions

A 1/2 is not a real typographical fraction as ½ is. Some software will automatically create fractions for you. If yours doesn't, you need to superscript the first number, use a real "bar" instead of a slash (if you have one) and then subscript the last number.

Shortcuts:

- **Ventura**

Hold down **Ctrl** and press **C**, then select Fraction or Equation from the menu, then enter the fraction normally; i.e., type **1 / 2** then hold down **Ctrl** and press **D** to save.

Or, place <$E*> in the text file, replacing the * with the fraction. Example: <$E½ >

- **PageMaker**

For ½, hold down the **Alt** key and type **189** on the keypad

For ¼, hold down the **Alt** key and type **188** on the keypad

For ¾, hold down the **Alt** key and type **190** on the keypad

- **WordPerfect**

For ½, hold down **Ctrl** and press **V**, then type **/2** and press **Enter**

For ¼, hold down **Ctrl** and press **V**, then type **/4** and press **Enter**

Gray pages

Gray pages full of nothing but body text are like unending days of gray skies to most people—depressing. If you don't add a little sunshine to your text with elements such as drop caps, subheads, or pull quotes, your readers will read some sunny travel brochures about Florida instead.

This doesn't mean you can't have text-only pages now and then. It just means that there are plenty of ways to add interest to a page, which will entice your readers to keep reading once they've begun.

An old adage says if you put a dollar bill on a page it should touch a heading, subhead, or substantial white space, otherwise your page is probably too gray. (This does not apply to novels or other fiction books that are all text—see *Fiction*.)

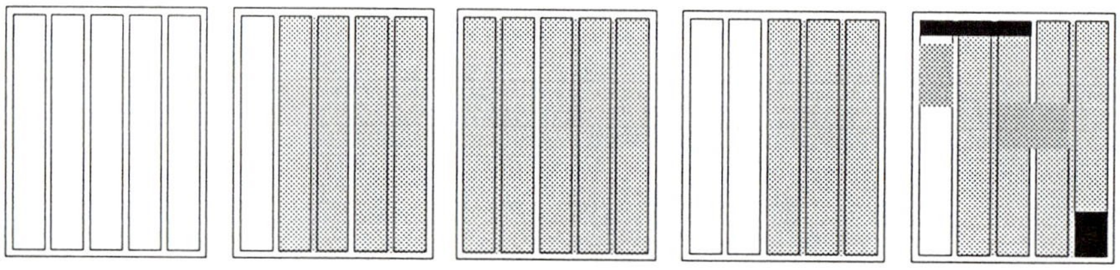

Grid

A grid is simply a basic unit of measurement that helps a publication maintain consistency. If you choose a six-column grid, it doesn't mean you must have six columns of text (which would be too narrow on an 8½ by 11inch page). It means that the width of each of those narrow columns is your main unit of measurement. Then you can combine two or more columns so that they are not so narrow, and use a single narrow column or two for white space. You also can use the width of a single column for vertical measurement as well, to give an overall uniform look.

While grids can get complicated and esoteric, the best grids are simple and obvious, so that both the designer and the reader benefit from their clear organization.

You don't have to be a slave to the grid. Use it as a point of reference but don't feel guilty if you have to bend it to suit your material.

Hyphenation

No Hyphenation
Always hyphenate if you justify. Otherwise you can be left with enormous gaping rivers of white space. It's difficult to read a n d ugly—simultaneously.

Hyphenated
Always hyphenate if you justify. Otherwise you can be left with enormous gaping riv-ers of white space. It's difficult to read and ugly—simultaneously.

Goudy Old Style.

I don't like to see text with more than two successive lines in a row hyphenated. Some software programs allow you to regulate the number of successive hyphens. If your software gives you this option, use it. Always hyphenate if you justify. Hyphenation can also make unjustified paragraphs look neat and allow you to fit more text on a page. People with last names like Will-Harris are very sensitive about being called a "hyphenate."

Indent style paragraphs

The accepted size of a paragraph indent is one em. That means if your body type is 12-point, you indent the first line 12 points or about .17 inches, or the width of two spaces (but don't use spaces, use tabs). If your software doesn't allow you to enter measurements in points (and most of them do if you know how), then approximate. Some programs allow you to set the indent through a style sheet.

The depth of the indent is relative to the width of the column. You can use a larger indent for effect, but a smaller one will look like a mistake. Don't use deep indents on narrow columns. If you are setting short paragraphs, don't use an indent because it's too distracting. It's traditional to skip the indent on the first paragraph of an article, story, or chapter.

Always indent using tabs (or by setting your software's style sheet). *Never, ever, ever* indent using spaces.

Italics

What should be italicized in body text? Titles of books, movies, magazines, plays, artwork, etc., can be italicized. I feel *strongly* that italics should be used for emphasis. Italics are also important for inflection. Just as you *subtly* emphasize certain words when you talk, italics help the reader to read the word to themselves the same way they would understand them if you *read* the text to them. The *trick* is not to *overdo* italics, *otherwise* they *lose* their *meaning* as *well* as *making* the text *tedious* and *slow* to *read*.

Because italics tend to be more ornate than roman styles, they can be more difficult to read, so don't use them for long blocks of text.

Justification

(See *Alignment*). If you justify you *must* hyphenate. Even the best computerized hyphenation sometimes needs manual help. If you see a big gap in a justified line, or a big space at the end of an unjustified line, see if you can hyphenate a word manually.

Don't justify if your lines are short, or your type is big.

Kerning

AWARE Unkerned
AWARE Kerned

ITC Avant Garde

Kerning moves pairs of letters closer together or further apart to make them look more evenly spaced. Most modern software has automatic kerning, and usually that's sufficient for body text. Bitstream provides more kerning pairs than most font companies, which means finer quality typesetting. If you've got automatic kerning, use it. Manual kerning is seldom necessary for body text.

Leading

Leading should always be one to two points larger than the type size, or about 20% larger. This means that with 10-point body text, you need about 12 points of leading (also written as 10/12 and called "10 on 12"). At the very least, add one point extra leading, such as 10/11 (10 on 11). You can make type smaller, but never skimp on the leading. If you don't use enough leading your readers will make you feel guilty about it.

Be consistent with the leading. All your body copy should have the same amount of leading. Don't add extra leading just to fill out a page.

Some programs will add extra leading if you do something as simple as making the first letter of the paragraph large for a raised cap. If that happens, make sure you set the leading (sometimes erroneously called "line spacing" or "line height") to fixed or manual, rather than automatic.

10/9
At the very least, add 1 point extra leading, such as 10/11 ("10 on 11"). You can make type smaller, but never skimp on the leading. If you don't use enough leading your readers will make you feel guilty about it.

10/10
At the very least, add 1 point extra leading, such as 10/11 ("10 on 11"). You can make type smaller, but never skimp on the leading. If you don't use enough leading your readers will make you feel guilty about it.

10/11
At the very least, add 1 point extra leading, such as 10/11 ("10 on 11"). You can make type smaller, but never skimp on the leading. If you don't use enough leading your readers will make you feel guilty about it.

10/12
At the very least, add 1 point extra leading, such as 10/11 ("10 on 11"). You can make type smaller, but never skimp on the leading. If you don't use enough leading your readers will make you feel guilty about it.

Various amounts of leading shown set in ITC Galliard.

Lemons

If you're handed a lemon, make lemonade. That's an invaluable tip to remember when working with type. You'll often bump into the limitations of the real world, but type is flexible enough so that you can work around them.

If you can't find or afford the exact typeface you want or need, then find something similar. If your printer can't print large size type, then use white space creatively, or add extra letter spacing between each letter of your smaller-than-you-really-wanted headline. If you want text at an angle but your software or hardware can't do it, paste it on by hand. No one is keeping score. There are no points taken away for manual pasteup. We all do what we have to do to get the job done.

Line length

When you read, you really don't read one word at a time. You scan the line, pausing to read groups of three or four words.

There is a theoretical "optimal" length, and then there are general suggestions. The magic number is supposed to be 50 characters per line, but you don't have to try to format everything to be 50 characters long. Two flexible and useful ways to look at it are:

- **About 70 characters long**

Lines shouldn't be more than about 70 characters long. When lines get longer than that, they get tiring, and the reader has a hard time finding the beginning of the next line.

- **About 30 characters short**

Too short
This column is too nar-row, so it would be difficult to read in long stretches.

Lines shouldn't be shorter than about 30 characters. Any shorter than that and sentences are broken into so many lines they can be hard to read. Also, justified paragraphs tend to have large, unsightly gaps in them when they are this narrow.

Short lines often occur unexpectedly when you run text around a graphic. Either re-size the graphic, or reconsider its placement. Very narrow lines of text are not only ugly, they're difficult to read. When you use a condensed typeface you can also use narrower columns. That's the long and short of it.

This line is too long
Lines shouldn't be more than about 70 characters wide. When lines get longer, it is tiring for the reader, and it's harder to find the beginning of the next line.

- **10 words for serifs**

Your average line should be about 10 words long.

- **8 or 9 words for sans serif**

Sans serif lines should be a little shorter.

Lines

(See *Ruling lines*) Don't you hate it when these lists say "See such and such" instead of just telling you what you want to know? So do I. What's my line? In the wacky world of typography, "lines" are called "rules" or "ruling lines."

Margins

Rule of "thumb." If your thumb covers text when you hold the page, then the margins may be too small.

Mortal sin

Always make sure there is blank space between block style paragraphs. Never set paragraphs without either space between them (block style) or an indent at the start, or they will all look like one long paragraph. (See illustration on page **8**-4.) This is one rule with *no* good reason to break it. Violating this rule is a mortal sin; you don't want to know what will happen to you if you do. Really.

Numbers/Figures

Typographers call numbers "figures." Of course, this is the same bunch that calls lines "rules." Whatever *you* call them, here are some tricks to making a few numbers look like a million.

- **Faking old style figures**

You're probably used to numbers all being in the same size, like this:

1 2 3 4 5 6 7 8 9 0

These are called *Lining* figures. But there used to be "old style" numbers that had something similar to lowercase. Old style figures are appropriate for fine typesetting such as elegant books or stationery but are inappropriate and unnecessary for things such as forms or price lists with many rows of numbers. Old style numerals look old-fashioned, so use them only when it's appropriate.

Few typefaces include old style figures, but here's a way to fake it so they look almost exactly like the "real thing:"

I 2 3 4 5 6 7 8 9 o

With 11-point body text, the 2 was set at 9-point, while the 3, 4, 5, 7, and 9 were set at 11-point but were subscripted 1.38 points. The 6 and 8 were left alone, and the 1 was replaced with a 9 point uppercase "I," and the 0 was replaced with a lowercase "o" (oh!).

While it can be tedious to make all those font changes, some software, such as Ventura Publisher, will allow you to specify the size of "small" caps and subscripts, as well as the exact amount of subscripting. Using those programs, you need only to mark some letters small, others as subscript, and replace the 0's with o's.

Normal numbers.

Avant Garde Theatre
10101 10th Street
New York, NY, 10001

The letter "O" as a zero.

Avant Garde Theatre
1O1O1 1Oth Street
New York, NY, 1OOO1

"O" as a zero and "L" as a one.

Avant Garde Theatre
IOIOI IOth Street
New York, NY, IOOOI

One	***"L"***
1 Avant Garde	l
1 Franklin Gothic	**l**
1 Futura	l
I Hammersmith	l
1 Swiss	l
1 Swiss Comp.	**l**
1 Zapf Humanist	**l**
1 Zurich	l
1 Zurich Bold	**l**

Many word processing programs will allow you to search and replace formatting codes, so it's possible that you could automate the entire process.

▪ Extra Leading

Often when you set an address it consists of lines of upper and lower case words, followed by lines of nothing but numbers. When you do this, the line with the numbers can look like it has less leading than the other lines. This is because the lowercase letters permit more white space to show through, while the all-cap numbers don't. The effect is to make your line spacing *look* uneven, even though it really *is* even.

To alleviate this, add a point or two of extra leading above the all-numeral line.

▪ Sometimes substitutions

Some typefaces, such as Avant Garde, have very wide O's and narrow 0's. So when you set words and numbers together, the 0's look too narrow. Replacing them with O's makes the text look more even.

In some sans serif faces, you'll notice that the figure 1's really *do* have serifs. While these help to distinguish the 1 from a lowercase "L" they are sometimes distracting. If they are, substitute a lower case "l" for the 1 and the distracting serif will be eliminated.

Of course, these tricks are taboo if you are using a spreadsheet program, or if the numbers are used in calculations.

Hammersmith is one of the few sans serifs which doesn't have a serif on the 1. This is fine *unless* the difference needs to be clear, as in the case of keystrokes.

In Illinois, press 11

Does that say "one el" or "el one?" What the 'el, you can't tell. In this case you would have to substitute another typeface, such as Zurich (Univers) for the number 1.

7. In numbered paragraphs the number should be decimal aligned.
8. Decimal align numbers.
9. Decimal align numbers.
10. Decimal align numbers.

Numbered paragraphs

Use decimal or right aligned numbers for numbered paragraphs.

Paragraph length

Shorter paragraphs are easier to read (less intimidating and more inviting) than longer ones.

Paragraph style

Use either a block style with a blank line between each paragraph or an indent style where the first line is indented. Don't use both. And *never* set paragraphs without one or the other. One big advantage of block style is that it adds more white space to a page. The advantage of indented paragraphs is that they permit more words on the page. (See illustration on page 8-4.)

Periods

IMPORTANT: Don't use double spaces after periods. This isn't typing, it's typesetting, and typesetters place only one space after periods. It looks better. The same rule applies for colons, exclamation points, question marks, quote marks, or any other punctuation that ends a sentence.

Double space after periods
Don't use double spaces after periods. This isn't typing, it's typesetting. Typesetters place only one space after periods. It looks better. The same rule applies for any other punctuation which ends a sentence.

Single space after periods
Don't use double spaces after periods. This isn't typing, it's typesetting. Typesetters place only one space after periods. It looks better. The same rule applies for any other punctuation which ends a sentence.

Activa (Trump Mediaeval)

Printer control

Laser printers tend to print too dark, making light typefaces look medium and medium faces look bold. The subtleties of type can be lost in all that toner.

Type always looks best when you set the laser printer to the lightest setting where blacks still come out solid black. On printers with Canon engines, such as the LaserJet, LaserWriter, or QMS-PS series, the normal setting is 5, but type will look better if the printer is set to 7 or 9. If parts of the characters disappear or break up, turn the printer to a darker setting (or see an optometrist).

Proofreading

It doesn't matter how brilliant your typography is if you have misspelled or missing words, misplaced punctuation, or other errors of writing. In fact, when your pages *look* perfect, errors seem to jump right out at you (but usually only after you've printed several thousand copies).

I strongly recommend that you print *all* drafts in the same typeface as your final manuscript. *Don't* use a monospaced font such as Courier for proofing text. It's a fact that it's easier to find mistakes on a typeset page or galley than on a typewritten page. In the past it used to be expensive to correct typeset galleys, but now all your drafts can be as easy to read as a galley, and *should* be.

Quotation marks

Neutral "Quote"

Typographic “Quote”

Dingbat ❝Quote❞

Use “real” quotes whenever possible instead of neutral inch mark typewriter quotes. Many programs will automatically convert typewriter quotation marks into real quotation marks.

If you don't want to enter a special character, you can also create quote marks by using two single ‘ marks (usually under the ~ on your keyboard) as an open quote, and two single ’ marks (usually under the quote mark key) as a closed quote mark.

- **Shortcut keys for PC Ventura & PageMaker**

For an opening quote, hold down **Shift** and **Ctrl** and press [
For a closing quote, hold down **Shift** and **Ctrl** and press]

- **Ventura/Place in the text file:**

For an opening quote, place <169> in your text file
For a closing quote, place <170> in your text file

■ WordPerfect

For an opening quote, hold down **Ctrl** and press **V**, then type **4,32**
For a closing quote, hold down **Ctrl** and press **V**, then type **4,31**

■ Mac

For an opening quote, hold down **Option** then press **[**
For a closing quote, hold down **Option** and **Shift** and press **[**

Raised caps

The first letter of a body of copy set in a display type for decoration or emphasis is called a raised cap. Often used to begin each chapter of a book, it can be any size. But leave ample white space above a paragraph with a raised cap. Also make sure that the raised cap is different enough from the body text, in both size and weight, that it doesn't look like a mistake.

Readability

Most people do not read letter by letter. They look at the shape of a word, and then recognize the word. This is why words set in upper- and lowercase are easier to read than words set in all caps. Upper- and lowercase words have more variation in shape. The top half of a letter contains more visual clues as to what the letter is than the bottom half. The left half is generally more distinctive than the right half.

Reverses

Reversed text, white text on a black background, is harder to read than black text on a white background. If you reverse any text, make sure it is large and bold enough to be read. Bold type is always easier to read when reversed than lighter weights. Sans serif faces also retain their true outlines and reverse better than serif faces. Never reverse tiny, light, or tiny and light type. The black will often bleed into the white type area during the printing process and make the type virtually invisible. I've seen people break this rule who should know better, and it always looks bad. Always.

Ruling lines or rules

The only thing you have to remember about horizontal rules is that they *separate* elements by forming a visual barrier. Use them any place you want to divide space, but don't use them between two items that are related.

Serif vs. sans serif

People find it easiest to read the type they grew up reading. Most Americans grow up reading serif type. Most Europeans grow up reading sans serif type. That doesn't mean Americans balk at reading sans serif, or Europeans recoil in horror if presented with serifs. Just remember: when in Rome...

Sidebar

While pull quotes do just what they say, sidebars are shorter articles that supplement the main text. While their purposes are different, pull quotes and sidebars follow many of the same rules, such as using a contrasting typeface and being set apart from the other text through white space or ruling lines.

Sidebars need to look different from body text, the same way pull quotes do. Otherwise people will confuse them with the main text, and read directly from the main text into the sidebar with unexpected (and possibly disastrous) results.

Size

How big is the page? How close is the reader? Big/Far=Big type. Small/close=smaller type. About 10- or 11-point type is normal in a book people read at a close distance. I think 9 point is as small as you should ever go for book, magazine, or newsletter text, and then only when you're sure it will be sharp enough. While 18- to 24-point type may seem large, it would be considered small body text in a large poster.

Space bar

The only time you should use the space bar is between words. Don't use it to indent paragraphs or align columns of numbers. The columns of numbers almost certainly will not align when printed, and if you need to change the amount of the indent, it won't be easy or accurate.

Small caps

If you have to set words in all caps, set them in *small* caps. This will keep them from being too OBTRUSIVE. Small caps used to be specially designed caps, not just normal caps set in a smaller size. But few digital typefaces include real small caps, so you can just set them in a smaller size instead.

Spell checking

Always spell check one final time before you print the final draft. It's *extremely* easy to introduce errors during typography and layout. See *Proofreading*.

Subheads

Use subheads to break text into more manageable chunks. They act as signposts to help readers find what they're looking for. They also keep pages from looking "gray."

Tabs

Always use tabs to line up columns of numbers. *Never* use spaces. With proportional typefaces, spaces will only align when the stars are also aligned and this happens all too infrequently. Tabs will always align, no matter what your sign is.

Tracking

Some programs call it tracking, others letterspacing, but what it means is the amount of space between all characters. You want to make sure the letters are close enough together so that it's easy to tell where the words begin and end. Usually the factory defaults are just right, but "tightening" (bringing the letters closer together) can sometimes save space and make text easier to read, particularly in display sizes. Be careful to make sure the letters don't touch, or you'll decrease readability. "Loosening" (making the letters farther apart) can lighten a page and make it look less dark and intimidating, but too loose and the reader can't tell where words end and spaces begin.

Type size

Body text set in 11-point type looks better at 300 dots per inch (dpi) than 10-point does.

Typeface

Use an *appropriate* typeface. Don't use something flamboyant for a serious subject or something too serious for a lighthearted subject.

- **Always use the same typeface for all your body text.**

Don't set one article in one typeface and another article in a different typeface. Conversely, sidebars, pull quotes, and other special text should almost always be a different typeface.

- **Body copy is normally between 9- and 12-point.**

While 11-point type is the easiest to read, body copy within a single document or publication should always be the same size.

Underlining

Don't underline. Use *italics* instead of underlines. Remember that underlines are proofreader's marks that signify "italics."

Vertical column rules

These are the vertical lines you often see between columns of text. These help create a straight vertical on the right side of unjustified paragraphs. In general, these work best with unjustified text. If you justify text you don't need ruling lines. You can use them, but often they are overkill and just make the page busier.

Vertical justification

Some programs can perform "vertical justification" to align the top and bottoms of columns. Ventura Publisher can either add space between paragraphs in one line increments (carding), or add tiny amounts of leading spread throughout a column (feathering). Despite the rule about not varying leading, feathering is preferable to carding because it is less obvious.

Wake up

Quick, before someone notices you were snoring. Besides, we're reaching the end of the body-text section and you will need to be wide awake and have all your wits about you to complete the test at the end of the chapter. A good grade could make the difference between your getting into the college of your choice or having to work for peanuts all your life. (I thought that would wake you up.)

Weight

Choose a medium weight for body text. Light typefaces start to look thin, and dark typefaces can look so heavy that the words lose their shape. However, if you know that your printer (the person, not the machine) tends to print dark, or the ink tends to spread on your paper, then a light typeface will help because it will print medium, whereas a medium typeface might end up dark.

Widows and orphans

Beware of the widow, a single word on a line by itself at the end of a paragraph. It's unattractive and makes the text harder to read. An even worse typographical horror is the orphan. That's the last word or line of a paragraph stranded at the top of a column of text. Or the first line of a paragraph stranded at the very bottom of a column of text. Many software programs automatically help you eliminate these outcasts of the type world. If yours does, take advantage of it.

White space

First, it's always called white space, no matter what color the paper is. Second, there are no hard and fast rules here but the importance of white space cannot be stressed enough. I'd like to put each of you in a room where the words "white space" repeat over and over until they've sunk into your unconscious mind.

White Space
White Space
White Space
White Space
White Space
White Space
White Space

White Space White Space White Space
White Space White Space White Space
White Space White Space White Space
White Space White Space White Space
White Space White Space White Space
White Space White Space White Space
White Space White Space White Space

Leave enough of it and your page looks inviting. Leave too little and your page looks oppressive, heavy, brooding, scary.

I'll give you several ways to think about it—you pick the one that makes the biggest impression in your brain tissue or soul, wherever you store this type of information.

- **Think of type as people and white space as *breathing room.***

If you pretend you are looking down on a room filled with people, with each letter being a person, make sure that there's room for everyone to walk around.

- **Scientific**

For every action there is an equal and opposite reaction, so for all type there must be white space.

- **Threats**

If you don't leave enough white space, your page will look too dark. People are frightened by dark pages because at one time or another everyone's mother was frightened by a newspaper during her pregnancy.

However you remember it, white space is vital.

Word spacing

Too much Word Spacing

Perfect Word Spacing

Too little WordSpacing

How much space do you need between words? When asked how long a man's legs should be, Abe Lincoln replied "long enough to reach the ground." In the case of word spaces, long enough so that the words look like distinct entities, and not so long that you can't quickly read from word to word. Generally speaking ¼ em (an em is the width of the letter M) is standard.

If you turn a page upside down, you'll get a better idea of the spacing between the words because you'll be less distracted by reading the text.

Subheads

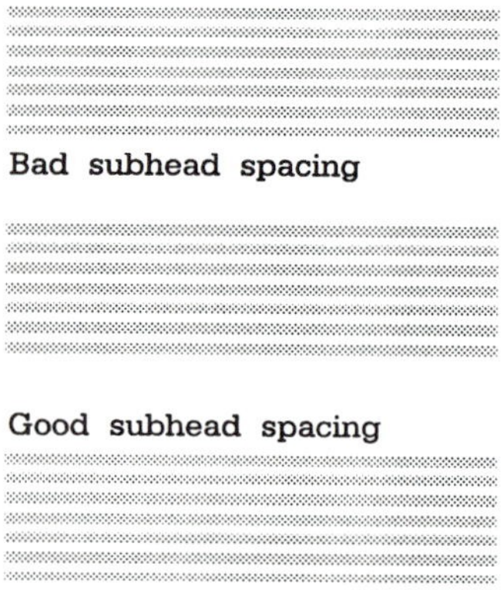

Signposts along the way to break up the gray

Use subheads liberally. These visual clues help the reader find what they are looking for more quickly. Long stretches of gray body copy *bores* readers, and a bored reader is an ex-reader. Subheads break information into more manageable, less intimidating chunks.

Subheads give readers something to anticipate. It's almost a money-back guarantee that you will improve the quality of your publication by adding subheads. (Novels or other book-type prose excluded. Subject to prior sale and the laws in your state. Void where prohibited. Your mileage may vary.)

Alignment

Left-aligned text is very easy to read and adds extra white space to the page. Centered subheads often don't look precisely right with unjustified text, but are OK with justified text.

Page breaks

Subheads should never fall on the last line of a column or page. Always keep at least two lines of body text after a subhead. Some programs allow you to mark a subhead as "keep with next" so that it will automatically move to the next column or page if it can't stay with at least one line of the next paragraph. If your software has this feature, *use it.* It will save you time and make everything you produce look better.

Justification

Don't fully justify subheads. Flush left subheads are the fastest and easiest to read.

Size

Make subheads at least two points larger than the body text, or set them in a different and darker typeface that will stand out.

Spacing

Place more space above a subhead than below it, so it's clear it goes with the paragraph that follows.

Ruling lines and underlines

Don't put a line or rule *under* a subhead—it separates the subhead from the text it is supposed to go with. Put lines *above* subheads. Don't underline a subhead either.

Typeface

Subheads should *always* be in a different font from the body text. Either they should be different typeface entirely, or the same typeface in another style such as bold, italic, bold italic, or small caps. If you set subheads in the same font as the body text, they will not stand out, which will defeat their purpose. Subheads are often in the same typeface as headlines.

Avoid using two different serif faces together, or two sans serif. For example, if your body text is serif (Dutch/Times Roman), use a sans serif for subheads (Swiss/Helvetica).

Type size

In general, subheads should be a minimum of two points larger than the body text. In order to save space, if the subhead typeface you choose is bold enough, it can be the same size as the body text.

Uniformity

Be consistent about the design of your subheads. That way the reader always knows what they are. Choose a specific size and alignment (such as 14-point, flush left), and stick with it.

Pull quotes

Highlighting and repeating important text

A pull quote is a section of text that is used as a graphic element. It pulls out a quote or statement from the text and displays it in a larger typesize than the body copy. Pull quotes make sure that people read the most important parts of the text, even if they don't read the whole piece. You can use up to three per page; after that they lose some of their impact.

Differentiation

Pull quotes are not headlines or subheads, but are most often duplicates of sentences or paragraphs of body copy used for emphasis. A pull quote must be set apart from the body text by using white space, ruling lines or some type of graphic device such as giant quote marks or decorative dingbats.

Length

Pull quotes should never be more than a few lines long. Otherwise they stop being pull quotes and start being a sidebar (a short article that supplements the main text).

Reverses

Reversed text (white text on a black background) is harder to read than black text on a white background. If you do reverse any text, make sure it is large and bold enough to be read. Bold faces are always easier to read when reversed than are lighter weights. Sans serif faces also reverse better than those with serifs.

Ruling lines and boxes

Ruling lines above, below, or both are also a good idea because they separate the pull quote even more. You can also put ruling lines along the left edge, to create a visual starting point, or place a box around the pull quote. Make sure to leave ample white space between any lines or boxes and both the pull quote and body text.

Solidarity

Pull quotes must *never* be broken by column or page breaks. Some programs help you eliminate this by allowing you to mark a paragraph as "keep together" or surround it with block protect codes.

Typestyle

Make sure a pull quote's typeface or type style is different enough in size and weight so that it clearly stands out from the text. Bold or italic typefaces are good because they contrast with the body text. If you use a different typeface from the body text, try to use the same one used for headlines and subheads. This will keep the page from becoming too busy.

Type size

Pull quotes are generally at least 14-point or larger.

White space

You can use white space alone to separate a pull quote from the body text if you don't use any type of ruling lines or graphic devices. Even if you do use lines or graphics, you still need to leave ample white space around the pull quote so it doesn't look crowded.

Headlines

Alignment

Left alignment is best for headlines. Centering headlines works with justified text. Right alignment is rare. Headlines should be consistently aligned throughout a publication or document, all left or all centered, otherwise the page can start to look messy.

Headlines need to relate to the rest of the page in a really big way, otherwise they just look like they've been haphazardly scattered on the page.

If you stand back a little and look at a page, the headlines should line up with the text. If they are flush left, then the left edge of the headline should line up with the left edge of the body text. If a headline is off by as little as 1/10th of an inch, it will be clearly noticeable. If you don't want the headlines to align for some reason, make it *obvious* or it will just look like a mistake.

Breaks

If a headline is more than one line long, the way the text breaks is *extremely* important. Always check headlines and break them for sense, rather than just any old way the computer wants to break them.

***The good, the
bad, and the
ugly***

***The good,
the bad,
and the ugly***

Caps

Be wary of setting headlines in all capital letters. They're harder to read and don't necessarily look more important. If you do set a headline in all caps, pay particular attention to the spacing between the letters. All caps often need hand kerning to make them look evenly spaced.

You can set headlines in initial caps (the first letter of each word in caps) or with only the first letter of the headline capitalized. Whichever you choose, be consistent.

Centered lines

One of the easiest mistakes to make while centering text is to leave a space character at the beginning or end of the line. Because the computer counts that space just like any other character, the headline really isn't centered.

Computers center type mechanically. While this works most of the time, sometimes the shapes of letters make this mechanical centering look off-center. This often happens when the text begins and ends with punctuation (which the eye does not consider part of the words themselves).

So if "centered" type looks off-centered, the easiest way to correct it is to do what you're not supposed to do: add an extra space at the beginning or end of the line. Some programs even allow you to insert spaces in different widths, such as "thin," "en," "em," and "figure" (the width of a number).

Copy fitting

Getting headlines to fit in their allotted space sometimes goes beyond being a craft and starts being an art. Still, the best way to get them to fit is to write them to fit.

Headlines that are too short look dumb, as if you couldn't think of anything else to say. Headlines that are too long just plain don't fit, and using multiple lines (not always bad in itself) can take a lot of space.

If your headline *almost* fits, many desktop publishing programs will help you get them to fit perfectly in ways only dreamed of in the past. You can easily make the type bigger or smaller, or add or remove space between letters.

Shortcuts

- **Ventura Publisher**

Larger/Smaller: Highlight the text, hold down **Shift** and press ↑ to make the text one point larger, or hold down **Shift** and press ↓ to make it one point size smaller.

Add/Remove space between letters: To move the letters of the highlighted text a bit farther apart (.02 ems, up to 1.27 ems), highlight the text and hold down **Shift** then press →. To move the letters of the highlighted text a bit closer together (.02 ems), hold down **Shift** and press ←.

- **PageMaker**

Larger/Smaller: Highlight the text and press **F3** to make it one point smaller, or **F4** to make it one point larger.

- **Note**

While these shortcuts work on scalable font printers, if your printer has set font sizes, Ventura and PageMaker will jump to the next larger or smaller size.

Coverage

A headline should be like a full head of hair: it should cover the width of the entire article it is above. If the article is four columns wide, its headline shouldn't barely cover three columns. The text of the article should *never* run next to or over the headline at any point. You will see some newspapers using three-column heads with four column stories, with the fourth column for running text next to the head. They do this because it saves space, but that doesn't make it look good (or easier to follow). Remember, just because someone else does something doesn't make it right. See the "Is Busy Work Unproductive" headline on page **9-16** for a good example of bad coverage.

Hyphenation

Don't hyphenate headlines. Ev-er.

The-
rapist to
the stars

Uh-oh.

Justification

Never fully justify a headline. It adds space between words or characters, robs the page of white space, and just plain looks bad.

Kerning

When you kern, strive to make the spaces between the characters appear equal. Because of the different shapes of letters, you often have to give them *un*equal spacing to make them *look* equal.

Properly kerned headlines look like distinct words rather than just a long string of letters. In most cases your software's automatic kerning is good enough, but sometimes you need to manually perform "optical spacing." This means that you manually kern certain pairs of letters closer together or farther apart to make them look like they are equally spaced.

For display titles (large text that aren't headlines) you may need to kern the punctuation so that it is closer to the text.

- **HE**

Characters formed of verticals placed next to each other need very little space between then.

- **HO**

Vertical characters next to curved characters need less space.

- **OO**

Two curved characters next to each other need very little space.

- **To**

You can tuck a small letter or punctuation under a "T."

- **WA**

The shape of certain characters creates extra space around them. These often need extra kerning, but don't kern them so close that they start looking like a ligature rather than distinct letters.

Leading

While body copy usually requires 20% extra leading, headlines don't. In fact, too much leading weakens the strength of headlines.

Lines/Rules

Don't put lines under headlines—it separates the headline from the text. Put lines *above* them.

Length

A headline that is too short looks like it's too short. It's not only obvious, but then the headline doesn't cover all the columns of text the way it should. If the headline is too short, either use an expanded typeface, or rewrite the headline and add extra words. Headline writing isn't easy, but a good headline motivates people to read the article.

Letterspacing/ Kerning

Touching Letterspacing
Tight Letterspacing
Normal Letterspacing
Loose Letterspacing
Very Loose Letterspacing

Futura Light

Set headlines tighter than normal copy, but not so tight that the letters touch. Letters that touch are harder to read.

Placement

For newsletters or newspapers with several headlines on a page, the most important articles should be near the top of the page, and their headlines should be bigger than those on the other articles.

Headlines should never be on the last line of the page. Always keep at least three lines of body text after them or they look silly.

Punctuation

Headlines should not end with a period.

Side-by-side heads

Try not to place headlines side-by-side. The reader may read them as one single headline, and this could be embarrassing, as well as confusing. This kind of mistake is called "bumping heads" or "tombstoning." It can usually be alleviated by moving a graphic or making the page design more horizontal. See the full-page example on page 9-16 for a good example of bad headline placement.

Typeface

Headlines should contrast with the text either by their size, their weight, or their typeface. Headlines should always be bigger, generally darker, and often in a completely different typeface from the body text. Sometimes headlines are different in all three ways.

The reason many headlines are sans serif is because sans serif is more legible (not readable, legible). This means that each character is more distinct—a blessing when setting short blocks of text such as headlines or subheads. When you set serif type in large sizes it's wonderful to see all those typographic details, but it can also be distracting.

Two different typefaces are usually sufficient for most publications: one for body text, and another for headlines, subheads, pull quotes, etc. Using more than two is going to make the page design more complicated and possibly confused. (Once you become typographically experienced you may be able to get away with it.)

Many magazines and newsletters take advantage of additional display faces to give headlines a specific personality that goes with a particular article or story.

An old adage goes, "Never mix, never worry." You can play it safe by using the same typeface for both body and heads. But even when you use the same typeface, make sure to vary the type*style*, using bold or italic for headlines rather than just the same roman/medium/book weight you used for the body text.

Size

Headlines are usually at least twice as big as the body text. The bigger they are, the more important they are. If you would rather use smaller type, use extra white space to add importance.

Spacing

Headlines should have more space above them than below them, otherwise they get separated from the text with which they belong.

Special effects

Don't use too many special effects, such as outline or shadow type. Save special effects for special occasions.

Underline

Don't underline a headline. If you want to use a line, put it *above* the headline.

TYPE*Tips*

These aren't traditional typesetting tips, but they are useful for the anyone who sets type on a computer.

Font fiche

Here's a good way to conserve resources. Did you know you can create a microfiche on your laser printer? It's amazing, but you can read 3-point type from a LaserJet III if you use the right typefaces. This method can pack the equivalent of 20 pages onto a single 8-column page and is a way to archive info without requiring the removal of more trees from our dwindling forests.

If your eyesight is good enough, you can read these pages with the naked eye, or you can use a magnifying glass. If you print on clear acetate sheets (make sure they're laser compatible or xerographic, or they'll melt and ruin your printer) you can even put them into fiche readers.

Sans serif typefaces work best because at that tiny size there simply aren't enough dots to reproduce the serifs accurately. Swiss and Zurich are good choices for this, with Zurich having the edge because it's a bit lighter than Swiss.

This type is so small that it won't reproduce well on a copy machine or offset press, so you must use the originals.

Giant type

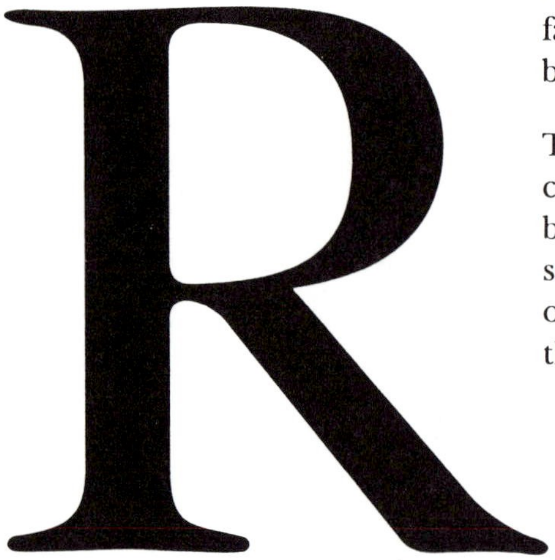

This is a 254-point Baskerville character.

Many DTP programs have a type-size limit of about 254 points, far smaller than the gigantic letters sprinkled throughout the backgrounds on many of the examples shown in this book.

The way around this is to use a draw program. Such a programs can take fonts and turn them into graphics. The graphics can then be placed in a page composition or word processing program and sized as large as you want. Because the graphics are object-oriented line art, they will not lose quality no matter how large they are scaled.

LaserJet limitations

LaserJet printers (except for the III) normally can't print reverses (white text on a black background), exceptionally large type sizes, or text running in two different orientations (portrait and landscape) on the same page.

But there are ways to get around these limitations. Most of them involve a draw program, such as Corel Draw or Micrografx Designer on the PC, Adobe Illustrator on the PC or Mac, and Aldus Freehand on the Mac.

Corel Draw and Micrografx Designer allow you to work directly with Bitstream typefaces and turn them into graphics. Then you can import them into your desktop publishing or word processing software and make them full-page size. Because they are graphic and not text, you *can* create reverses, run text in several orientations, and print giant type.

Even with the wonders of draw programs, the one remaining limitation is *printer memory*. Everything on the page requires memory, including graphics from draw programs. If you print a page that requires more memory than your printer has, the printer gives you an error message, and your page is broken into two or more pages.

■ When you can't make it big

Make the best of what you have. What, you don't have a PostScript printer? You don't have two megabytes of LaserJet memory? Money doesn't grow on trees? Gee, without big type you can't possibly produce anything that looks attractive and professional, right?

Wrong. While PostScript printers or large quantities of LaserJet memory offer you power with a lot of options, you can do without them if you just use a little imagination.

Some noted designers avoid large type, believing that smaller sizes force the reader to pay attention. (About an equal number of designers think that you can't grab a reader's attention without using large type, but quoting them would only negate the intention of this section, so I'll simply pretend they don't exist.)

While size is a quick way to garner attention, it's not the only way. You can spruce up pages with small type by simply using ruling lines and white space. Ruling lines don't take up much printer memory and white space takes *none*.

▪ Rule this

Heavy ruling lines above headlines attract the reader's eye and make the type seem larger and more commanding. When designing documents with related material, such as newsletters and newspapers, remember to use ruling lines above, not below, headlines. This is because lines are a form of separation and a line under a headline breaks the connection between the headline and the text beneath it. Also, make sure there's enough space under the line and above the headline.

▪ Spaced out

One way to make type appear larger is to simply put a space or two between each letter—also known as *letterspacing*. Make sure to add at least twice as much space between each word as you did between each letter, and be consistent with the amount of space you've added. If your software allows it, the letterspacing feature gives you much more control than just pressing the space bar between letters.

▪ Rules in space

Of course, the ultimate bit of trickery involves both ruling lines and white space. A thick black rule over widely spaced text will take up the most space and grab the greatest attention when using small typesizes.

Lest you think that all this work leads only to artificially filled pages, the results, you will be pleased to know, are extremely attractive.

Paper

All papers are not alike. The relatively inexpensive standard copier "bond" papers most people use in laser printers tend to be on the thin side, somewhat rough, not very opaque, and not very white. This paper is fine for drafts, but not the best choice for your final camera-ready pages, or for the times when your originals are used straight out of the laser printer. High-quality bond papers are available, and these often have a rag content that gives them a richer feel.

When choosing paper for originals, always test the paper in your own laser printer with the fonts you plan to use. "Text" grade papers come in many colors and textures but are also more expensive.

Some stationery paper doesn't work well in laser printers. Many papers with visible fibers tend to expand and look frightening when they come out of laser printers, while other papers with fibers work just fine.

Many paper companies, including Hammermill, James River, Weyerhaeuser, Crane, Strathmore, Wausau, and Fox River, make special high-quality paper for laser printers.

When selecting paper for reproductions, look for paper that is very smooth, so that none of the printed details is obscured. Smooth paper is also more reflective, so it looks whiter and provides more contrast for the black letters.

You can even run thick card stock through a laser printer as long as you have a straight paper path. Printers based on Canon SX engines, including the LaserJet II, LaserJet III, LaserMaster 1000, QMS PS printers and Apple LaserWriter II printers, all have a virtually straight paper path if you pull down the "face up" exit tray located in the back of the printer.

Saving resources

Computers were supposed to decrease the amount of paper used by businesses. Instead, they've made it easier to use *more* paper than ever before. Money may not grow on trees, but paper does. Still, trees are a precious resource. They purify the air, provide homes for animals, and act as a watershed.

Remember, too, that there are many types of paper that aren't made from trees. Cotton makes great paper, as does linen (from flax seeds).

In the future, paper *may* be obsolete and we may read everything from high resolution electronic pages. Until that time, when you are printing drafts of your work, always *use both sides of the paper.* When you've printed on both sides, recycle it. You'll save money and you'll help save the planet. You can't argue with that.

In the past, trees may have been cheap, but now we can't afford to waste them.

Reduction

The *easiest,* cheapest way to up the resolution of your type is to photographically reduce the page before having it printed. Most print shops don't charge anything extra to shoot the page "at a percentage."

An 8½- by 11-inch original can be reduced by 18% and yield a 7- by 9-inch page (typical book size). Instead of photographing the page at 100%, the camera can be set to 78%. This reduction raises the resolution of the page from 300 to 400 dpi—a very noticeable difference.

The more you reduce the page, the higher the resolution gets. If you are creating booklet-size pages that are half the size of normal 8½- by 11-inch pages, you end up with 5¼- by 8½-inch pages. Instead of printing these at the final size on your laser printer, print them full size, then have the printer reduce them at 65%. The result will be pages with a resolution of about 461 dpi.

This tactic can reach colossal proportions by printing "tabloid" size pages and reducing them to regular 8½- by 11-inch size. Many page layout programs can create tabloid size pages by printing four 8½- by 11-inch pages which you paste together manually. Shooting these pages down to one 8½- by 11-inch page means you are shooting the page at 25%, a 75% reduction. The result is an apparent resolution of 1200 dpi, that of a typesetter. Of course, this isn't suitable for an entire book, but it works fine for a single page.

Resolution enhancements

While 300 dpi is standard for most laser printers, it's not really high-resolution, but it's more than acceptable for most applications. Some printers, such as the LaserJet III, have resolution enhancement features to remove jaggies and increase the *apparent* resolution. Here are some other ways of increasing the real resolution.

- **Add-on boards**

All LaserJet printers, and most other laser printers, can be upgraded to higher resolution through add-on products. These usually consist of a pair of boards: a full-sized one that fits inside your computer, and another smaller one that fits inside the printer.

These products provide much higher resolution than standard laser printers. While not as high-resolution as traditional imagesetters, these cost-effective alternatives can produce results so good that they are almost indistinguishable from more expensive alternatives.

These products are manufactured by various companies, but the best known of this kind come from LaserMaster in Minnesota. LaserMaster boards increase both the performance and resolution of the printer, raising resolution from 800 dpi to 1000 dpi.

- **Service centers**

If your final pages are to be printed on very smooth or shiny paper, or you need the very highest quality and most professional output, you should consider using a service bureau.

A service bureau is a company that offers very expensive high-res typesetting (also called "imagesetting") equipment capable of typesetting from 1200 dpi to 2450 dpi. This equipment is often "Linotronic."

These imagesetters generally use the "PostScript" page description language, so the files you send them must be in PostScript format. The staff at these centers are usually experienced and will be able to tell you the specifics for creating files in this format.

As well as printing on high-resolution photographic paper, these machines can also print directly onto the film used by commercial printers to make offset plates.

Before you send a job to a service bureau, you need to know if they have the typefaces you want, and if the typefaces are from the same foundry as the ones you are using. All of Bitstream's typefaces have the same metrics (character widths) and spacing, no matter what type of printer or output device you use. If you format your page for a LaserJet, the line and page endings will remain the same, even when printed on a high-res typesetter.

Service bureaus tend to charge by the page, although on large jobs they can charge by the hour. It's best to show them a printed draft of your entire project and get estimates before handing over your files.

9

The logic of design

You can't get answers unless you ask questions

You've read the rules. You've seen the movie. Now it's time to experience the thrill of using your brain.

The logic of design

You can't get answers unless you ask questions

Where do you start? At the beginning, of course. Some people are frightened when they look at a blank piece of paper knowing they have to fill it. But if you have clear goals, know your audience, and ask the right questions, the answers will follow.

You've read the rules. You've seen the movie. Now it's time to experience the thrill of using your brain. (Oh no, please don't make me use my brain, please, it's tired.) Yes, it's time to start *thinking* for yourself.

Type is one of those areas, like music, sports, or art, where you can't just read a book and become an instant expert. You have to *do it.* You have to work with type, play with type, and experiment until you are comfortable.

Because of this, I use what I call the Think System. Just thinking about type is enough to make a difference in the way you work with it. Start realizing that type is something more than just a bunch of letters and know that it can have a major impact on your finished pages.

I know this probably sounds like yet another flaky idea from California, or you may even recognize it as a method first expounded by Professor Harold Hill in River City, Iowa. If you do, you'll get a good laugh, but the truth is that this system *works.*

You've probably seen those four-year-old Japanese violin prodigies on television, who learned to play using a similar technique, the Suzuki method. Basically the method is that if you do it, and think about doing it, you'll learn it. All this may sound terribly obvious, but it's not. It's not good enough just to sit around thinking; you have to think about type in particular.

So to get started, find a comfortable chair, pour yourself a glass of whatever it is you like to drink, put your feet up, and if anyone asks what you're doing, tell them you're working. They don't have to know that all you're really doing is thinking.

THINK
THINK
THINK
THINK
THINK
THINK
THINK
THINK
THINK
THINK
THINK
THINK
THINK
THINK
THINK
THINK
THINK
THINK
THINK
THINK
THINK
THINK
THINK
THINK
THINK
THINK
THINK
THINK
THINK
THINK
THINK

More secrets

You've already discovered most of the secrets in Chapter 8. Some of those rules may seen arbitrary or even clichéd, but they do work. Now for the rest of the secrets. Even if you forget some of the rules in the previous chapter, the next clues will help you do the right thing instinctively.

- **Everything is on the page for a reason.**
- **Everything is relative.**
- **Play around until it works.**

Let me explain:

Everything is on the page for a reason

Here's one of those secrets that sounds so much like common knowledge it's deceptive. Some people sit down at the computer and just pour type on a page. They never ask themselves "who, what, when, where, why, or how," they just start working. This is not advisable.

With type, the overriding reason is always to make the text more understandable and enticing.

My dictionary says enticing means "being extremely and often dangerously attractive," and I like that. The idea of people being unable to stop themselves from reading the pages you create is kind of amusing, don't you think?

But creating an enticing page isn't the *only* reason for your decisions concerning type. There are always many reasons, and they change with every different page you create. If you don't ask who, what, when, where, why, and how, your page may end up looking pretty, but brain-dead.

Every professionally-designed page you've seen in your life was designed for a reason: to grab your attention, to convey a specific message, to distract you from something else. It's important to sit down and think about what really attracted you to that page in the first place.

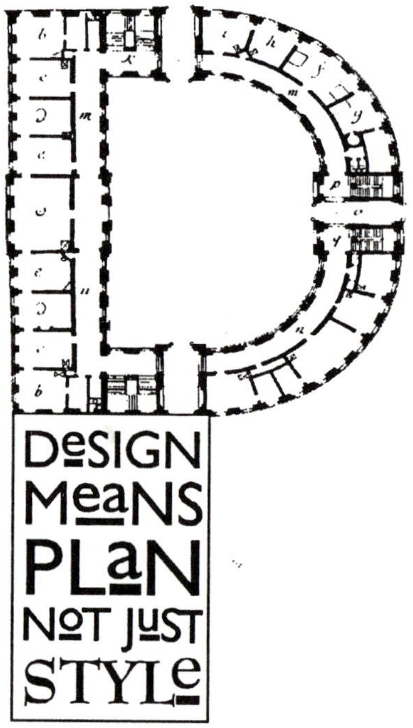
DESIGN
MEANS
PLAN
NOT JUST
STYLE

"Design" means structure, blueprint, plan, strategy, aim, intention, and purpose, as well as style.

Every page you produce should have some goal. Print it in big letters and put it up someplace where you can see it. You don't have to stare at it; seeing it out of the corner of your eye works just fine. I can hear some of you saying "He's goal-oriented and I'm growth-oriented," which means that either you've read too many self-improvement books or you've been in therapy.

Working with type (or playing with type) is much easier if you have a specific goal. Make defining the goal part of the process. Having a goal to focus on will make finding answers and finishing the project smoother and faster. Rather than forcing yourself to decide on an arbitrary typeface, you just have to *aim* at that goal.

You may still have to work for answers, but at least with a goal you'll quickly be able to eliminate those choices that are completely off target; you'll be able to narrow the field and have a more focused group of choices.

Aim towards a clear, focused goal

Now I'll admit, sometimes the hardest part is coming up with a clear goal. Sometimes it's very clear, like,"We want to sell 900 pairs of shoes this week," or "We want to move this piece of property." But often it's not nearly so obvious.

One good way to clarify your goal is to come up with a *TV Guide* blurb. That's one of those short paragraphs (less than 20 words) that explains the essence of your project. Distill the idea into a single sentence, such as, "To help people choose, use, and understand type" (the goal of this book).

I apologize if any of this sounds like "How to find happiness in 30 days," but the fact is that you can't come up with the best typographic solutions until you've asked the best demographic questions—who, what, when, where, why, and how.

Typographic answers require demographic questions

If you're the artistic type and balk at something that sounds so clinical, think again. Most of the time when we do something that works, we have a reason. Often it's difficult to articulate what that reason is, but if you *can,* then you can use it again later.

Finding reasons also helps you avoid overdesigning a page and making it distracting. You can strip away elements, one by one, until you end up with something reasonable.

If you're a very intuitive person, the kind who does things because they "just look right," then "reasons" might seem hard for you to handle. But give it a try. If you're a logical person and all this type business seems too enigmatic, asking questions and coming up with answers will turn type into something simple and straightforward.

A good reason *isn't* something you concoct after the fact, when someone asks you why you've done something and you really don't know.

"I like the way it looks" is a good reason—if the way it looks relates to and supports what your page is supposed to say, *and* if your readers share your opinion of what looks good.

"I want to" is only a good reason if you really do know what you're doing.

"Just to be different" is only a good reason if you're very talented.

Being cheap is never a good enough reason. Being thrifty or environmentally sound is.

Everything is relative

There is no one right typeface. There is no one right choice. If there were, then computers could do it all for you.

Everyone is different and the answers they come up with will be different. If you give two people the same text, the same "goal," and the same choices, they probably will develop two different solutions. Both solutions can be right as long as they fulfill the original intent. One person might choose Zapf Humanist (Optima), while another selects Goudy Old Style. Both can be right.

Of course, both can also be wrong. While some people will tell you that there are no wrong choices when it comes to type, I'm not one of them. Wrong type choices are either those that make the text harder to read or those that are inappropriate.

"Appropriate" is the key word in choosing the right typeface.

The "right" type is always relative to the intended purpose. You probably wouldn't use the same typeface for an elegant invitation as you would for a final notice. You wouldn't use the same size type in a card that you place in your wallet as you would for a giant poster.

Before you can really think about what typeface to choose or how to use it, you first have to decide *who* is the reader, *what* you are producing, *when* it needs to be completed, *where* the reader will find and read your material, and *how* you will produce and distribute it.

Who?

Who is the reader: young, old, employee, boss, stockholder, internal staff, general public? What's their age, rank, serial number, IQ? Your job is to entice your audience to start reading and keep them interested once they've begun. Just as there's rarely a single solution that appeals to everyone, there's rarely a single "right" way. There are many bad ways and many good ways. And there's always a "better" way.

What?

What will they be reading: large magazine, small booklet, narrow flyer, sign? Is the material timely, like today's newspaper; trendy, like advertisements or catalogs; or timeless, like a novel? Your choices about type will be based on the application.

When?

When is your audience reading your message? During a busy work day, where they need to find information fast, or on a leisurely Saturday for pleasure? When is your deadline? If you miss your deadline, you'll realize that yesterday's news is old news.

Where?

Where is your audience reading your message? From a car looking at a billboard 200 feet away, or from a quick reference card pulled from a wallet? *Where* will people find your publication? Does it have to stand out from many other competitors on a shelf or through the mail? How close are your readers to your publication? Are they holding it in their hands?

Why?

Why are they reading? They're all reading for a reason—necessity, curiosity, business, pleasure, fear, love. Do they *want* to read or do they *have* to? Do you have to sell them on something or are they already convinced? Are they going to be reading every single word or skimming and jumping from topic to topic?

How?

How is the document printed and distributed? Is it xeroxed and delivered by hand or does it involve expensive four-color printing? How is it bound? Is postage a concern?

Your design decisions will be based on questions like these and on any other special circumstances your work might encounter.

Where to start?

A book should look like a book

So how can you decide what to do? As my wife Toni loves to tell me, "Put yourself in the other person's shoes." What do *you* want to see? What would persuade you? What would inform you?

While not everyone in the world shares your tastes, it's a reasonable starting point. If you find something attractive, chances are other people will, too.

If you're the intuitive type, now's the time to start exploring your options. If you have several typefaces at your disposal, try them all. See how they look at all sizes, in all their various styles. Get to know them. Look through other printed material to help you crystalize what you do and don't like.

If you're the structured type, this is when you should start scouring through other publications, sorting them into stacks of ones you *do* and *don't* like. Do that research you love so much.

There's nothing wrong with starting out by emulating a publication you like. It isn't possible to copyright type selection, page layout, margins, columns, and other typographic elements, so you don't have to worry about infringing on anyone's rights.

For beginners, choosing a model is a good way to start. When the more experienced do it, it's called "finding stimulus." Studying something you like helps you see *how* it's put together, and *why* you like it. You don't have to copy the design line for line, but find the best elements and try to adapt them to your application. After a while, maybe you can even improve on the original design that influenced you.

People *expect* magazines to have a certain "look" and books to have another. The more your publication resembles other similar publications, the better it will be accepted. You don't have to be a slave to tradition, but you should realize that if your design doesn't bear some resemblance to similar publications, you'll have to work harder to get your message across.

Remember your number one concern: communication. It doesn't matter how flashy your publication looks if it doesn't get your message across. Don't compromise readability for the sake of design. It's better to have someone say "I read it" than "Oh, doesn't that look hip, doesn't that look modern, doesn't that look pretty."

Organization

The more organized your text is, the easier it will be to create a design which emphasizes that organization.

By organized, I don't mean that your desk has to be neat and tidy or that you have to have a place for everything. It would be nice if you could be that organized, but some people (me included) can't, no matter how hard we try or how many *How to Be Organized* books we read.

If there is an outline or table of contents for the material, use it to help you see how the text is organized. You may have hated outlines in school (I did), but once you start to use them without a teacher looking over your shoulder, you'll appreciate them (as I do now). Working without an outline puts you in danger of succumbing to the old "Can't see the forest for the trees" trap. An outline allows you to see both the forest and the trees (and even the roots and leaves).

With an outline, you'll be able to see at a glance whether or not the work is broken up into digestible bits (to switch from the tree metaphor to something easier to swallow). You'll see if chapters have subheads (which often are placed in a table of contents or outline) or whether you'll need to add them.

If there isn't an outline or table of contents, make one.

Sometimes during the design process you may discover that the material is not well organized. If this happens, discuss it with the person responsible for the text (if it's you, talk to yourself). Either you don't understand how the material is organized, or else it's disorganized.

Hierarchy or anarchy: the choice is yours

In a book, organization may mean various levels of headings: chapter titles, chapter subtitles, main headings, and subheadings.

People generally equate size with importance—with bigger inevitably being better, except in the case of bugs, snakes, or warts.

For a book, the size order goes like this: the type for the chapter title should be bigger than for the subtitle. The subtitle should be bigger than the subheads. The subheads should be bigger than the body text.

In a newsletter or newspaper where each story is its own little entity, it's a little different. A kicker (short text above the headline) would be perhaps 14-point. The headline would be 36-point. The deckhead (lines in larger type under the headline that contain more info about the story) would be 14- or 18-point. If the body copy is 11-point, the byline and subheads would probably be 12- to 14-point bold or bold italic. Newspapers and newsletters have an additional dimension: placement on the page. The most important stories are generally placed near the top of the page.

On your own: tools for doing it yourself

Be organized or be sorry

Now that you know the do's and don'ts, you've got to concentrate on putting it all together. To help you make sure you ask all the pertinent questions and don't ignore the answers, here is a form I find indispensable. Photocopy it and *use* it, and your life will be easier. Ignore it and you're on your own.

Runsheet

I've helped many people put together many publications, and no matter how organized people seem to be, they rarely keep a list of all the ingredients of their publication. Complex documents that contain many different text files and graphics could also benefit from a *runsheet.*

A runsheet is simply a list of every single piece of text or graphics that will be in your publication, its designated location, and length or size. A runsheet not only helps you keep track of the text and graphics in your publication, but just as importantly, helps you keep track of *who* is responsible for each item and when it is due. Even if you're doing it all yourself, the form on the opposite page can help you.

RUNSHEET Project: Date: Pg#

AUTHOR	TITLE/SUBJECT	PG#	ART	K	HEAD			

When to start

One thing that I've learned over and over again (the hard way), is that you shouldn't begin setting type until all the text elements are complete. I know, I know, this is the *real* world and everyone does everything at the last minute. Now that everyone knows you're using a computer, they also think they can make more changes, up to the very last second.

It's true that you can make changes up to the last second if it's a real emergency or if you're working on time-sensitive material that *must* come in right at deadline. But don't do it unless you have to. Put your foot down. Set deadlines and stick to them. That's often a difficult thing to do if you're working *for* someone. But you need to make it clear to them that if they miss their deadline you can't promise to make yours.

The more embryonic the text, the more time you'll waste. The more complete the text, the less time it will take to format it.

Once you start setting the type, each change in the text will ripple through your pages, causing more and more changes: widows, orphans, bad hyphenation, strange text breaks, going a word or more over your page limit—the list is endless.

If you can start with finished text, it's easier to concentrate on the typography. Even if you start typesetting a little later, perfecting the typography will take less time if the text is complete.

Play around until it works

This is not the same as "fool around," because play isn't foolish. Call it "experimentation" if you're too embarrassed to call it "play." Once you've finished your homework, it's playtime, the moment when you put everything together and see how it looks, shuffle things around, try new ideas.

This is a *very important* step, because it takes you from the theoretical to the real—from ideas to reality. Few people make that jump perfectly the first time. What "seemed like a good idea at the time" often requires rethinking, modulating, and, always, much fine tuning.

You *can* do it. I'm a firm believer that many great things have been accomplished by people who didn't know better—people who had never heard that it *couldn't* be done.

So don't allow type to scare you unless it says "Boo."

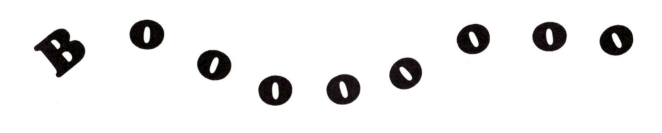

Boooooooo

On your mark

When you're in the midst of your project, the last thing you need to do is search through this book to find important points. So use these two lists to help remind you of what's really important. Actually, your health and sanity are *really* the most important things, but as far as type is concerned, these are the top 10.

Top 10 Type Tenets

Content first! Type must enhance the message of the text—never obscure or confuse it (eschew obfuscation). If possible, make sure the text is complete before you start designing, so you don't have to make changes later on.

Remember your audience. Ask yourself who, what, when, where, why, and how. If you consider the content and audience, the design will follow.

Design everything for a reason. *Design* means "structure, blueprint, plan, strategy, aim, intention, and purpose," as well as merely "style."

Use type to provide organization. Design the project so that it is easier to read and use.

Use an appropriate typeface. Type is your personality on paper. If it's a serious subject, be serious. If it's a casual subject, be casual. Don't send mixed signals to readers.

Be consistent. The design and structure act as signposts for the readers. Changing the typeface or format at random throughout a document will confuse readers.

Keep it simple. Unexpected complexity will arise anyway despite your good intentions. Use as few styles or tags (or whatever your program calls them) as possible.

Accept your limitations. Work with what you have. If you are handed a lemon, make lemonade.

Use spell checking and a proofreader! It doesn't matter how typographically perfect a page is if it contains stupid spelling errors.

If at all possible, have fun. If you have fun, the chances of your readers having fun are greatly increased. People learn more when they aren't bored.

Get set

Top 10 Type Techniques

Be generous with leading. Add at least 1 or 2 points to the type size.

Keep line lengths reasonable. Optimum size: Over 30 characters and under 70 characters. Or about 10 words long for serif, 8 or 9 words long for sans serif.

If you justify you must also hyphenate.

Use either indent or block style for paragraphs, but not both, and use only one space after a period, not two.

Use italics instead of underlines, but don't set long blocks of text in italics because it's harder to read.

Leave more space above headlines and subheads than below them, and avoid setting them in all caps.

Don't underline headlines or subheads, since those lines would separate them from the text to which they belong.

Use subheads liberally (Unless you're typesetting a novel) to help readers find what they're looking for.

Use enough white space. Think of the page as a room, the letters as people sitting in rows. Give them enough room to move around, or they will start a riot. Rule of thumb: Always leave at least enough room to place your thumbs at the edges of the page without touching the type.

In case of emergency—*break rules.*

GO!

While working with type can be fun, it can also be hazadous to your health. After I created the bad example on the next page I was almost ill. See how many mistakes you can detect (before turning away in horror). Then turn the page to check your observations.

GOVERNOR'S PEN IS RED THIS YEAR.

IS BUSY WORK UN-PRODUCTIVE?

*T*o coin a phrase. The moment you've all been waiting for -- "The real thing". Today's the first day of the rest of your life. The long and short of it. Tell it like it is. Out of the mouths of babes...

That's the way it was. Something for everyone. It's always darkest before the dawn. When it rains it pours. Every cloud has a silver lining. The light at the end of the tunnel. Good things come in small packages. Let's put on a show. All systems are go. One giant leap for mankind. It's a once in a lifetime opportunity. Only you can prevent forest fires.

Hold everything. Down to the wire. Don't touch that dial. On the edge of my seat. I'll get to the bottom of this if it's the last thing I do. What do you take me for? A word to the wise. Word of mouth. Food for thought. Soul food. 99.44% pure. I can resist everything except temptation. That's the way the cookie crumbles. Do you want fries with that? Let's do lunch.

SUBHEAD

It seems like only yesterday. Time flies. What do you want to be when you grow up? You're only as old as you feel. You're not getting older you're getting better. It's just a phase. Another day older and deeper in debt. Are we having fun yet? Time is money. You've got to pay your dues. Do you take American Express? Nothing succeeds like success. Nothing exceeds like excess. Go for broke. Rags to riches. If they could see me now. That's when a million dollars was worth something. Value for money. The check is in the mail. The bottom line.

Subject to prior sale. Void where prohibited by law. Subject to change without notice. Hail to the Chief.

Famous last words. Expletive deleted. Hail to the Chief. Expletive deleted.

SOME ASSEMBLY REQUIRED. BATTERIES NOT INCLUDED. COLLECT 'EM ALL. SO EASY EVEN A CHILD CAN DO IT. FOOLPROOF. YOU CAN'T MISS IT. SO NEAR YET SO FAR. YOUR MILEAGE MAY VARY. SUBSTANTIAL PENALTIES FOR

I'm going to teach you a thing or two. Gimme an "F." Don't make a federal case out of it. United we stand, divided we fall. We must all hang together or surely we will all hang separately. The moment of truth has arrived. The majority rules. To tell the truth. You have the right to remain silent. Throw in the towel. Soon to be made into a major motion picture. Art imitates life. No redeeming social value. What you see is what you get. Look out for number one. With friends like that, who needs enemies. What are friends for? A friend in need is a friend indeed. A friend in need is indeed a pest. People in glass houses shouldn't throw stones. Speak softly and carry a big stick. What you don't know won't hurt you. Ignorance is bliss. Don't get smart with me. Keep it down to a dull roar. You're cruisin' for a bruisin' and skating on thin ice. Is there a doctor in the house? Feed a cold, starve a fever. Don't let the bedbugs bite. Duck and cover. Just what the doctor ordered. Nice guys finish last. I never met a man I didn't like. She speaks 14 different languages and she can't say "no" in any of them. Tell it to the Marines. When you've seen one, you've seen 'em all. How can I miss you if you won't go away? This will hurt you more than it hurts me. How can you believe me when I tell you that I love you when you know I've been a liar all my life? Once upon a time. Boy meets girl. Pure as the driven snow. To know him is to love him. One bad apple don't spoil the whole bunch, girl. He made me an offer I couldn't refuse. For better or for worse. Sign on the dotted line. A lifetime guarantee. Don't knock it till you've tried it. Man does not live by bread alone. Builds strong bodies 12 ways. Bring home the bacon. What's for dinner? I'll pretend I didn't hear that. The honeymoon is over. Nothin' says lovin' like somethin' from the oven. We reserve the right to serve refuse to anyone. Meanwhile, back at the ranch. Father knows best. I leave those decisions to my wife. The rules of the road. Don't chew with your mouth open. You never call, you never write, you never say "hello." This is your mother speaking. Where did we go wrong? Trip down memory lane. What I did on my summer vacation. Having a wonderful time, wish you were here. If you can't stand the heat, get out of the kitchen. A nice place to visit but I wouldn't want to live there. Keep those cards and letters coming.

Do as I say, not as I do.

What's wrong with the page?

Everything is wrong with the previous page. It's a typographic nightmare come true. I doubt that you could *ever* do anything this awful with so many errors on a single page, but it's common to see at least one of these errors on an average page. Let's start at the top.

First, there's *no white space* anywhere on the page. All the columns are too narrow. There isn't enough room between the columns, and the vertical lines not only are overkill with justified text, but each one is a different thickness.

The "Governor" headline: *Never set headlines in all caps,* underlined, *or* justified. Don't put periods in headlines. There's too much white space under the headline. *And* the headline is set in Zapf Calligraphic (Palatino), while the body text for this article is Baskerville.Two faces that are too similar look like a mistake. A sans serif face would have been a better choice for the headline.

"To coin a phrase..." First paragraphs actually *can* be set in a different typeface for effect, but in this case, ITC Avant Garde isn't a good choice because it's not easy to read. There's not enough leading, the drop cap isn't big enough and doesn't sit on the baseline.

There's no hyphenation anywhere in the first column, so you end up with big, ugly gaps, and there's a double hyphen (- -) instead of a real em dash (—).

This article commits the mortal sin of using indents (which are too deep) *and* space between the paragraphs. It's 11-point body text with only 11-point leading, which isn't enough, so it looks dark. Once again, there's no hyphenation.

The second column starts with an orphan. It looks awful and could have been eliminated automatically just by setting the software to avoid leaving one line by itself at the top or bottom of a column.

The subhead is dreadful, yet I see these *all* the time. It's the same face as the body, though it should be bold or italic or a different typeface altogether. It's indented like the body text when it should be flush left. And it's underlined. Bad, bad, bad. Never underline subheads. And never leave as much (or more) space under a subhead as you have above it because it should be a lead-in for the text that follows. Had enough? Wait, there's more. Keep reading.

Too much italicized text here. Yes, Baskerville has pretty italics, but it's harder to read.

The next two paragraphs have no space in front of them. This is actually good, but it's inconsistent with the rest of the article.

Not leaving any white space between the box and the text inside it is a *very* common mistake. It's also a very ugly mistake. Not to mention that the ALL CAPS makes it harder to read.

Bumping heads. Not only does it look bad, but this example shows the *danger* if someone accidentally reads across the two headlines as if they were one. This headline is also justified (wrong, wrong, wrong) and hyphenated (never, never, never), and ITC Bookman (yet another serif and yet another typeface on the page for no good reason). And it runs into the intercolumn rule! Add all that to the fact that this headline doesn't span both columns of the story and it's enough to make you nauseous.

The first article had indents *and* blank spaces, the second article has neither. It looks like one giant, boring paragraph. *Always* use either one or the other, but *never* both or neither.

Why is this article set in Century Schoolbook? *All* body text (except for separately boxed text such as sidebars) should be in the same face. The type here is 10/10.5, a different size from the first article with, once again, not enough leading. They should both have been 11-point.

The pull quote is so bad it's scary. It runs into the body text, it's left aligned when centered would have separated it more from the text, the white space around it is uneven, *and* it's ITC Galliard italic, yet another typeface. The whole thing is too wide, so it makes the text in the adjacent columns look horrifically spaced out.

Never underline. Use *italics* instead.

Never, *never* add extra leading to a paragraph or two just to fill out the column. If you are sure you need all your column bottoms to align, spread the space out evenly, in tiny, imperceptible amounts. If your software has a vertical justification feature, set the amount of additional space to the minimum. Or, better yet, just leave the column bottoms ragged.

Did you notice? All the text had two spaces after the periods instead of just one. Another no-no.

10

The elements of Type*Style*

Drop caps
Subheads
Pull quotes

Drop caps, subheads, and pull quotes can transform a page from mundane to magnificent. Follow my example.

Drop caps

Swiss Compressed

Don't touch that dial. To coin a phrase. The moment you've all been waiting for. The real thing. Today's the first day of the rest of your life. The long and short of it. Tell it like it is. Out of the mouths of babes. That's the way it was. Something for everyone. It's always darkest before the dawn. When it rains it pours. Every cloud has a silver lining. The light at the end of the tunnel. Good things come in small packages. Let's put on a show. All systems are go. It's a once in a lifetime opportunity.

Bernhard Modern

Run, don't walk. Hold everything. Down to the wire. Don't touch that dial. On the edge of my seat. I'll get to the bottom of this if it's the last thing I do. What do you take me for? A word to the wise. Word of mouth. Food for thought. Soul food. 99.44% pure. I can resist everything except temptation. That's the way the cookie crumbles. Eat your heart out. Thanks, but no thanks.

Kaufmann Bold

Only yesterday. Time flies. What do you want to be when you grow up? You're only as old as you feel. You're not getting older you're getting better. It's just a phase. Another day older and deeper in debt. Are we having fun yet? Time is money. You've got to pay your dues. Do you take American Express? Nothing succeeds like success. Nothing exceeds like excess. Go for broke. Rags to riches. Concept by Al Masini. If they could see me now. That's when a million dollars was worth something. Value for money. The check is in the mail.

ITC Tiffany Bold

Put all your eggs in one basket. Some assembly required. Batteries not included. So easy even a child can do it. Foolproof. You can't miss it. So near yet so far. Your mileage may vary. Substantial penalties for early withdrawal. Subject to prior sale. Void where prohibited by law. Subject to change without notice.

Futura Light, 8 pt. outline

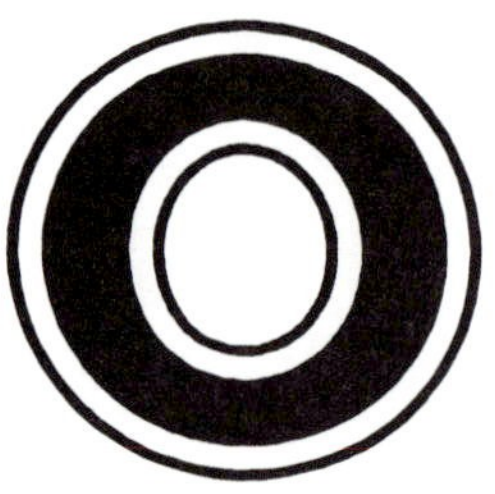

Futura Extra Black inline

Baskerville Bold Italic

Bodoni Bold rotated 45°

Broadway

Collect 'em all. Nice guys finish last. I never met a man I didn't like. She speaks 14 different languages and she can't say "no" in any of them. Tell it to the Marines. When you've seen one, you've seen 'em all. How can I miss you if you won't go away? This will hurt you more than it hurts me. How can you believe me when I tell you that I love you when you know I've been a liar all my life?

University Roman

Art imitates life. What you see is what you get. Look out for number one. With friends like that, who needs enemies. What are friends for? A friend in need is a friend indeed. A friend in need is indeed a pest. People in glass houses shouldn't throw stones. Speak softly and carry a big stick. What you don't know won't hurt you. Ignorance is bliss.

ITC Galliard

Pure as the driven snow. Once upon a time. Boy meets girl. To know him is to love him. One bad apple don't spoil the whole bunch, girl. He made me an offer I couldn't refuse. For better or for worse. Sign on the dotted line. A lifetime guarantee. Don't knock it till you've tried it. Man does not live by bread alone. Builds strong bodies 12 ways. Bring home the bacon. What's for dinner?.

Futura Extra Black

Soon to be made into a major motion picture. Nothin' says lovin' like somethin' from the oven. We reserve the right to serve refuse to anyone. Meanwhile, back at the ranch. Father knows best. I leave those decisions to my wife. The rules of the road. Don't chew with your mouth open. Do as I say, not as I do. Wait 'til your father gets home. It's 10 p.m., do you know where your children are? My, how you've grown.

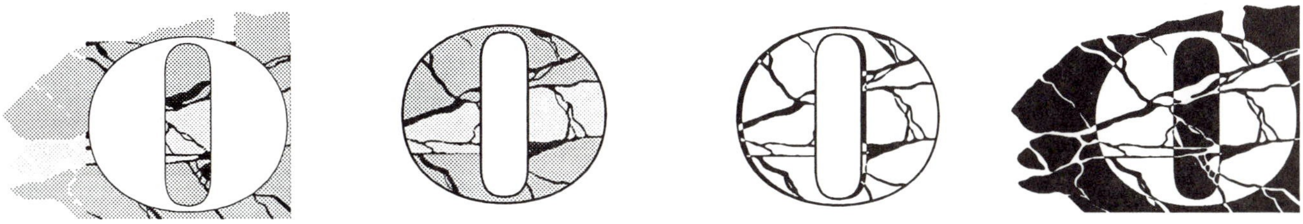

ITC Tiffany Bold combined with treatments of *Natural Images* backgrounds by Artbeats. Assembled in Corel Draw.

Subheads

ITC Avant Garde

To coin a phrase

The moment you've all been waiting for. The real thing. Today's the first day of the rest of your life. The long and short of it. Tell it like it is. Out of the mouths of babes. That's the way it was. Something for everyone. It's always darkest before the dawn. When it rains it pours. Every cloud has a silver lining. The light at the end of the tunnel. Good things come in small packages. One giant leap for mankind. It's a once in a lifetime opportunity.

Zurich Black Extended

To coin a phrase

Hold everything. Down to the wire. Don't touch that dial. On the edge of my seat. I'll get to the bottom of this if it's the last thing I do. What do you take me for? A word to the wise. Word of mouth. Food for thought. Soul food. 99.44% pure. I can resist everything except temptation. That's the way the cookie crumbles. Eat your heart out. Thanks, but no thanks.

Baskerville Bold

■ TO COIN A PHRASE

It seems like only yesterday. Time flies. What do you want to be when you grow up? You're only as old as you feel. You're not getting older you're getting better. It's just a phase. Another day older and deeper in debt. Are we having fun yet? Time is money. You've got to pay your dues. Do you take American Express? Go for broke. Rags to riches. If they could see me now. Value for money. The check is in the mail. The bottom line.

Futura Bold

To Coin A Phrase

Some assembly required. Batteries not included. Collect 'em all. So easy even a child can do it. Foolproof. You can't miss it. So near yet so far. Your mileage may vary. Substantial penalties for early withdrawal. Subject to prior sale. Void where prohibited by law. Subject to change without notice.

Serifa Black

To coin a phrase. Hail to the Chief. Let me make one thing perfectly clear. I am not a crook. Famous last words. Expletive deleted. I'm going to teach you a thing or two. Don't make a federal case out of it. United we stand, divided we fall. We must all hang together or surely we will all hang separately. The moment of truth has arrived. The majority rules. To tell the truth. You have the right to remain silent. Soon to be made into a major motion picture. Art imitates life.

Futura Condensed

To coin a phrase. Nice guys finish last. I never met a man I didn't like. She speaks 14 different languages and she can't say "no" in any of them. Tell it to the Marines. When you've seen one, you've seen 'em all. How can I miss you if you won't go away? This will hurt you more than it hurts me. How can you believe me when I tell you that I love you when you know I've been a liar all my life?

Swiss Compressed

To coin a phrase. What you see is what you get. Look out for number one. With friends like that, who needs enemies. What are friends for? A friend in need is a friend indeed. A friend in need is indeed a pest. People in glass houses shouldn't throw stones. Speak softly and carry a big stick. What you don't know won't hurt you. Ignorance is bliss. Keep it down to a dull roar.

Bitstream Amerigo

To coin a phrase

What's for dinner? I'll pretend I didn't hear that. The honeymoon is over. Nothin' says lovin' like somethin' from the oven. We reserve the right to serve refuse to anyone. Meanwhile, back at the ranch. Father knows best. I leave those decisions to my wife. The rules of the road.

Handel Gothic

To coin a phrase ....

Once upon a time. Boy meets girl. Pure as the driven snow. To know him is to love him. One bad apple don't spoil the whole bunch, girl. He made me an offer I couldn't refuse. For better or for worse. Sign on the dotted line. A lifetime guarantee. Don't knock it till you've tried it. Man does not live by bread alone.

Baskerville Italic

❖ *To coin a phrase*

Do as I say, not as I do. You've got to watch him every minute. I can't take you anywhere. Wait 'til your father gets home. It's 10 p.m., do you know where your children are? My, how you've grown. You never call, you never write, you never say "hello." This is your mother speaking.

Franklin Gothic Condensed

To coin a phrase

Trip down memory lane. What I did on my summer vacation. Having a wonderful time, wish you were here. If you can't stand the heat, get out of the kitchen. A nice place to visit but I wouldn't want to live there. Keep those cards and letters coming. To make a long story short. That's life. From all of us to all of you. And many more.

Pull quotes

To coin a phrase. The moment you've all been waiting for. The real thing. Today's the first day of the rest of your life. The long and short of it. Tell it like it is. Out of the mouths of babes. That's the way it was. Something for everyone. It's always darkest before the dawn. When it rains it pours. Every cloud has a silver lining. The light at the end of the tunnel. Good things come in small packages. Let's put on a show. All systems are go. One giant leap for mankind. It's a once in a lifetime opportunity. Only you can prevent forest fires. Hold everything. Down to the wire. Don't touch that dial. On the edge of my seat. I'll get to the bottom of this if it's the last thing I do. What do you take me for? A word to the wise. Word of mouth. Food for thought. Soul food. 99.44% pure. I can resist everything except temptation. That's the way the cookie crumbles. Eat your heart out. Do you want fries with that? Thanks, but no thanks. Let's do lunch.

Time is money. You've got to pay your dues. Go for broke. Are we having fun yet?

Bernhard Modern

Time is money. You've got to pay your dues. Go for broke. Are we having fun yet?

It seems like only yesterday. Time flies. What do you want to be when you grow up? You're only as old as you feel. You're not getting older you're getting better. It's just a phase. Another day older and deeper in debt. Are we having fun yet? Time is money. You've got to pay your dues. Do you take American Express? Nothing succeeds like success. Nothing exceeds like excess. Go for broke. Rags to riches. Concept by Al Masini. If they could see me now. That's when a million dollars was worth something. Value for money. The check is in the mail. The bottom line.

Zurich Black

Time is money.
You've got to pay your dues.
Go for broke. Are we having
fun yet?

ITC Galliard Italic

Some assembly required. Batteries not included. Collect 'em all. So easy even a child can do it. Foolproof. You can't miss it. So near yet so far. Your mileage may vary. Void where prohibited by law. Subject to change without notice.

TIME IS MONEY. YOU'VE GOT TO PAY YOUR DUES. GO FOR BROKE. ARE WE HAVING FUN YET?

Futura Medium

Hail to the Chief. Let me make one thing perfectly clear. I am not a crook. Famous last words. Expletive deleted. I'm going to teach you a thing or two. Gimme an "F." Don't make a federal case out of it. United we stand, divided we fall. We must all hang together or surely we will all hang separately. The moment of truth has arrived. The majority rules. To tell the truth. You have the right to remain silent. Speak softly and carry a big stick. People in glass houses shouldn't throw stones. Throw in the towel. Soon to be made into a major motion picture. Art imitates life.

What you see is what you get. Look out for number one. With friends like that, who needs enemies. What are friends for? A friend in need is a friend indeed. A friend in need is indeed a pest. People in glass houses shouldn't throw stones. Speak softly and carry a big stick. What you don't know won't hurt you. Ignorance is bliss. Don't get smart with me. Keep it down to a dull roar. Is there a doctor in the house? Feed a cold, starve a fever.

t ime is money. You've got to pay your dues.

ITC American Typewriter

Nice guys finish last. I never met a man I didn't like. She speaks 14 different languages and she can't say "no" in any of them. Tell it to the Marines. When you've seen one, you've seen 'em all. How can I miss you if you won't go away? This will hurt you more than it hurts me. How can you believe me when I tell you that I love you when you know I've been a liar all my life?

"Time is money.
You've got to pay your dues.
Go for broke. Are we having fun yet?"

ITC Korinna Italic with
ITC Zapf Dingbat quotes

Trip down memory lane. Having a wonderful time, wish you were here. If you can't stand the heat, get out of the kitchen. A nice place to visit but I wouldn't want to live there. Concept by Al Masini. Keep those cards and letter coming. To make a long story short. That's life. From all of us to all of you. *And many more.*

T*ime is money. You've got to pay your dues.*
Go for broke. Are we having fun yet?

Goudy Old Style Italic

11

Where there's type there's art

Letters *are* graphics

Type is decorative. The shapes of the letters are visually interesting, even when they aren't spelling anything.

Where there's type, there's art

Letters are graphics

Futura Extra Black "D" combined with circles.

You've now read chapter after chapter saying that type isn't just decorative and that its purpose here on earth is to serve "the message." But while that's true, type *is* graphic. Type *is* decorative. The shapes of the letters *are* visually interesting, even when they aren't spelling anything.

Type is a wonderful way to add interest to a page when you don't have a graphic at your disposal. For instance, you might use a big drop cap, a giant but light initial cap floating subliminally in the background, or just the pure shape of a letter.

Type tools

The best way to manipulate type as graphics is with a draw program. For PCs, Micrografx Designer directly accepts Bitstream fonts in *Speedo* format, and Corel Draw converts Fontware fonts using its WFNBoss program (which I call "Esperfonto"). For Macs, Aldus Freehand and Adobe Illustrator can access Bitstream's *Type 1* fonts using utility programs such as Altsys Metamorphosis.

Kaufmann "neon."

The wonderful thing about these programs is that they allow you to use type as both text and graphics. You enter words and select the typeface; the program sets the type.

You can overcome basic limitations of page composition programs like type size, because these programs rarely limit character size. You also have the power to rotate text; fill it with colors, patterns or shades of gray; outline it; inline it; compress it; expand it; skew it; slant it; and set it to "paths" such as circles, arcs, boxes, or wavy lines. Creating a 720-point (10 inches tall) letter rotated 12 degrees and filled with light gray is no trouble at all.

You can even break type down into its basic curves and manipulate it as pure graphics, allowing for the creation of the kind of custom characters that are the mainstay of logo design.

Goudy Old Style distorted.

Corel Draw is a real standout when it comes to manipulating text. One thing that makes Corel's text control so special is that you can edit text even after it has been compressed, expanded, or automatically set to paths. Everything about the text can be changed: the typeface, size, kerning, word spacing, and vertical

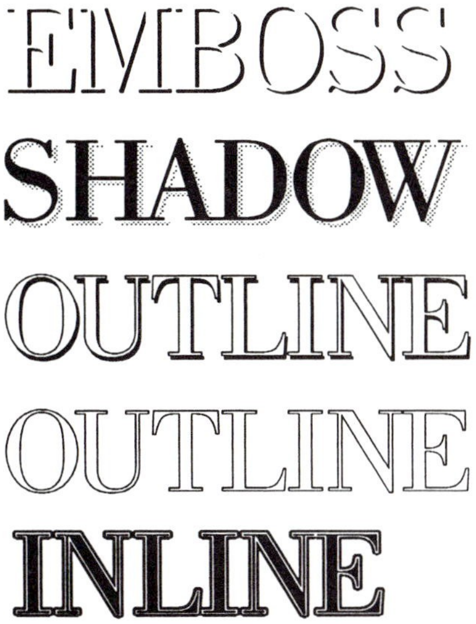

Basic special effects.

Futura Extra Black as op-art (S combined with circles).

Futura Condensed "neon," set using "text to path."

alignment. Corel's kerning feature is especially impressive because it allows for infinitesimal control over characters, which typographers need. Corel's kerning is so good that I often use it for creating large headlines, and then import the headline into a page composition program as a graphic. The only time you lose the ability to edit text is when it's converted to curves for manipulation of character shapes.

Hammersmith combined with squares.

Corel Draw's "text to path" feature will set text along any path you draw. Setting text around circles or arcs is difficult and tedious to do manually, but Corel Draw does it accurately in seconds. The letters remain perfectly kerned. Text can be made to fit inside or outside the circle or shape, and can be straightened and re-pathed at any time.

Export license

Once you've had your way with your text, you export it to a graphic file. These programs can export to many different formats, but it's best to choose a *line art* format such as EPS (Encapsulated PostScript), CGM (Computer Graphic Metafile), or GEM (Graphic Environment Metafile). Line art graphics consist of shapes such as lines and curves, so they can be scaled to any size without any loss of quality and will always print at the highest resolution of the printer or typesetter.

Futura Extra Black with a new wave treatment from Corel Draw.

The other basic graphic format is called "bitmapped" because it is made up of tiny dots (or bits). A bitmap file is basically a grid of dots; this one is black, this one is white. When you scale these images to make them larger, the dots get bigger too, resulting in "the jaggies." Scanned images are bitmapped.

Scanning for type

Another great way to add decorative type is to use a scanner. Now let's get this straight: I'm not talking ransom notes here. I don't mean to suggest that you laboriously string together hundreds of characters you've scanned from other sources to make paragraphs of text. What I mean is to use a scanned letter as a decorative element, such as a drop cap or first letter of a headline, or even as type that is simply decorative.

From New Art Deco Alphabets by Marcia Loeb (Dover).

While Bitstream has a large type library, and thousands of typefaces have been digitized, there's still 500 year's worth of type that isn't yet available for computers. And yet, with any scanner, whether a hand scanner or a flatbed, you can bring hundreds of years of type into your computer.

As with anything you scan, the trick is to avoid getting hauled into court for copyright infringement. Fortunately, there's a huge spectrum of unusual, attractive, distinctive, and copyright-free decorative type that you can scan and print until the cows come home.

If you can find magazines that are over 75 years old, you can scan anything in them. Garage sales and libraries are an Aladdin's cave for finding these old publications. Some old publications may be expensive, even at garage sales, but others can cost a quarter and still be chock full of fascinating possibilities. It's not unusual to find beautiful specimens of type you've never seen before. Most libraries won't permit you to check out old magazines because they're too fragile, but most will allow you to photocopy pages, which you can then scan.

Books of type

Copyright free, virtually free

From New Art Deco Alphabets by Marcia Loeb (Dover).

By far the most extensive, easiest to find, safest, and most reasonably priced collection of copyright-free decorative type is available from Dover Publications. Up to ten illustrations may be taken from each book for any one project, free and without permission.

Those clever folks at Dover scoured old magazines and books from around the world and filled scores of volumes with fabulous fonts. Dover's "Pictorial Archive" books are famous for their line art. And because of the high-quality printing, images from Dover publications always scan very well, usually requiring little or no cleanup.

From Decorative Letters (Dover).

With the help of a paint program, you can quickly customize these beauties into something that looks like it was designed just for you.

Just as remarkable as the books are their low prices. The average price of a Dover publication ranges from $3.50 to $7, and the books are even available by mail order if your local bookstore doesn't carry the complete line. I've been addicted to Dover books since I was a child, and the price of one of my early Dover discoveries has gone up only $1 in 16 years. That makes them an even better value today than they were back then.

The best book to start with is from the "Ready to Use" series and is called *Decorative Letters,* edited by Carol Belanger Grafton. This $3.50 wonder has over 800 letters in a totally eclectic mix of styles ranging from Renaissance to Art Deco, with forays into Victorian and Art Nouveau along the way. There are anywhere from 20 to 40 specimens for each letter of the alphabet, but no numbers.

From New Art Deco Alphabets by Marcia Loeb (Dover).

Most of Dover's books concentrate on one style or period of design. These books are wonderful if, for example, you're an Art-Decoholic as I am, or an Art Nouveau-aficionado as my wife is. Don't expect to find complete alphabets in every typeface, however; some books offer only a single character from a specific typeface.

While most of the books take type from old sources, one of my favorites consists of 38 original alphabets. *New Art Deco Alphabets* by Marcia Loeb is absolutely essential for anyone even remotely interested in the period. Many of the designs are clearly inspired by well-known typefaces. Every design includes a complete alphabet, and many include numerals. The type ranges from streamline to sunburst. Type with a starry background, palm trees, moons, dots, and zig-zags abounds. These fun faces are astoundingly creative, endlessly useful, and an absolute steal at $4.95.

Some of the wackiest typefaces you'll ever see can be found in *Bizarre & Ornamental Alphabets,* edited by the prolific Carol Belanger Grafton. This book includes fairly complete alphabets resembling animals, architectural drawings, Victorian, medieval, even surrealistic collage. My personal favorites are the extraordinary "blueprint" letters that appear to be the floor plans for Versailles. (See illustrationon page 9-4.)

From Bizarre & Ornamental Alphabets (Dover).

Art Nouveau fans will go wild over *Art Nouveau Display Alphabets,* selected and arranged by Dan X. Solo from the Solotype typographer's catalog. This book contains 100 sets of capital letters, 75 lowercase sets, 90 sets of numbers/symbols, and 20 ornamental

From Decorative Letters (Dover).

From Decorative Letters (Dover).

From Treasury of Art Nouveau Design & Ornament (Dover).

designs. This orgy of organic letterforms is authentic (including the set from the Paris Metro), well presented, and can be yours for only $4.95.

A few more noteworthy volumes include *Treasury of Art Nouveau Design & Ornament,* selected by your friend and mine, Carol Belanger Grafton. This book contains gorgeously decorated initial caps as well as fancy ornaments and borders.

Treasury of Authentic Art Nouveau Alphabets, Decorative Initials, Monograms, Frames and Ornaments, edited by Ludwig Petzendorer includes 137 complete alphabets, 23 uppercase fonts, 33 complete sets of decorative initials, 1,951 monograms, 146 colophons, and 179 ornaments and borders. The monograms are especially comprehensive and unique.

Art Nouveau & Early Art Deco Type & Design from the Roman Scherer Catalogue, edited by Theodore Menten, is full of unusual designs and useful dingbat-like characters, but most of the alphabets are incomplete.

Scanned art to line art

All of the type from these books can be easily scanned. However, scanners create bitmapped files, while line art files scale better and print sharper. If you have a draw program you're in luck again. All these programs contain a feature called "autotrace" that allows you to turn scanned images into line art, which prints razor sharp, even on a Linotronic.

Adobe sells a stand-alone program called Streamline, which does a better job than the autotrace features of some draw programs. Corel Draw includes Corel Trace, a similar stand-alone program.

So send for the free Dover catalog this very minute. Nowhere else can you buy so much great type for such a small amount of money.

Dover Publications Inc.
31 East 2nd Street
Mineola, NY 11501
516-294-7000

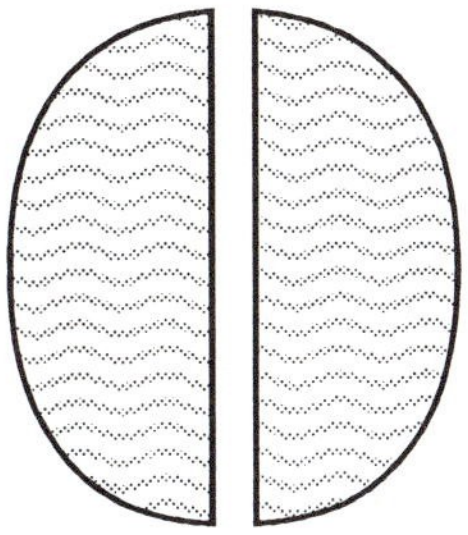

Futura Black with "wave" background.

Futura Bold combined with squares.

Futura Light combined with squares.

From Bizarre & Ornamental Alphabets (Dover).

Baskerville "embossed."

From Bizarre & Ornamental Alphabets (Dover).

ITC Galliard.

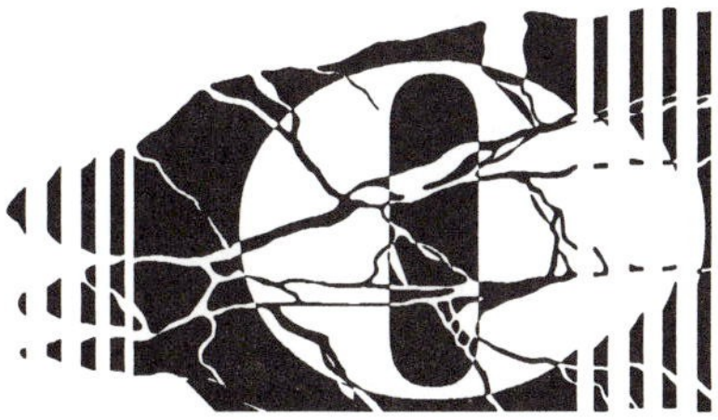

ArtBeats marble background combined with Tiffany Bold "O," cut to shreds.

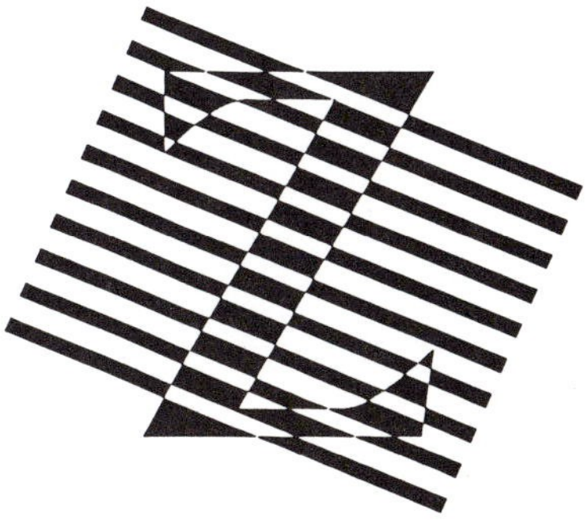

Amerigo combined with rectangles.

12

Seen in the best company

Corporate identity

If people never actually meet you, or see your office, they form their opinion of you solely on the correspondence and other printed material they receive from you.

Seen in the best company

Corporate identity

We live in a shallow society. We often judge people and things merely by how they look, instead of what they say or do. I have to admit that sometimes I find all this superficiality repugnant, but it's a fact of life. That's why a corporate identity is so important. If people never actually meet you, or see your office, they form their opinion of you solely on the correspondence and other printed material they receive from you.

A corporate identity is your company's face on paper—instant recognition—and includes everything having to do with the *look* of a printed page. A corporate identity doesn't just mean sticking your company logo on everything (although I have more to say on that subject in next chapter). Building an identity requires a methodical unification of all existing documents to conform to a company's design philosophy.

Having a corporate identity means that there is consistency among all the printed material emanating from a business. This consistency covers typefaces, type sizes, margins, whether text is set justified or ragged right, even the company's logo—where it appears on the page, and how big it is.

Sometimes a corporate identity is limited to materials that leave the company, such as business cards, correspondence, reports, proposals, forms, and newsletters. Other times, it's all inclusive and covers every type of printed matter, including internal forms, memos, even message pads.

Not only will a specific corporate identity give your business distinction, but it can make it faster and easier to produce documents. You can even set up template files for these documents so that everyone spends less time formatting and still achieves consistently attractive results.

Capitalistic connotations

You can capitalize on a typeface that someone else has endowed with connotations, or you can conjure up connotations of your own.

IBM has an established corporate image that runs through every piece of printed material it produces. If you've ever studied IBM's print advertisements, you'll notice that it always uses the same typestyle (a special version of Bodoni), and usually the same ad layout: a big picture on top with copy running along the bottom. This high recognition factor means that you only have to glance at the ad, not even read it, to know who it's from.

Identity

Bodoni

You also may have seen, but not realized, that smaller companies often copy this format, right down to the typeface. At first you may look at one of their ads because you think it's from IBM. But even after you realize that it's not (and not everyone will), you may still subconsciously link the company or product with IBM.

While it's illegal to use IBM's logo (or even its name without proper trademark disclaimers), there has yet to be any type of "look and feel" legal case for printed pages, unless an actual name or logo was involved. A strategy often used by new, small companies involves emulating an already established firm's design. They aren't creating an image of their own, but people immediately identify the look of the page with something they've seen before and respected.

But if you're a new small company and you're out to make a name for yourself, you may not want to look like or be confused with someone else's business. If you're self-confident, then develop your own style. When people start to copy it, then you'll know it's successful.

Big corporations regularly spend huge sums of money hiring designers or ad agencies to create an image for them, but you don't have to. No matter what size your business, there are some basic things you can do to establish a corporate identity for yourself.

Find your own typographic identity

First and foremost, choose a typeface to represent you or your company. This isn't always as easy as it sounds, because the typeface you choose should be one that works on every kind of printed matter your company uses, from business cards to overhead slide shows. This means you need to select a "body text" typeface that works well at any size from small text sizes to large display ones. If you choose a typeface and start to use it for everything, soon people will associate that typeface with you and your business.

Identity

Bitstream Amerigo

IBM wisely chose a classic but distinctive typeface in Bodoni, and you could do the same thing. That doesn't mean you have to use the same typeface, but it is a warning to not choose a typeface that's overused. Swiss and Dutch (Helvetica and Times Roman) no longer project a distinct identity, and if you use them, you are doomed to look like everyone else who got them for free.

Identity

Activa

The same sad fate of overuse has befallen all the fonts built into the original PostScript printers. Palatino, while lovely, isn't truly distinctive anymore because too many people use it. Century Schoolbook, Avant Garde, and even Zapf Chancery have been used so often that they no longer stand out. Still, if you have to choose one of the built-in faces, I'd recommend Palatino or New Century Schoolbook. I don't much care for Century Schoolbook, but it's a readable face that looks different enough from Times Roman to at least have some identity.

Identity

Bitstream Charter

Identity

ITC Cheltenham

In your quest for the perfect typeface, *don't* choose one that is so trendy that you'll have to redo your company image in a few years. Be careful about using anything too extreme. That might be alright for your logo because it's unique, but using an extreme typeface for all your other material will not only be impractical, but, once again, will become dated.

Identity

ITC Clearface

If you want a serif face, try Amerigo, Activa (Trump), Baskerville, Bodoni, Charter, ITC Cheltenham, ITC Clearface, Cooper, ITC Galliard, ITC Garamond, Goudy Old Style, ITC Korinna, Serifa, ITC Souvenir, Zapf Calligraphic (Palatino), or Zapf Elliptical (Melior). Any of these would be a good face for a corporate identity.

Identity

Bitstream Cooper

Identity

ITC Galliard

If you want a modern sans serif look, try Futura, Hammersmith (Gill Sans), Zapf Humanist (Optima), or even Zurich (Univers).

Important: You can, but don't have to, use your corporate typeface for your logo. You also aren't locked into a single typeface. You need one main typeface that you use for the bulk of your work, but you can also choose another complimentary typeface. The advantage of using only one face is that it keeps pounding that identity into people's brains rather than diluting the identity by using another typeface.

Details, details

Developing a corporate identity for all your printed material requires much thought and planning, and some trial and error. But it's worth it when you've worked out a system and need to add a new type of document. You'll already know:

- Whether the margins should be justified or ragged.
- Whether you use intercolumn rules or no rules.
- Whether you use indented paragraphs or block style, and if block style, how much space you use between paragraphs.
- What your default bullet character is.
- Whether your logo is centered, left aligned, right aligned, or always slightly off-center.
- Whether you use headers or footers, or both.
- Whether you have ruling lines in these headers or footers. If you use Ruling Line Above, you'll know whether it should be margin wide, column wide, or text wide, and how thick the line should be.

Remember, a corporate identity covers everything, down to the last detail, so it's important to be consistent. We're talking picky. But don't do any of this at the expense of practicality. If you always want the footer to be 1.5 inches in from the left of the page, set it up correctly in the style sheet so that it's easy to create a new document using the "Save As" command when you make a new chapter and style sheet.

Don't come up with nonsensical requirements, such as having the "RE:" line start 2 inches down and a tenth of an inch to the right of the end of the date line. Those kind of arbitrary rules can drive people nuts when they're trying to get paperwork out the door by 4 o'clock. Of course, if you have some cosmic reason for wanting it that way, it's OK, as long as you make it easy by using a style sheet.

Identity

ITC Garamond

Identity

Goudy Old Style

Identity

ITC Korinna

Identity

Serifa

Identity

Souvenir

Identity

Zapf Elliptical

Don't get into any "i before e except after c" kind of stuff either. Make the rules simple and make sure they make sense. "The left margin will begin at the right edge of the logo" makes sense. It's a concrete visual mark that the eye can relate to, and it's not impractical if your style sheet is complete. "I like wide left margins because it leaves room for notes." OK, that's another good reason for a design decision, and you might expand it to include other printed matter, such as your business card, giving it a wide right margin too. After all, people might want to make notes on your business card.

Documenting your identity

It's important to keep track of those seemingly unimportant little details, so if you really want all your documents to be uniform you can create a design guide for your corporate identity. Include information about the typefaces, preferred type sizes, the manufacturer of the typeface (typeface names can differ from foundry to foundry), the margins, types of paper, logo specs, color choices with Pantone references, or whatever you think is important.

The main reason to do this is that your business is not static. In six months or six years, when you want to create a new form or send out an invitation, instead of guessing you can bring out the guide and easily check all the specific formatting details.

Now that I've bombarded you with the importance of being consistent, controlled, uniform, and regular, I'll tell you to be flexible. You can't possibly think of all contingencies in advance, so don't hold the handbook up like a shrine and make people pray to it. Your design guide is just that, a guide. If you decide that you really should have used 11-point type with 13-point leading instead of 9-point type on 10-point leading, fine. Change it.

Even once you think it's set in stone, you still have to be able to adapt. If you do a poster, it may not make sense to set the type 11 on 13. On a poster that could be considered fine print. Go ahead, do what looks right, use 18- or 24-point body text and don't worry about it.

13

Logos to go

What's black and white and *you* all over?

No, it isn't you dressed as a penguin for Halloween. It isn't even you dressed as a nun. The correct answer is: your logo.

Logos to go

What's black and white and you all over?

No, it isn't you dressed as a penguin for Halloween. It isn't even you dressed as a nun. The correct answer is: your logo. Logos don't have to be just black and white, but because of their versatility, some of the best logos *are* black and white. The simpler and more graphic the logo, the better.

A logo is a form of graphic shorthand and it can be very important to your image because it helps give you or your company a *signature*—one single graphic that represents an entire business. A good logo is a good first impression. And I'm sure you've heard the cliché, "You never get a second chance to make a first impression."

The same graphic gets two different type treatments. This one uses Cooper Black.

An effective logo can be used on *everything* you produce. And the more you use it, the more powerful it becomes. This doesn't mean that you should use it 25 times on the same page (unless you do in a subtle way, such as in a very light gray as a background image), but it does mean that you should use it constantly and consistently on all your documents.

A good logo needs to be generic and simple enough to use in various media, including paper-based and electronic. The best logos show up equally well on paper and on screen, be it a computer monitor or television. And the very best logos work well in black and white. Color printing is often expensive or impractical. So if your logo works in black and white, it won't require any special print runs.

This logo combines Swiss Compressd with a Tiffany Bold "5."

Famous word logos include: IBM's striped logo, which looks sort of like the scan lines on a monochrome monitor; the word "Disney" set in a script taken from Walt's signature; Ford's famous script, set in an oval. Then there are initial logos. Hewlett-Packard's logo consists of the letters H and P, inside a white circle, inside a rounded rectangle. Hewlett-Packard's logo isn't the most striking or clever, but the company uses it on *everything* it does, and it's an important part of HP's image. The Xerox logo consists of the Xerox name, set in the company's own specially designed typeface.

Bernhard Modern "STYLE" with Swiss Extra Compressed "TYPE."

Swiss Compressed with triangle overlays & ITC Galliard Italic.

Swiss Compressed & ITC Galliard Italic.

It takes all kinds

Jones & Sons

Swiss

JONES (& SONS)

ITC Avant Garde

Jones & SONS

Bitstream Amerigo

JONES&SONS

Futura Bold, Medium, Light

There are three types of logos: text only, graphic only, and a combination of text and graphics. The text-only logo is the most basic. It consists of your name (or your company name) or initials. Text-only logos live or die by their typeface, since they consist of a few letters or a word. Naturally, these work best with distinctive names and distinctive typefaces. Logos are a good place to try out those flashy/strange display faces. "Jones & Sons" set in Swiss is about as exciting as two-day-old oatmeal. No one will even see it. If you absolutely must use Swiss, then take the same words and arrange them in a more interesting way, with the "& Sons" inside the "O" of Jones. Still better, set it in a more interesting sans serif such as ITC Avant Garde.

Now set the same characters in a typeface with a strong personality, such as Bitstream Amerigo, Futura, or Bodoni. Instantly even the most prosaic name looks more exciting. You could also use just the initials "J&S" alone. Initials often make for a more graphic and distinctive logo. If all else fails, a name change could be in order (no offense intended).

J&S

Futura Extra Black

J&S

Bodoni Bold

J&S

Bodoni Bold

J&S

Bodoni Bold

Be specific

CA$H

Tiffany Bold

If you or your company has a long name, something like "Cooperative Association of Software Hackers," then you're better off using initials. Logos are meant to be read very quickly; anything over seven or eight letters is too long. In the case of our hackers, CASH is nice and catchy. Even catchier is CA$H. While you could set a word as interesting as CA$H in any typeface, using one such as Tiffany Heavy makes it even more effective because Tiffany is reminiscent of the typefaces used on the money we all know and love.

The best way to create text-only logos is to use a draw program. These programs give you almost infinite control over spacing, kerning, shading, outlines, shadows, and the letterforms themselves. The most effective text-only logos usually manipulate the typeface in some way. Draw programs can't be beat for this purpose because they allow you to easily break typefaces into their basic curves and change the faces in subtle or extreme ways.

Remember that a good logo should work at *any* size, from tiny to gigantic. Consequently, most logos usually won't have much intricate detail, since detail would be lost in smaller sizes.

Your company logo does not have to use your corporate typeface, but it should work *with* your corporate typeface, since a good logo will appear on almost everything you do.

Be consistent about placement as well. It makes a difference whether your logo is always in the upper right corner, always centered, or always printed on the backside of the paper so it shows through tantalizingly. The more consistent the placement, the more recognizable the logo becomes.

A text-only logo set in Bodoni reverse.

A text and graphic logo set in Bernhard Modern Italic reverse.

Get the picture

Graphic-only logos are effective because they require no reading, just a recognition of shapes. The disadvantage of graphic-only logos is that they don't immediately convey the name of your organization. That's why graphic-only logos are usually paired with the company name.

Dynamic duo: type and graphics combined

The most common type of logo uses both text and a graphic. A logo like this can perform triple duty, with the text alone, the graphic alone, or both combined.

For a logo with text and graphics to be truly effective, each element should be able to stand on its own. This is tricky, because if either element is too distinctive, the two may clash when joined together. If you have a great graphic that can stand on its own and simple text that can't, use common sense and use the graphic alone, or the graphic and text combined, but not the text alone.

A text and graphic logo set in Hammersmith (Gill Sans) and ITC Zapf Dingbats.

A text and graphic logo set in Bodoni.

Over and over again

For a logo to gain recognition, you have to use it consistently. Studies have found that most people don't notice an advertisement until the third time they've seen it; logos work in much the same way. Once you've established a logo, don't mess with it. While minor variations or additions are OK, don't make radical alterations unless something in your business has changed, or you feel you can vastly improve the logo.

If your logo is composed of both a graphic and text, use it as a unit, or, after establishing the whole logo, use the separate elements for emphasis within a single document or across various documents.

Follow our examples

In order to illustrate several points, I've created some mock-up logos for fictional companies. The logo for the "Characters" Typeface Corporation is an excellent hybrid—a text-only logo that looks like a graphics-only logo. Single letters of the alphabet are called "characters"; the double meaning is inherent in the logo as well as the name. It shows how type can be stretched noticeably in Corel Draw, as well as how the letter "A" has been changed subtly.

For the graphic element, the word "typeface" is broken into its basic parts, "Type" and "Face," and uses the letters "CTC" to create a face made out of type. This logo works at *any* size, with or without the type around the edge.

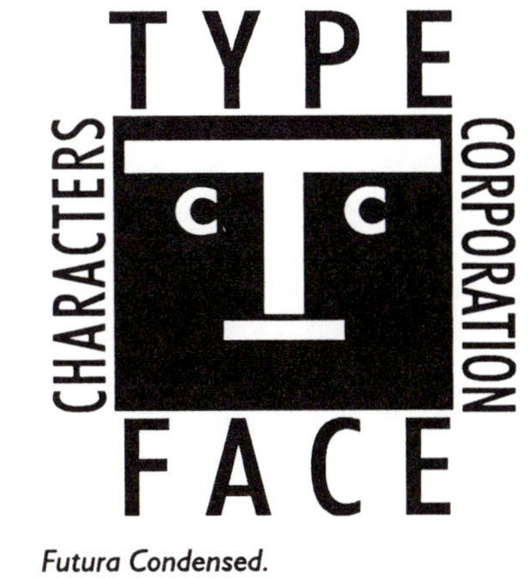

Futura Condensed.

Futura Condensed and Bodoni. The two "Characters" elements can work separately, but they also work well together, with the final "E" grasping the graphic like a vise.

Original set in Bodoni.

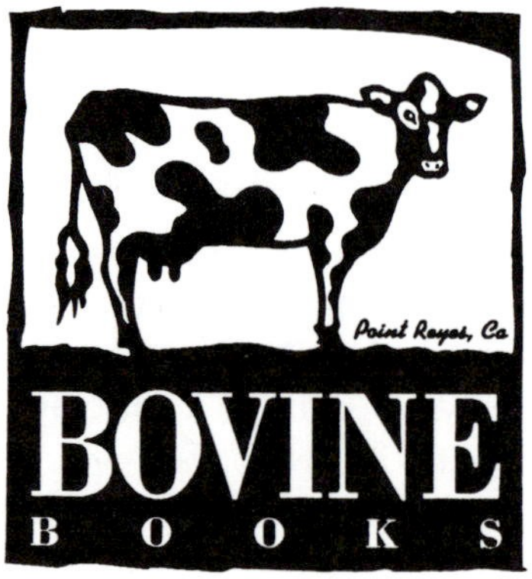

Bodoni Bold

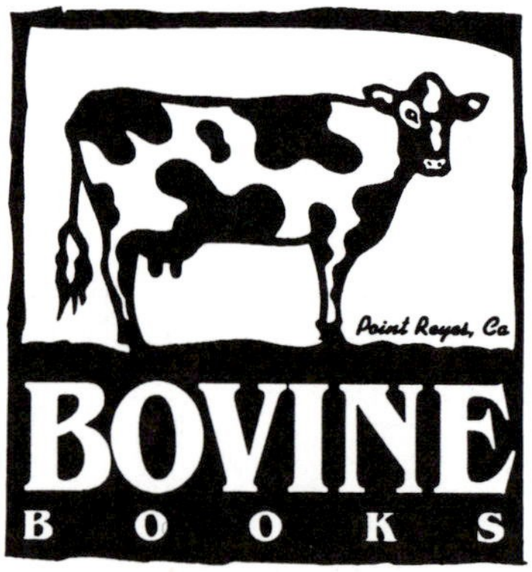

ITC Benguiat Bold

The first "Bovine Books" example contains too much detail to be effective and too many elements that don't work well together. The cow-pattern text is so strong that it could be used as a text-only logo by itself. And while the wonderful cow graphic from Metro ImageBase would look good in a large format, when printed small its charming detail is lost.

Serifa

I decide to simplify the background of the graphic and remove the distracting cow pattern from inside the text. You could also wipe out the border and use the cow atop the name all by itself. Metro ImageBase offers a wide variety of silhouettes and individual images that can provide a good starting point for logo design. (Metro ImageBase, 18623 Ventura Blvd. #210, Tarzana, CA 91356; 800-843-3438.)

Examine the same graphic with various typefaces. They each have a slightly different feeling. If you don't like any of them and want to go to the other extreme, simplicity, take a look at the oval "Bovine" logo on the next page. University Roman is whimsical, so it's clear this company doesn't publish books about cows exclusively. The curved text isn't boring, but it still wouldn't really stand on its own, and the logo would look naked without the cow.

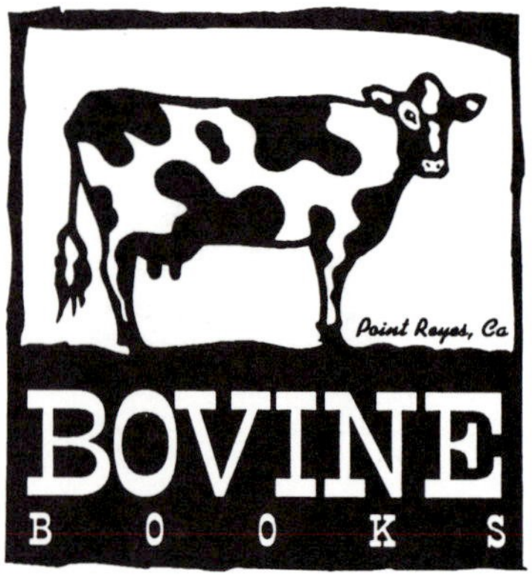

P.T. Barnum

A logo can't be too simple. Well, a single line might be too simple. But for most logos, simplicity means that it will reproduce well under all conditions. It's easy to imagine this logo reduced, and printed on the spine of a book, or giant-sized, over the door at company headquarters.

The cow graphic on the next page is from DesignClips' *Habitat Collection*. DesignClips, from LetterSpace, offers clean, sharp, striking libraries of graphic symbols specially suitable for logo design. Focusing on trees, flowers, and animals, the images are not a bit fussy or old fashioned. Each disk of the Natural Environment

Cooper Black

Series contains 50 images and is available in either draw or paint formats. (LetterSpace, 100 Wooster St., New York, NY 10012; 800-933-9095, ex. 100.)

The light bulb concept for the "Idea Books" logo is a good one. But, because the type is used to simulate the filament, it's tiny. If the logo were used in a small size it would just look like an illustration of a light bulb. The second logo screams "books" and uses type to spell out ideas. The type itself is fairly large, so this logo would work in miniature, and the books are a strong enough image to be used without the type. Both use Bernhard Modern, which has very distinctive uppercase letters with dramatic serifs.

Getting a second opinion

University Roman

When designing a logo, don't stop after the first try. In fact, you should try to design as many variations as possible. It's not uncommon for a designer to create over a dozen different logos for the same company. As you design one, it may make you think of something else. The design evolution can mean the difference between a boring, obvious logo, and a subtle, effective one that will still be interesting in ten years.

Once you've created a slew of logos, start narrowing the field, but don't always try to decide by yourself. If you show other people a dozen different logos, they may be overwhelmed. Choose the ones you like best and show them to other people.

As the designer, you know what you had in mind when you designed a particular logo. But other people will only know how it strikes them. If you fall in love with a design but everyone else says it looks like a tombstone, believe them.

Bernhard Modern

Bernhard Modern

Actually, I have a theory. If one person tells you something, think about it, then take it or leave it. If two people tell you the same thing, think about it really hard before making a decision. If three people tell you the same thing, pay attention, they may be onto something. Of course, as with everything else, the trick is *which* three people. If four people give you the same criticism, either start over or see if you can't convince/fool four other people. Try not to ask just anybody; ask people whose opinion you trust, or those who have demonstrated to you through their use of graphics that they know what they're doing.

Revising your image

A good logo should serve you for years. And because it becomes part of your image, changing it can be difficult. In the case of our *Designer Disk* style sheet software, in 1987 I came up with a simple logo. I created a "dashed" diskette image to symbolize a designer's graph pad and rotated it 45 degrees, setting the words "Designer Disks" in Futura Extra Black, a strong typeface.

The old logo.

What my wife (and partner in more ways than one) and I discovered after using the logo for awhile was that while it said "design," it didn't say "mail order." Since the business is mail order only, we decided a logo that suggested "style by mail" would be more effective. Equally important, we wanted something bolder, to stand out from the growing field of DTP products advertised in magazines.

I used Corel Draw to create the new logo. Because I wanted to retain a sense of continuity, I used the basic disk, but made it solid black so it would stand out. Then I clipped the edges to make it look like a stamp, and added "cancel" marks to give it some movement. The text is set in Hammersmith, which I edited, adding small protrusions to the "E" and "R" to make them more distinctive. The words "Style by Post" can appear on the logo when it's large enough or be removed when it's printed small. The new logo, which should last us for many years, now graces everything related to the *Designer Disks,* from ads to disk labels (it also appears on the template order form in the back of this book).

The new logo.

A good logo is its own reward. But it can also reward you with greater recognition and a better image.

Technical tips

Because logos are used at so many different sizes, it's best to get them into a line art, draw-type format, rather than a bitmapped paint-type format. Paint graphics get jagged when enlarged, and mushy when reduced, while draw-type graphics look good no matter how large or small you make them.

If your logo has already been designed but is not yet computerized, the easiest way to use it within a page composition or word processing program may be to digitize it by means of scanning.

If you scan your existing graphic, be sure to convert it into a draw format. Programs such as Adobe Streamline and Corel Trace allow you to convert any scanned image to line art. Of course, even after these sophisticated programs have done their work, it's often a good idea to use a draw program to perfect the images.

If you are using a PostScript printer, export the graphics to .EPS format. If you're using a LaserJet or LaserMaster, export the graphics to .CGM or .GEM formats. If you're working under Windows, you can also use a metafile from the Windows clipboard.

The Point Reyes Light is my local newspaper, and I have taken the liberty of redesigning its logo with Corel Draw. This Pulitzer Prize–winning paper serves a community of about 1500 people (and countless cows). Its name is based on the lighthouse at Point Reyes, hence, beams of light project from Bernhard Modern.

14

As a matter of fax

The font fax of life

It used to be that the page you printed was the page other people saw. Now, the page they see may just be a very rough picture of the page you created, and that poses all sorts of special problems.

As a matter of fax

Font fax of life

It used to be that the page you printed was the page other people saw. Now, the page they see may just be a very rough picture of the page you created, and that poses all sorts of special problems.

Fax machines send pictures. The pages that appear to be type are actually pictures. Unlike laser printers, which print at 300 dpi, a fax machine in normal mode prints at only 100 dpi. Making type look acceptable at this low-resolution requires special, sometimes drastic measures.

For faxing, the correct choice of typeface is not just a matter of aesthetics, it's a necessity if your message is to be readable. Some typefaces are extremely difficult to read when faxed at low-resolution while others are surprisingly clear. People will struggle to read a fax, but they won't enjoy it. And as I've said before, the more people *like* the appearance of something, the better they respond.

Size: Bigger is better

The one constant element in fax typography is *size.* While 10-point may be standard in normal printed correspondence, 10-point type in faxes can be sadistic. While 11-point is better, 12-point is better still. If the fax message is short, there's nothing wrong with using 13- or 14-point body text. In normal printed matter 14-point type could look huge. But in a fax, people are relieved to be able to read it easily.

Of course, the length of time it takes to send a fax determines its cost, and if you have more than a memo, 14-point type could turn a three page fax into five pages, almost doubling the cost to send it.

Fine mode

One way to instantly improve the quality of your faxes is to press the "Fine" button (if your machine has one). This doubles the resolution from 100 x 100 dpi to 100 x 200 dpi. That's still rough, but it's also only half as rough, or twice as sharp (depending whether you're a "half-empty glass" or "half-full glass" type of person). Judging from the majority of fax messages I receive, most people either don't know their fax machines have a fine mode or don't want to pay for it. Fine mode is not only twice as sharp, it can take twice as long to send, so the cost goes up.

Of course, if you're interested in making a good impression, then you'll want your faxes to look better. If you pay a high price for custom stationery and then send your faxes on normal resolution to save a few bucks, it won't make the best impression.

When you set your fax to fine mode, the facsimile of your original is automatically received in fine mode, regardless of the model of the receiving fax machine. This means that when your fax arrives it instantly looks good.

Fax faces

Even with fine mode, some faces reproduce better at low resolution than others. Generally, faces with large x-heights do better because they don't get as "clogged up." Very light faces don't do well because they lose bits and pieces, and dark faces tend to become blobs. Faces designed for newspapers, such as Dutch (Times) or Zapf Elliptical (Melior) do well because they are designed to withstand poor printing.

The results are *very* subjective, so you'll have to judge for yourself. Photocopy some of the specimen pages in Chapter 15 and run them through your fax machine on "copy" mode. If you're still not sure, I'd recommend Bitstream Charter (designed especially to withstand low-resolution printing).

Cover pages & fax etiquette

One of the first things you learn about when you start sending faxes is the cover page. A cover page should contain your name, company name, voice number, fax number, the date, the person and organization to whom you are sending the fax, and the number of pages you are sending. It's important to include the number of pages so that the recipient will know whether he or she received all the pages you sent.

Cover pages have become a big source of waste of both fax paper and phone time. Most cover pages only take about a quarter of a page, leaving the rest as blank white space. What's worse, fax paper is *not* recyclable. It's expensive for the recipient and bad for the environment. What can you do about it? Use some common sense.

You need a cover page if:

- You are sending to a fax machine that is shared by *many* users, in order for your fax to be routed to the right person.
- Your fax is confidential and you want the cover page to conceal information.

You don't need a cover page if:

- You are sending to a fax machine that is not shared.
- You have spoken to the recipient and he or she is waiting at the machine as it arrives.
- You integrate the routing and "number of pages sent" information into the address of the correspondence.

Being reasonable

I've found that unless a document is confidential, the best way to handle cover pages is to simply include the information at the top of the document, as you would in a memo. All you need is:

FROM: (your name, company, voice #, fax #)

TO: (the recipient's name, company voice #, fax #)

PAGES: (number of pages in this transmission)

RE: (what this is in regard to)

The illustration opposite shows a page format that integrates the cover page information in a clean, efficient, and easy-to-read way. Many business letters will fit on this single page. Because you are sending one less page, you'll be able to send your fax on fine mode in the amount of phone time it used to take to send your wasteful cover page.

This is my standard fax page, and it uses Zurich Black Extended 14-point for the main headings, Zurich Condensed 12-point for the details.

Fax	10-29-90	From:	To:	CC:	Re:	Pages:
DWH		Daniel Will-Harris v: 415-555-1212 f: 415-555-1313	Pauline Ores v: 212-555-8453 f: 212-555-4738	Lurlaine Oswego	*Current Project*	1, including this one

Pauline:

Thanks for your words of encouragement.

When I was working on designs for the format of this project, I tried what seemed like hundreds of variations. Different typefaces, different margins, different arrangements. I even tried things I thought would look horrible. Sometimes they did—but sometimes they surprised me and looked great. Since you can throw away your mistakes, no one has to see them but you.

The final sizes for some of the headings, subheadings, and other type elements in this project are smaller than I would recommend for a page of this size. But when more than one person is involved in reaching a decision regarding the design of a document, often a compromise must be reached. An easier-to-read design would use larger type for the headings and other type elements. Maybe next time.

Box 1235, Point Reyes, CA 94956

15

Setting a good example

Featuring
Bitstream typefaces

Over 50 full-page examples and type specimen pages illustrate how to make type work for you.

Activa™

The Bitstream version of the Trump Mediaeval® typeface.

Roman

abcdefghijklmnopqrstuvwxyz
ABCDEFGHIJKLMNOPQRSTUVWXYZ
1234567890&$£%.,:;-!?''åçëîñòšúß

Italic

abcdefghijklmnopqrstuvwxyz
ABCDEFGHIJKLMNOPQRSTUVWXYZ
1234567890&$£%.,:;-!?''åçëîñòšúß

Bold

abcdefghijklmnopqrstuvwxyz
ABCDEFGHIJKLMNOPQRSTUVWXYZ
1234567890&$£%.,:;-!?''åçëîñòšúß

Bold Italic

abcdefghijklmnopqrstuvwxyz
ABCDEFGHIJKLMNOPQRSTUVWXYZ
1234567890&$£%.,:;-!?''åçëîñòšúß

15 point

Bitstream is an independent digital typefoundry. Using the latest computer graphics tools, Bitstream's designers maintain the traditional essentials of good type design. Shape, weight and spacing rhythm are expertly controlled *to produce digitized letterforms of the highest quality in all font formats. In addition to making definitive versions of existing faces, Bitstream introduces creative new designs.*

9 point with 10 point lead

Bitstream is an independent digital typefoundry. Using the latest computer graphics tools, Bitstream's designers maintain the traditional essentials of good type design. Shape, weight and spacing rhythm are ***expertly controlled to produce digitized letterforms of the highest quality in all font formats. In addition to making definitive versions of existing faces, Bitstream introduces creative new designs.***

Business Stationery

The stationery reflects a coordinated system where the letterhead, business card, and envelope possess a strong, unified design. This unity is achieved by consistent use of a single type size, and all copy is set flush left with a generous amount of white space.

Instead of highlighting the company name by setting it in bolder and larger uppercase characters, the designer chose to emphasize it in a quiet restrained manner. The company name is set in Activa Bold and further emphasized by setting it apart from other copy.

Type specifications:
The address block is set in 7/10 Activa; the company signature in Activa Bold.

Logos such as this are best created in a draw program. In fact, all this could easily have been created in a draw program.

P.O. Box 8330, FDR Station
New York, New York 10010
(212) 555-5200

Zero-zero Corporation Inc.

P.O. Box 8330, FDR Station
New York, New York 10010
(212) 555-5200
Anne R. Sheridan, System Engineer

Zero-zero Corporation Inc.

P.O. Box 8330, FDR Station
New York, New York 10010

Zero-zero Corporation Inc.

ITC American Typewriter®

Medium

abcdefghijklmnopqrstuvwxyz
ABCDEFGHIJKLMNOPQRSTUVWXYZ
1234567890&$£%.,:;-!?''åçëîñòšúß

Bold

abcdefghijklmnopqrstuvwxyz
ABCDEFGHIJKLMNOPQRSTUVWXYZ
1234567890&$£%.,:;-!?''åçëîñòšúß

Medium Condensed

abcdefghijklmnopqrstuvwxyz
ABCDEFGHIJKLMNOPQRSTUVWXYZ
1234567890&$£%.,:;-!?''åçëîñòšúß

Bold Condensed

abcdefghijklmnopqrstuvwxyz
ABCDEFGHIJKLMNOPQRSTUVWXYZ
1234567890&$£%.,:;-!?''åçëîñòšúß

15 point

Bitstream is an independent digital typefoundry. Using the latest computer graphics tools, Bitstream's designers maintain the traditional essentials of good type design. Shape, weight and spacing rhythm are expertly controlled to produce **digitized letterforms of the highest quality in all font formats. In addition to making definitive versions of existing faces, Bitstream introduces creative new designs.**

9 point with 10 point lead

Bitstream is an independent digital typefoundry. Using the latest computer graphics tools, Bitstream's designers maintain the traditional essentials of good type design. Shape, weight and spacing rhythm are expertly con**trolled to produce digitized letterforms of the highest quality in all font formats. In addition to making definitive versions of existing faces, Bitstream introduces creative new designs.**

Calendar

Friendly and legible, ITC American Typewriter is used for this promotional calendar because it has an old-fashioned feeling, but in reality is a typeset face with plenty of curve appeal.

Throughout this calendar, type is used in an illustrative manner. Contrasting typefaces are combined in the logotype to create a distinctive, memorable image.

The reversed type for the days of the week provides a graphic emphasis and detail. Rules in the calendar organize information and enhance legibility.

Type specifications:
In the logotype, *HaLig*, *H* is set in 48-point Hammersmith and *alig* is set in 18- and 33-point Dutch. The calendar is set in 9-point ITC American Typewriter Medium with the days of the week in Bold; *mar.* is set in ITC American Typewriter Medium.

HaLig

S	M	T	W	T	F	S
		1	2	3	4	5
6	7	8	9	10	11	12
13	14	15	16	17	18	19
20	21	22	23	24	25	26
27	28	29	30			

mar.

1 9 8 8

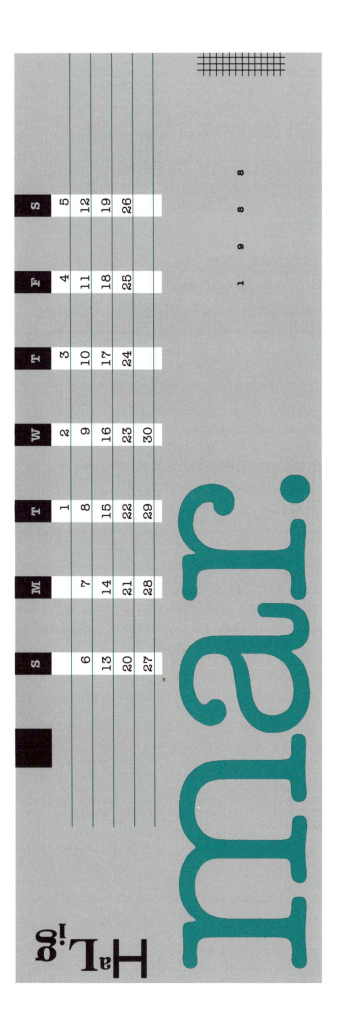

Bitstream Amerigo®

Roman

abcdefghijklmnopqrstuvwxyz
ABCDEFGHIJKLMNOPQRSTUVWXYZ
1234567890&$£%.,:;-!?“åçëîñòšúß

Italic

abcdefghijklmnopqrstuvwxyz
ABCDEFGHIJKLMNOPQRSTUVWXYZ
1234567890&$£%.,:;-!?“åçëîñòšúß

Bold

abcdefghijklmnopqrstuvwxyz
ABCDEFGHIJKLMNOPQRSTUVWXYZ
1234567890&$£%.,:;-!?“åçëîñòšúß

Bold Italic

abcdefghijklmnopqrstuvwxyz
ABCDEFGHIJKLMNOPQRSTUVWXYZ
1234567890&$£%.,:;-!?“åçëîñòšúß

15 point

Bitstream is an independent digital typefoundry. Using the latest computer graphics tools, Bitstream's designers maintain the traditional essentials of good type design. Shape, weight and spacing rhythm are *expertly controlled to produce digitized letterforms of the highest quality in all font formats. In addition to making definitive versions of existing faces, Bitstream introduces creative new designs.*

9 point with 10 point lead

Bitstream is an independent digital typefoundry. Using the latest computer graphics tools, Bitstream's designers maintain the traditional essentials of good type design. Shape, weight and spacing rhythm *are expertly controlled to produce digitized letterforms of the highest quality in all font formats. In addition to making definitive versions of existing faces, Bitstream introduces creative new designs.*

Corporate Identity Manual

This page from the corporate identity manual, organized on a three-column grid, presents the company logotype and subsidiary signatures. The accompanying text explains both elements.

Bitstream Amerigo, which reproduces well at small and large sizes, works well as a logo typeface. The abundant white space frames the logotype on the page for maximum emphasis.

Type specifications:
The text is set in 9/13 Bitstream Amerigo (9-point type with 13 points leading); the logotype, *Arcadia*, is set in 118-point Bitstream Amerigo Bold; the headline and subheadline in 9-point Hammersmith Bold.

2.3 A new corporate identity

Company logotype

The most fundamental element of the Arcadia identity is the company logotype. Use of *Arcadia* as a single word serves to identify the entire company with all its subsidiaries. The logotype will be used in conjunction with the legal signature of each subsidiary, e.g.: Arcadia Pharmaceutical Research, U.S.A., Inc.

The logotype has been designed to project an image of rationalism, representing the research side of the company, with an approachable, humanist feeling corresponding to Arcadia's involvement with health care. The logotype is set in a typeface called Bitstream Amerigo Bold.

Arcadia

Subsidiary signatures

The individual signatures, or legal operating names, for each of Arcadia's five companies will appear in conjunction with the Arcadia logotype.

In business papers the signature will appear as the first line of an address block. The signature will set in 9-point Amerigo Bold. The address will set in 9/13 Amerigo as shown below.

Arcadia Pharmaceutical Research, U.S.A., Inc.
Arcadia Pharmaceutical, Inc.
Arcadia Pharmaceutical of Canada, Ltd.
Arcadia Pharmaceutical Mexicana, S.A.
Arcadia Pharmaceutical Nederland NV

Arcadia Pharmaceutical Nederland NV
Rijnlandstraat 67
Utrecht
Postbus 3137

Telefoon 020-76 55 55
Telex 55713

ITC Avant Garde Gothic®

Book

abcdefghijklmnopqrstuvwxyz
ABCDEFGHIJKLMNOPQRSTUVWXYZ
1234567890&$£%.,:;-!?"åçëîñòšúß

Medium

abcdefghijklmnopqrstuvwxyz
ABCDEFGHIJKLMNOPQRSTUVWXYZ
1234567890&$£%.,:;-!?"åçëîñòšúß

Demi

abcdefghijklmnopqrstuvwxyz
ABCDEFGHIJKLMNOPQRSTUVWXYZ
1234567890&$£%.,:;-!?"åçëîñòšúß

Bold

abcdefghijklmnopqrstuvwxyz
ABCDEFGHIJKLMNOPQRSTUVWXYZ
1234567890&$£%.,:;-!?"åçëîñòšúß

15 point

Bitstream is an independent digital typefoundry. Using the latest computer graphics tools, Bitstream's designers maintain the traditional essentials of good type design. Shape, weight and spacing rhythm are expertly controlled to produce digitized letterforms of the highest quality in all font formats. In addition to making definitive versions of existing faces, Bitstream introduces creative new designs.
9 point with 10 point lead

Bitstream is an independent digital typefoundry. Using the latest computer graphics tools, Bitstream's designers maintain the traditional essentials of good type design. Shape, weight and spacing rhythm are expertly controlled to produce digitized letterforms of the highest quality in all font formats. In addition to making definitive versions of existing faces, Bitstream introduces creative new designs.

Schedule

The multi-tabular schedule organizes complex information in a rational manner. The ITC Avant Garde Gothic typeface reinforces the simplicity and helps keep the document from overwhelming the reader while still getting its point across. A harmonious balance of type and white space is created.

Use of varying type weights creates a hierarchy, which is reinforced by the rules. A solid horizontal rule separates programs; within these programs, leader dots separate time bands.

Type specifications:
The logotype, *NEWFANE*, is set in 27-point Bodoni Book; *ACADEMY* is in 8-point ITC Avant Garde Gothic Bold.
In the table, heads are set in 8-point ITC Avant Garde Gothic Bold; days of the week are in 8-point Book; program titles in 8-point Demi; event times in 6-point Medium; course lists in 6/7 Book.

NEW ENGLAND ACADEMY

Schedule

Seminar and Course List Spring 1989

		Monday	Tuesday	Wednesday
Professional Development Seminar	9:00-11:00am			
	9:30am-4:30pm		Improved Project Management Begins March 9 Project Scheduling and Budgeting Begins March 30	
	5:00-7:00pm	Uses of Computers in Facilities Planning and Management Begins April 11	Understanding the Massachusetts Building Code Begins March 2 Marketing Techniques Begins March 2 Operations Management Begins April 6 Computer Literacy for Design Professionals Begins May 8	
	5:30-7:00pm	Interior Restoration Techniques Begins April 20		Buying and Selling Real Estate Begins March 31 Financing Techniques for Residential Real Estate Begins March 3
	6:00-8:00pm		Real Estate Financial Analysis Begins March 2	
Architecture and Design	9:30am-12:30pm			
	10:00am-12:00pm			
	10:30-am-1:30pm			
	4:00-7:00pm		Introductory Architecture Design Studio A-1, Sect I Introduction to Design	
	5:00-7:00pm		Graphic Design Production Techniques for Graphic Designers	Introduction to Typography Basic Drawing History of Design in the Last 100 Years
	5:30-7:30pm	Landscape Analysis		Plant Materials
	5:45-7:45pm	Architectural Rendering II	Basic Architectural Sketching	
	6:00-8:00pm			
	7:15-8:45pm	Landscape Aesthetics in Urban Design		
Interior Design Program	5:00-7:00pm	Basic Drafting Skills		Introductory Interior Design Studio/Oatman Intermediate Interior Design Studio/Burdette
	5:30-7:00pm	Art for Interiors Color Theory		
	6:00-8:00pm			Finishes for Interior Spaces
Materials/Tools/Methods	2:00-5:00pm			
	4:00-7:00pm	Furniture Conservation	Intensive Model Building	

Baskerville

Roman

abcdefghijklmnopqrstuvwxyz
ABCDEFGHIJKLMNOPQRSTUVWXYZ
1234567890&$£%.,:;-!?"åçëîñòšúß

Italic

abcdefghijklmnopqrstuvwxyz
ABCDEFGHIJKLMNOPQRSTUVWXYZ
1234567890&$£%.,:;-!?"åçëîñòšúß

Bold

abcdefghijklmnopqrstuvwxyz
ABCDEFGHIJKLMNOPQRSTUVWXYZ
1234567890&$£%.,:;-!?"åçëîñòšúß

Bold Italic

abcdefghijklmnopqrstuvwxyz
ABCDEFGHIJKLMNOPQRSTUVWXYZ
1234567890&$£%.,:;-!?"åçëîñòšúß

15 point

Bitstream is an independent digital typefoundry. Using the latest computer graphics tools, Bitstream's designers maintain the traditional essentials of good type design. Shape, weight and spacing rhythm are expertly *controlled to produce digitized letterforms of the highest quality in all font formats. In addition to making definitive versions of existing faces, Bitstream introduces creative new designs.*

9 point with 10 point lead

Bitstream is an independent digital typefoundry. Using the latest computer graphics tools, Bitstream's designers maintain the traditional essentials of good type design. Shape, weight and spacing rhythm are ex- ***pertly controlled to produce digitized letterforms of the highest quality in all font formats. In addition to making definitive versions of existing faces, Bitstream introduces creative new designs.***

Title Page

Here we have a contemporary resetting of John Baskerville's 1757 design for his printing of Virgil's *Bucolics, Georgics, and the Aeneid.* At a time when most European printers relied heavily on ornament, John Baskerville made an early argument for less being more.

Baskerville's contemporaries commonly combined many point sizes and typefaces on a single page, which often resulted in visual confusion. Here, Baskerville's judicious use of type sizes and a single type family create an enduring argument for restraint.

The design is simple and orderly. The title and the author's name receive the greatest emphasis. The city, printer, and date are treated in a secondary way through use of a smaller point size.

Baskerville's restrained monumental capitals set with open spacing and generous undecorated margins create an appropriately classical feeling for Virgil's works.

Type specifications:
The text is set in Baskerville. Baskerville Italic is used for *ET* and *BIRMINGHAMIAE*. The type sizes used are 14-, 18-, 24-, and 42-point.

PUBLII VIRGILII

MARONIS

BUCOLICA,

GEORGICA,

ET

AENEIS.

BIRMINGHAMIAE:

Typis JOHANNIS BASKERVILLE.

MDCCLVII.

ITC Benguiat®

Book

abcdefghijklmnopqrstuvwxyz
ABCDEFGHIJKLMNOPQRSTUVWXYZ
1234567890&$£%.,:;-!?"åçëîñòšúß

Book Italic

abcdefghijklmnopqrstuvwxyz
ABCDEFGHIJKLMNOPQRSTUVWXYZ
1234567890&$£%.,:;-!?"åçëîñòšúß

Bold

abcdefghijklmnopqrstuvwxyz
ABCDEFGHIJKLMNOPQRSTUVWXYZ
1234567890&$£%.,:;-!?"åçëîñòšúß

Bold Italic

abcdefghijklmnopqrstuvwxyz
ABCDEFGHIJKLMNOPQRSTUVWXYZ
1234567890&$£%.,:;-!?"åçëîñòšúß

15 point

Bitstream is an independent digital typefoundry. Using the latest computer graphics tools, Bitstream's designers maintain the traditional essentials of good type design. Shape, weight and spacing rhythm *are expertly controlled to produce digitized letterforms of the highest quality in all font formats. In addition to making definitive versions of existing faces, Bitstream introduces creative new designs.*

9 point with 10 point lead

Bitstream is an independent digital typefoundry. Using the latest computer graphics tools, Bitstream's designers maintain the traditional essentials of good type design. Shape, weight and spacing rhythm are expertly controlled ***to produce digitized letterforms of the highest quality in all font formats. In addition to making definitive versions of existing faces, Bitstream introduces creative new designs.***

Gift Certificate

ITC Benguiat is used for its informal yet traditional feeling. Elements from twenty-dollar bills suggest monetary value in a playful way. Contrasting serif and sanserif faces are combined in the logotype, *IQ inc*.

Type specifications:
IQ is set in 64-point ITC Benguiat Book; text in 10-point ITC Benguiat Book and Book Italic; *inc* is set in 11-point Zurich Bold. The large triangle is from the ITC Zapf Dingbats collection available in the Bitstream *Symbols 1* typeface package.

Note: Graphic images were scanned into the system. They might also be imported from a paint or draw program or added by means of manual paste-up (see *Paste-up* in the Glossary).

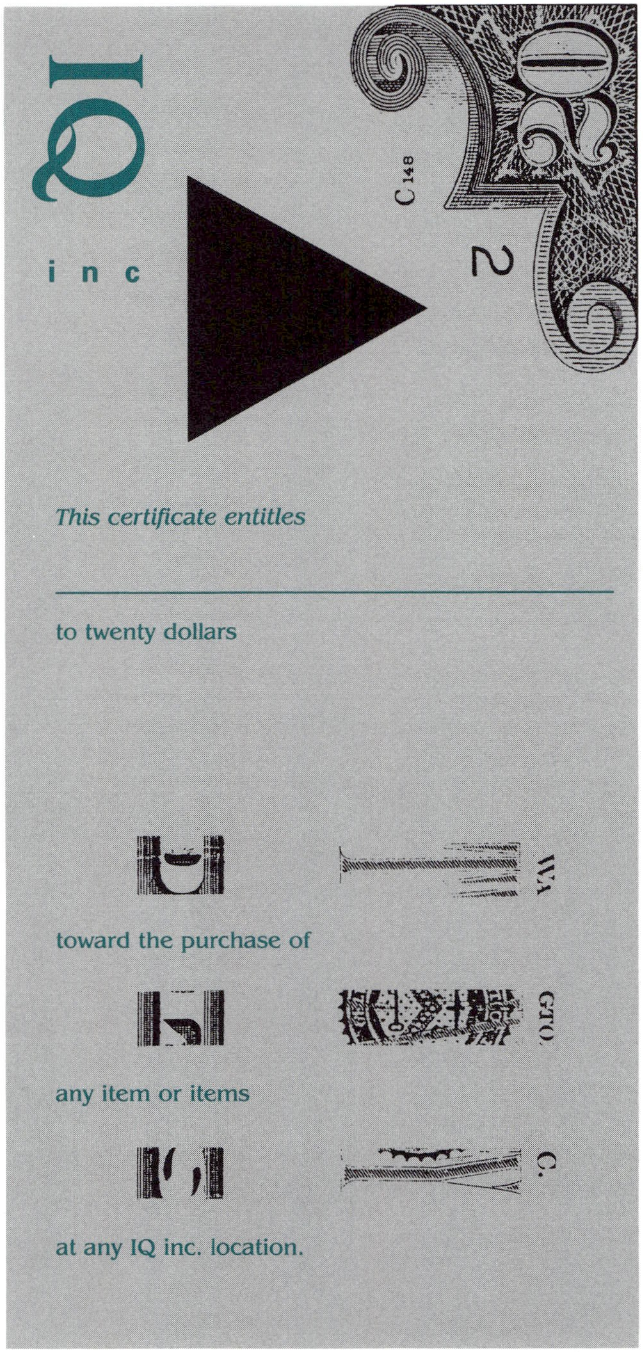
IQ
inc
2
C 148
This certificate entitles
to twenty dollars
toward the purchase of
any item or items
at any IQ inc. location.
WA
GTO
C.

Bernhard Modern®

Roman

abcdefghijklmnopqrstuvwxyz
ABCDEFGHIJKLMNOPQRSTUVWXYZ
1234567890&$£%.,:;-!?‘’åçëîñòšúß

Italic

abcdefghijklmnopqrstuvwxyz
ABCDEFGHIJKLMNOPQRSTUVWXYZ
1234567890&$£%.,:;-!?‘’åçëîñòšúß

Bold

abcdefghijklmnopqrstuvwxyz
ABCDEFGHIJKLMNOPQRSTUVWXYZ
1234567890&$£%.,:;-!?‘’åçëîñòšúß

Bold Italic

abcdefghijklmnopqrstuvwxyz
ABCDEFGHIJKLMNOPQRSTUVWXYZ
1234567890&$£%.,:;-!?‘’åçëîñòšúß

15 point

Bitstream is an independent digital type-foundry. Using the latest computer graphics tools, Bitstream's designers maintain the traditional essentials of good type design. Shape, weight and spacing rhythm are expertly controlled to produce digitized letterforms of the highest quality in all font formats. In addition to making definitive versions of existing faces, Bitstream introduces creative new designs.
9 point with 10 point lead

Bitstream is an independent digital type-foundry. Using the latest computer graphics tools, Bitstream's designers maintain the traditional essentials of good type design. Shape, weight and spacing rhythm are expertly controlled to produce digitized letterforms of the highest quality in all font formats. In addition to making definitive versions of existing faces, Bitstream introduces creative new designs.

Magazine

This magazine page is organized on a three-column grid. The large headline, which relates to both articles, straddles all three columns. The primary article fills the first two columns and is continued on another page; the sidebar occupies the third column.

Visual variety is achieved by mixing three typefaces: Bernhard Modern, Franklin Gothic Extra Condensed, and Goudy Old Style. Bernhard Modern is used for the major headline and initial caps because of its classical, monumental feel. But with its extremely high ascenders and low x-height, it's not easy to read in small point sizes in lengthy articles. Therefore Goudy Old Style is used for the longer primary article, and Bernhard Modern is used in a larger point size for the sidebar articles.

The pull quote, beginning in the left margin and continuing into the first column, breaks the grid and keeps the page from becoming static.

In the third column, the sidebar heading mixes a sanserif, Franklin Gothic Extra Condensed, with a serif, Bernhard Modern Bold and Bold Italic. The contrast of a Franklin Gothic helps to identify this as a separate article. Use of a larger point size and Bernhard Modern for the sidebar text further emphasizes that this is a related, but separate, story.

Type specifications:
The large headline is set in 131-point Bernhard Modern; the primary text is in 11/13 Goudy Old Style; the pull quote is in 24/24 Bernhard Modern Bold. In the sidebar head, *healthguide* is set in Franklin Gothic Extra Condensed; *for* is in Bernhard Modern Bold Italic; *Seniors* is in Bernhard Modern Bold. Text for the sidebar is in 12/14 Bernhard Modern. Bernhard Modern is also used for the page folio and magazine name in 8- and 6-point to effect the look of large and small caps.

SENIOR CARE

"QUALITY CARE is what we are all about," says Sylvia LeBourveau of the Elder's Aid Home. Early in 1987, the Women's Junior League began working with the Fielding Hospital to create the Elder's Aid Home. The Elder's Aid Home is a retirement home for independent seniors over 65. The Elder's Aid Home is a 35-person facility that allows seniors to live and socialize as a group providing the care and community so many seniors are missing.

Elder's Aid Home offers a family life and the dignity of choice.

"We allow residents to furnish their own rooms, to plan their own schedules, to live their lives the way they choose. But we also provide nutritious meals and excellent health care, we offer planned activities—we offer a family life and the dignity of choice," explains Elaine Kendall of the Elder's Aid Home.

LeBourveau, the home's director, says that the Elder's Aid Home is one of a new and growing field of non-hospital resident care programs. Health care homes have grown from just over 200 homes in 1985 to nearly 1,800 nationwide in 1988. This rapid growth is a response to America's increasing elder population.

As the senior population continues to grow, old methods of caring for the elderly become less and less feasible. America is realizing the need for better care and better treatment. Seniors can no longer be classified as sick people needing 24-hour hospital care. Seniors are healthier than in the past and are living longer. And with the division of family and community, children and neighbors are no longer taking the responsibility to care for the elderly.

"We saw the need for a quality option for seniors. At the Elder's Aid Home, seniors are able to live a better life. They are surrounded by people of their own age, they are treated with respect, and they also have the benefits of quality care," explains Vivian Shultz of the Women's Junior League. "Many healthy seniors were alone. They had no one to talk to, no one to be with. Many were also afraid. Living in a community alleviates this fear. They are no longer easy targets," continues Shultz.

continued on page 38

healthguide *for* Seniors

With more and more reports coming out telling people, seniors in particular, what types of food are bad for them, it is becoming harder to eat. Avoid foods with a high cholesterol level; avoid foods high in fat; avoid foods with high levels of preservatives and artificial ingredients. What can people eat? What can seniors eat? If melba toast and bran cereal are not enough, Donald Taylor, M.D., may have a book for you. *Eating For Seniors* examines the nutritional needs of the elderly, identifies problem areas and offers solutions for both healthy and tasty meals.

"I have kept the latest health reports in mind, along with good taste, and have developed a selection of meals seniors will enjoy eating and that will provide the nutrition they need."

ABCD

EFGH

IKLM

Bodoni Book

NOPR
STUV
WXYZ

Bodoni

Book

abcdefghijklmnopqrstuvwxyz
ABCDEFGHIJKLMNOPQRSTUVWXYZ
1234567890&$£%.,:;-!?"åçëîñòšúß

Book Italic

abcdefghijklmnopqrstuvwxyz
ABCDEFGHIJKLMNOPQRSTUVWXYZ
1234567890&$£%.,:;-!?"åçëîñòšúß

Bold

abcdefghijklmnopqrstuvwxyz
ABCDEFGHIJKLMNOPQRSTUVWXYZ
1234567890&$£%.,:;-!?"åçëîñòšúß

Bold Italic

abcdefghijklmnopqrstuvwxyz
ABCDEFGHIJKLMNOPQRSTUVWXYZ
1234567890&$£%.,:;-!?"åçëîñòšúß

15 point

Bitstream is an independent digital typefoundry. Using the latest computer graphics tools, Bitstream's designers maintain the traditional essentials of good type design. Shape, weight and spacing rhythm are ex*pertly controlled to produce digitized letterforms of the highest quality in all font formats. In addition to making definitive versions of existing faces, Bitstream introduces creative new designs.*
9 point with 10 point lead

Bitstream is an independent digital typefoundry. Using the latest computer graphics tools, Bitstream's designers maintain the traditional essentials of good type design. Shape, weight and spacing rhythm are expertly controlled ***to produce digitized letterforms of the highest quality in all font formats. In addition to making definitive versions of existing faces, Bitstream introduces creative new designs.***

Concert Program

An elegant, yet strong and distinctive typeface, Bodoni is used in the program to visually create a musical feeling. The use of contrasting weights, sizes, and white space modulated by indents evokes musical composition. The background of handwritten music further enhances the content.

On the right-hand page, the English translation of the Latin is set apart by use of italics and an indent.

Color is used to highlight titles, the composer's name, and the English translation and further enlivens the page.

Type specifications:
Baroque Music Society is set in 12-point Bodoni Bold Italic; *VIVALDI* is in Bodoni Book; musical titles are in 12-point Bodoni Book; concerto numbers are in 9-point Bodoni Book; *Allegro, Largo, Presto,* etc. are in 7/10 Bodoni Book; text is in 9/11 Bodoni Book and Italic.

Baroque Music Society

Elizabeth Avery, *Artistic Director*
Saturday, April 30 at 8:00 pm
St. James Hall, Sidney

VIVALDI *Lauda Jerusalem*

The Four Seasons

Concerto No. 1 in E Major (Spring)
Allegro
Largo
Allegro

Concerto No. 2 in G Minor (Summer)
Allegro non molto
Adagio-Presto
Presto

I N T E R M I S S I O N

Concerto No. 3 in F Major (Autumn)
Allegro
Adagio molto
Allegro

Concerto No. 4 in F Minor (Winter)
Allegro non molto
Largo
Allegro

Gloria

. . . . .

Arthur Ellwood, *violin*
Cynthia Briggs, *soprano*

Lauda Jerusalem

Lauda Jerusalem, Dominum.
Lauda Deum tuum Sion.
Praise the Lord, O Jerusalem;
praise thy God, O Sion.

Quoniam confortavit seras portarum tuarum
et bendixit filiis tuis in te.
For he hath made fast the bars of thy gates;
he hath blessed thy children within thee.

Qui posuit fines tuos pacem
et adipe frumenti satiat te.
He maketh peace in thy borders;
he filleth thee with the finest of wheat.

Qui emittit eloquium suum terrae,
velociter currit sermo euis.
He sendeth out his commandment upon earth,
and his word runneth very swiftly.

Qui dat nivem sicut lanam,
nebulam sicut cinerem spargit.
He giveth snow like wool;
he scattereth the hoar-frost like ashes.

Mitit crystallum suam sicut bucellas,
ante faciem frigoris eius quis sustinebit?
He casteth forth his ice like morsels;
who is able to abide his frost?

ITC Bookman®

Light

abcdefghijklmnopqrstuvwxyz
ABCDEFGHIJKLMNOPQRSTUVWXYZ
1234567890&$£%.,:;-!?"åçëîñòšúß

Light Italic

abcdefghijklmnopqrstuvwxyz
ABCDEFGHIJKLMNOPQRSTUVWXYZ
1234567890&$£%.,:;-!?"åçëîñòšúß

Demi

abcdefghijklmnopqrstuvwxyz
ABCDEFGHIJKLMNOPQRSTUVWXYZ
1234567890&$£%.,:;-!?"åçëîñòšúß

Demi Italic

abcdefghijklmnopqrstuvwxyz
ABCDEFGHIJKLMNOPQRSTUVWXYZ
1234567890&$£%.,:;-!?"åçëîñòšúß

15 point

Bitstream is an independent digital typefoundry. Using the latest computer graphics tools, Bitstream's designers maintain the traditional essentials of good type design. Shape, weight and spacing rhythm are ex-*pertly controlled to produce digitized letterforms of the highest quality in all font formats. In addition to making definitive versions of existing faces, Bitstream introduces creative new designs.*

9 point with 10 point lead

Bitstream is an independent digital typefoundry. Using the latest computer graphics tools, Bitstream's designers maintain the traditional essentials of good type design. Shape, weight and spacing rhythm *are expertly controlled to produce digitized letterforms of the highest quality in all font formats. In addition to making definitive versions of existing faces, Bitstream introduces creative new designs.*

Résumé

ITC Bookman was selected for its easy readability and open, friendly appearance. A strong flush left, two-column format is used to facilitate scanning. Note that the name and address are set flush left to align with the text below, rather than centered at the top of the page. This scheme provides a natural starting point for the reader.

To emphasize the individual's name, a number of options were available: setting it larger than the text; printing it in color; setting it in uppercase; or setting it in a heavier weight. Using all these options at one time would project brashness rather than the desired image of confidence. Emphasis was given in a more restrained and confident way by using ITC Bookman Demi and printing it in a second color.

The category heads, *Objective*, *Experience*, and *Education* are placed flush left in the first column and lead easily into the text of the second column. ITC Bookman Light Italic was used for the text following *Objective*.

Type specifications:
This résumé is set in 10/11 ITC Bookman Light; the name and category heads are set in ITC Bookman Demi; job titles are set in ITC Bookman Demi Italic.

Cody Seward Webb
32 Korman Drive
Apartment 3
Glendale, CA 91209

818-555-8378

Objective

Sales management position using expertise in motivating sales personnel, increasing sales and creation of effective programs contributing to higher organizational profits and market share.

Experience

Headquarters Account Manager
Fulton Food Co., Consumer Products Group. Glendale CA. October 1986—Present
National account management of a $3 million account.
Responsible for staff of fourteen, covering six states.
Responsibilities include formulating profit structure, constructing and formulating all promotional activities, setting up all co-op advertising, feature pricing, establishing goals, organizing inventory control of spoils and damages.

- Doubled promotional activity, which has increased sales by 12% and profits by 8%.
- Reinstated extender and merchandising program, increasing sales by over $20 thousand per month.

Sales Representative
Grocery Products Division. May 1983—October 1986
Serviced territory consisting of Northern and Southern California; concentration on independent and chain accounts. Complete control of service, sales and in-store promotional activity.

- Increased client base through prospecting by 28% or eight new accounts, for a total of $1.7 million in increased sales.

Sales Representative
Trevor, Inc., Institutional Sales Division. Cleveland OH. December 1980—May 1983
Responsible for horizontal and vertical sales growth of full line of food service products to accounts within a defined territory.

- Doubled sales volume and profit margin within first year. Number 2 salesperson in region.
- Voluntarily relinquished territory to establish new territory in unsold area. Within six months built sales to match original territory.

Manager
Marcos Restaurant, Dayton OH. June 1978—December 1980
Responsible for 20 employees. Duties included: bookkeeping, pricing, ordering and product inventory control, food planning, preparation and maintaining a daily schedule.
Implemented time study for daily operations.

- Reduced expenses and overhead by 20%.
- Maintained a 40% net profit.
- Increased business by 33%.

Education

Windsor Paine College
Cornwall, Vermont
B.S., Planning and Administration, *cum laude*
May, 1980

Century Schoolbook®

Roman

abcdefghijklmnopqrstuvwxyz
ABCDEFGHIJKLMNOPQRSTUVWXYZ
1234567890&$£%.,:;-!?“åçëîñòšúß

Italic

abcdefghijklmnopqrstuvwxyz
ABCDEFGHIJKLMNOPQRSTUVWXYZ
1234567890&$£%.,:;-!?“åçëîñòšúß

Bold

abcdefghijklmnopqrstuvwxyz
ABCDEFGHIJKLMNOPQRSTUVWXYZ
1234567890&$£%.,:;-!?“åçëîñòšúß

Bold Italic

abcdefghijklmnopqrstuvwxyz
ABCDEFGHIJKLMNOPQRSTUVWXYZ
1234567890&$£%.,:;-!?“åçëîñòšúß

15 point

Bitstream is an independent digital typefoundry. Using the latest computer graphics tools, Bitstream's designers maintain the traditional essentials of good type design. Shape, weight and spacing rhythm are expertly controlled *to produce digitized letterforms of the highest quality in all font formats. In addition to making definitive versions of existing faces, Bitstream introduces creative new designs.*

9 point with 10 point lead

Bitstream is an independent digital typefoundry. Using the latest computer graphics tools, Bitstream's designers maintain the traditional essentials of good type design. Shape, weight and spacing rhythm are expertly controlled to ***produce digitized letterforms of the highest quality in all font formats. In addition to making definitive versions of existing faces, Bitstream introduces creative new designs.***

University Catalog

Designed for use in reading primers, Century Schoolbook is serious, but not too formal. Easy to read, it is appropriate for applications with lengthy copy.

Here, text is set in a three-column grid. A clear hierarchy exists for each course: titles in bold, descriptions in roman, prerequisites in italic.

The letterspaced uppercase copy, *COURSE DESCRIPTIONS,* provides a contrasting texture. The large *H,* reminiscent of a varsity letter, provides contrasting scale and enlivens a dense page of text. Vertical rules at the bottom of the page add visual interest and acknowledge the underlying grid.

Type specifications:
Text is set in 8/9 Century Schoolbook; course titles are in Century Schoolbook Bold; prerequisites are in Century Schoolbook Italic; the name *Hampton College* is in 12-point Century Schoolbook; the side-head, *COURSE DESCRIPTIONS,* is in 8-point Century Schoolbook Bold Italic; the large *H* is 588-point Century Schoolbook Bold.

The large character “H” may require a draw-type program capable of creating such large type. To overlay this second color, you either need to manually create what's called an “overlay” (usually a piece of clear acetate with the image on it), or have your software create one automatically.

H

• Hampton College

CS-C-205 Assembly Language
Computer structure and machine language, representation of numeric and character data, mnemonic operations including data transfer, arithmetic, branching, and bit manipulation operations, symbolic addressing, addressing modes, subroutines and procedures, macros, and input/output especially as they are implemented on a VAX 11/785 machine. (3 credits)
Prerequisite: CS-C-201

CS-C-207 Programming in PASCAL
Introduction to the Pascal programming language. Topics include declaration of variables, assignment and decision statements, loops, declaration of user-defined types, arrays, procedures and function, recursion, sets, records, file manipulations, dynamic storage allocation and the pointer data type. (3 credits)
Prerequisite: CS-C-100 or equivalent

CS-C-209 C Programming
C is a widely used systems programming language. C provides an opportunity to learn many of the standard techniques of systems programming: recursion, dynamic storage allocation, file manipulation, and file handling. The objectives of this course are to provide the student with the ability to read and write C programs, including the use of C library routines, and to expose the student to techniques of systems programming. (3 credits)
Prerequisite: knowledge of data structures

CS-C-220 Data Structures and Algorithms
Basic concepts in representation and manipulation of data: internal representation of reals, searching techniques, linked lists, stacks, queues, trees, binary search trees, expression trees, sorting techniques, graphs, hashing, and directory organizations. (3 credits)
Prerequisite: CS-C-207

CS-C-225 Logic Design
Boolean algebra is introduced as a tool for the analysis of logic circuits. Procedures for the design and minimization of circuits using Karnaugh mapping techniques are presented. Integrated circuit logic elements fron TTL and CMOS families including memories, counters and arithmetic elements are studied and used as design components. (3 credits)

CS-C-305 Introduction to Compilers
Principles of compiler design, finite state machines, lexical analysis, pushdown machines, context-free grammars, syntax-directed processing, top-down and bottom-up processing, and error recovery. A project to implement the lexical and syntactical analysis-phases of compilation is required. (3 credits)
Prerequisite: CS-C-220

CS-C-332 Operating Systems
This course covers the basic principles of computer operating systems. The study includes memory management techniques, interrupt handling, multi-programming, data protection, and resource allocation. VAX/VMS will be used as a specific example of the implementation of some of the concepts. (3 credits)
Prerequisite: CS-C-220

CS-C-350 Software Engineering
A study of the nature of the program development task when many people, many modules, many versions or many man-years are involved in designing, developing, and maintaining the system. Both technical (e.g., design and specification) and administrative (e.g., cost estimation and elementary software management) are considered. The course will consist primarily of working in small teams on the cooperative creation and modification of software systems using the software life cycle approach. (3 credits)
Prerequisite: CS-C-220

CS-C-365 Microcomputer Technology I
A study of microprocessors and microcomputer technology with emphasis on the 16-bit 8086-8088 family of devices. The microcomputer instruction set, bus structure, control signals, memory, and peripheral chips are studied and utilized in laboratory experiments. (3 credits)
Prerequisite: CS/EE-C-225

CS-C-381 Database Principles
The study of the concepts and structures necessary to design and implement a data base management system (DBMS). Examples of specific database management systems will be examined and related to the data models discussed. Design consideration for a DBMS will be considered. Topics include file organizations, database concepts and characteristics, external, conceptual and internal schemas, hierarchical, network, and relational implementations, normalization, DDL and DML, concurrency control, security controls, database administration, recovery and restart procedures, and distributed databases. (3 credits)
Prerequisite: CS-C-220, Corequisite: CS-C-332

CS-C-432 Artificial Intelligence
A one-semester introduction to the concepts, techniques and tools of artificial intelligence. Topics covered include representation, vision and image processing, syntax and parsing, varieties of search, logic and deduction, elementary memory organization, expert systems, and planning. In addition to theoretical discussion, LISP programs illustrating major topics will be studied and used. (3 credits)
Prerequisite: CS-C-220

CS-C-472 Computer Architecture
The analysis and design of the major elements of a digital computer. The specification of the interconnection of these elements to form a digital computer. This specification is accomplished with the aid of a special purpose register-transfer language (similar to a programming language). Control of the register-transfer sequence is treated from both the hard-wired and microprogrammed viewpoints. Interrupts and I/O are treated. (3 credits)
Prerequisite: CS/EE-C-225

EC-C-201 Principles of Microeconomics
An introduction to economics that stresses the value of knowledge of the market and its alternatives in understanding current issues of social and public policy. The main focus is on how and why markets work, why they fail, and the implications of success or failure for social policy in such things as the control of industry, poverty, consumer choice, and the environment. (3 credits)

EC-C-202 Principles of Macroeconomics
An introduction to economics that examines the broad economic forces determining the level of unemployment and the rates of inflation and economic growth. The measurement of an economy's performance; the determination of the level of prices, output and employment; and the use of the monetary and fiscal tools by the central authorities make up the primary subject matter. (3 credits)

EC-C-311 Intermediate Microeconomics
An analysis of the price system in order to explain how, in the market, resources are allocated to the production of particular goods and how these goods and services are distributed among the population. Consumer behavior, producer behavior, market structures and welfare theory are the main topics covered. Economic analysis is also applied as a problem-solving tool. (3 credits)
Prerequisite: EC-C-201

EC-C-318 Money and Finance
An introduction to the analysis of the structures and behavior of financial and monetary institutions and their relationship to the aggregate performance of the economy. Policy options are discussed in terms of alternative analytical models and different social perceptions and values. (3 credits)
Prerequisite: EC-C-202

Bitstream Charter®

Roman

abcdefghijklmnopqrstuvwxyz
ABCDEFGHIJKLMNOPQRSTUVWXYZ
1234567890&$£%.,:;-!?"åçëîñòšúß

Italic

abcdefghijklmnopqrstuvwxyz
ABCDEFGHIJKLMNOPQRSTUVWXYZ
1234567890&$£%.,:;-!?"åçëîñòšúß

Black

abcdefghijklmnopqrstuvwxyz
ABCDEFGHIJKLMNOPQRSTUVWXYZ
1234567890&$£%.,:;-!?"åçëîñòšúß

Black Italic

abcdefghijklmnopqrstuvwxyz
ABCDEFGHIJKLMNOPQRSTUVWXYZ
1234567890&$£%.,:;-!?"åçëîñòšúß

15 point

Bitstream is an independent digital typefoundry. Using the latest computer graphics tools, Bitstream's designers maintain the traditional essentials of good type design. Shape, weight and spacing rhythm are expertly controlled *to produce digitized letterforms of the highest quality in all font formats. In addition to making definitive versions of existing faces, Bitstream introduces creative new designs.*

9 point with 10 point lead

Bitstream is an independent digital typefoundry. Using the latest computer graphics tools, Bitstream's designers maintain the traditional essentials of good type design. Shape, weight and spacing rhythm are expertly controlled to ***produce digitized letterforms of the highest quality in all font formats. In addition to making definitive versions of existing faces, Bitstream introduces creative new designs.***

Newsletter

The first page of your newsletter needs to be visually exciting and at the same time easy to read. This newsletter uses a decorative typeface, as well as ample white space. Remember that no one reads your pages in a vacuum (or even a blender)—your page has to compete with other pages. If this newsletter were on a cluttered desk, the white space would help to make it stand out from the competition—and get read.

The company name, *Republic*, has been reversed to provide emphasis. The large Cloister Black *herald* makes reference to blackletter faces commonly used for newspaper banners (the logo of a newspaper is *not* a masthead; the masthead contains the names of the staff). I always advise against underlining headlines; but this is not a headline, it's a nameplate (the name of the publication), so the 24-point rule under it works to *separate* it from the body of the newsletter and establish the column width for the story below.

The three-column grid of varying widths provides organization without monotony. The first line of each story uses large and small caps for emphasis, combining 7-point caps with 9-point text. Paragraphs are block format, with a blank line between each.

Type specifications:
The nameplate for this newsletter, *herald*, is set in 146-point Cloister Black; in the company name, *The* is set in 32-point Charter Italic with *Republic* set in Charter Black. Text is set in 9-point Charter with 12 points space between lines. Headlines are set in 14-point Charter Black. The page folio, date, volume, and issue numbers are set in Hammersmith Bold. The table of contents is set in 7/20 Charter with page numbers in Charter Black. The large pound sterling symbol is 740-point Charter Italic.

The Republic

herald

Sales and News Letter for Employees of Republic Financial

Volume 3
Issue #2

November 1991

Contents

A Good Place to Be

An unusally eventful year is winding down. It has been a year during which:

- *A far-reaching Tax Reform Act was implemented, bringing with it major adjustments for some and opportunities for others.*

- *Interest rates spiked a bit and then eased back; the dollar weakened, but our trade deficit showed slight improvements; our legislative leaders began to take seriously the problems created by our national debt.*

These events, and others, served as a reminder that The Republic has been a companion to history for more than 100 years and has grown and prospered through much more calamitous periods.

We are comforted more than ever by the values of The Republic that have evolved over time . . . integrity, quality, financial stability and respect for tradition. The Republic is a good place to be.

Keep the Sale Simple

"Keep it simple." In those three words, Phil Wolfe revealed his formula for success in selling life insurance.

"Simplicity's the most important point to remember in selling Life," he explained. And the second most important point?

"Maximize the Life sale. Start with a small Life sale—rather than walk away without a sale—to establish a client. Then build on this with good service and additional sales."

Can ideas this simple work? "They do," Wolfe said. "Basically, these are the two premises I keep in mind."

The importance of simplicity

Explaining the reason behind his position among the company's top producers, Wolfe said, "Life is a great door opener. It leads to the sale of a broad range of other products, including disability and equities." Though Wolfe practices very successfully what he preaches, some people might still wonder how such basic techniques qualify as a subject for "Master Methods." The answer lies in looking at some of the human race's achievements: They began with simple ideas that some people may have overlooked.

"Life sales are easy sales to make," Wolfe said. "The problem is that many agents think of the Life sale as complicated. They make the mistake of getting into the complexities and technicalities with their clients. So if you ask me what's the first piece of advice I can give a new agent selling life insurance, it's KISS."

Keep it simple, stupid. This blunt advice applies exceptionally well to the Life marketplace. While the keep-it-simple approach can sharply increase an agent's closing ratio, Wolfe stresses that it does

continued on page 6

ITC Cheltenham®

Book

abcdefghijklmnopqrstuvwxyz
ABCDEFGHIJKLMNOPQRSTUVWXYZ
1234567890&$£%.,:;-!?"åçëîñòšúß

Book Italic

abcdefghijklmnopqrstuvwxyz
ABCDEFGHIJKLMNOPQRSTUVWXYZ
1234567890&$£%.,:;-!?"åçëîñòšúß

Bold

abcdefghijklmnopqrstuvwxyz
ABCDEFGHIJKLMNOPQRSTUVWXYZ
1234567890&$£%.,:;-!?"åçëîñòšúß

Bold Italic

abcdefghijklmnopqrstuvwxyz
ABCDEFGHIJKLMNOPQRSTUVWXYZ
1234567890&$£%.,:;-!?"åçëîñòšúß

15 point

Bitstream is an independent digital typefoundry. Using the latest computer graphics tools, Bitstream's designers maintain the traditional essentials of good type design. Shape, weight and spacing rhythm are expertly controlled *to produce digitized letterforms of the highest quality in all font formats. In addition to making definitive versions of existing faces, Bitstream introduces creative new designs.*
9 point with 10 point lead

Bitstream is an independent digital typefoundry. Using the latest computer graphics tools, Bitstream's designers maintain the traditional essentials of good type design. Shape, weight and spacing rhythm *are expertly controlled to produce digitized letterforms of the highest quality in all font formats. In addition to making definitive versions of existing faces, Bitstream introduces creative new designs.*

Newsletter

ITC Cheltenham and Hammersmith are combined in this horizontal newsletter format. Both are easy-to-read typefaces. ITC Cheltenham is down-to-earth and friendly, but still serious and businesslike.

Both faces are combined in the nameplate, where the bold serif *Gazette* establishes a solid image to contrast with the lightness of the sanserif *The*.

An 18-point rule accentuates the nameplate and defines the overall width of the four-column grid, below. An 8-point rule sets the width of the first column and visually separates the letter from the three-column table beneath it.

The letter, set in Italic, has a conversational look to it. Hammersmith Bold drop caps introduce each story and provide a visual landmark for the text.

Type specifications:
In the masthead *The* is set in 96-point Hammersmith; *Gazette* is in 95-point ITC Cheltenham Bold. Headlines are set in 18-point ITC Cheltenham Bold; text is in 9/10 ITC Cheltenham Book; drop caps are in 22-point Hammersmith Bold; the letter is in 11/12 ITC Cheltenham Book Italic; the employee list is in 8/9 ITC Cheltenham Book and Bold.

Note: Graphic image was scanned into the system. It might also be imported from a paint or draw program or added by means of manual paste-up.

Newsletter of the
Bauer-Renwick Companies
Volume I Number I

June 1991

The Gazette

Dear Main Office Employees:

We are delighted to present the first issue of our monthly publication for all Main Office employees.

Its success will be determined by you—its readers. We will rely on you to inform your department correspondents (listed below) of news that would be appropriate to include in the newsletter. So, please, make it a point to keep your correspondents well informed so that the Main Office newsletter can present an accurate and timely picture of activities throughout our various departments.

We hope you will continue to read the publication each month. If you have any comments or questions pertaining to the newsletter, please direct them to Rebecca Honan in employee communications, ext. 5351.

Carol Wilson

Information Systems
Eva Cassava
Theresa LaBarge

Employee Relations
Alan Harap
Terry Turnblat

Human Resources
Ben Bonanno
Lea Menkens

...ications

Executive
Steve Wolf
Halley Barron

Corporate Planning
Ken Holzberg
Candace Chick

Insurance
Greg Weithman
Steve Masucci

Corporate Account-

Law
Sean Ng
Kurt Pettinga

Control
Colin Whitehouse
Amber Alexander

Planning
Sarah Davenport
Susan Turner

Benefits
Josh Williams
... Brown

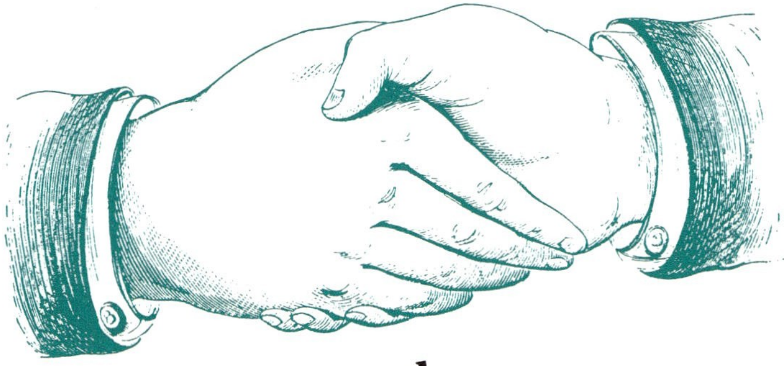

Welcome Aboard

This May, a "Welcome Aboard" program was launched for new Main Office employees by the Employee Relations Department. The program is designed to familiarize new employees with Bauer-Renwick and to extend a formal welcome via a luncheon each month for those new to the corporate staff. Tom Stevens, group employee relations manager, corporate staff, explains that the luncheons provide new employees with an opportunity to meet Bauer-Renwick's management (several senior officers of the Corporation are invited to attend each luncheon) and to learn more about Bauer-Renwick. For those new to the city, a "Welcome Aboard" packet includes information about the area, transit schedules and city and suburban maps.

During the luncheon, Stevens narrates a slide presentation on the company, and new employees are asked to introduce themselves and to give a brief description of their educational and professional backgrounds. All in all, the "Welcome Aboard" orientation luncheons are an excellent way for new employees to get to know the company.

Bauer-Re...
Moving
Experie...

What a diffe... make. Nov... Communication... Departments ha... their new quar... Newton Street, ... imagine the st... week precedi... weekend of M... coordination, ... effort was rec... tractor, furnis... movers and ... sonnel to pu...

The last c... Sunday afte... ness as usu... In spite of ... the move ... first day of ... with a rec... room at 4...

Reactio... have bee... there stil... up items... way of a... final tou...

ITC Clearface®

Regular

abcdefghijklmnopqrstuvwxyz
ABCDEFGHIJKLMNOPQRSTUVWXYZ
1234567890&$£%.,:;-!?''åçëîñòšúß

Regular Italic

abcdefghijklmnopqrstuvwxyz
ABCDEFGHIJKLMNOPQRSTUVWXYZ
1234567890&$£%.,:;-!?''åçëîñòšúß

Heavy

abcdefghijklmnopqrstuvwxyz
ABCDEFGHIJKLMNOPQRSTUVWXYZ
1234567890&$£%.,:;-!?''åçëîñòšúß

Heavy Italic

abcdefghijklmnopqrstuvwxyz
ABCDEFGHIJKLMNOPQRSTUVWXYZ
1234567890&$£%.,:;-!?''åçëîñòšúß

15 point

Bitstream is an independent digital typefoundry. Using the latest computer graphics tools, Bitstream's designers maintain the traditional essentials of good type design. Shape, weight and spacing rhythm are ex*pertly controlled to produce digitized letterforms of the highest quality in all font formats. In addition to making definitive versions of existing faces, Bitstream introduces creative new designs.*

9 point with 10 point lead

Bitstream is an independent digital typefoundry. Using the latest computer graphics tools, Bitstream's designers maintain the traditional essentials of good type design. Shape, weight and spacing rhythm are expertly controlled to ***produce digitized letterforms of the highest quality in all font formats. In addition to making definitive versions of existing faces, Bitstream introduces creative new designs.***

Classified Advertisement

ITC Clearface brings a businesslike but not stuffy feeling to this recruitment ad. The heavier Franklin Gothic headlines complement the text. The contrasting textures of white space, black bar, and text create a lively yet organized image.

Instead of following the conventional wisdom of setting classified ad text as large as possible to fill up the space, the designer has set the type in a size that is comfortable to read. Because the use of white space in this ad is conspicuously different from that in most newspaper ads, this ad stands out on the page. Note that the broad channel of white space along the left and bottom brings emphasis to the name *Moore.*

Because Clearface is slightly condensed, it took less space than some other typefaces and freed up white space. If a wider typeface was used it would probably have been set in a smaller size and that would have made it less effective and harder to read.

Type specifications:
The job title is set in 14/15 Franklin Gothic, the introductory text in 9/20 ITC Clearface Italic, the body text in 9/10 ITC Clearface.

At Moore, we're making things happen in the banking industry. As one of New England's largest and most successful financial institutions, we are ready to take full advantage of interstate banking as it unfolds. We are looking for a qualified professional to join our marketing department.

Marketing Research Associate

Becoming Moore
In this key position, you'll be involved in gathering and analyzing marketing information necessary for developing business strategy. You will test new products, conduct bank image and advertising awareness studies, measure market share and determine product penetration. At least 3 years of market research background is required, preferably in financial services. A college degree is required, and statistics and computer skills are preferred.

Offering Moore
Moore fosters individual achievement and recognition, and rewards personal efforts. As part of the Moore/Helmsley Financial Group, Moore National Bank offers competitive compensation including a full range of benefits and exceptional opportunity for advancement.

If you would like to be a part of this successful team, send your résumé to Donald Vaughn, Moore National Bank, 32 Howe Street, Providence, RI 02903.

Moore National Bank is an Equal Opportunity Employer M/F/H/V.

Moore

Bitstream Cooper

Light

abcdefghijklmnopqrstuvwxyz
ABCDEFGHIJKLMNOPQRSTUVWXYZ
1234567890&$£%.,:;-!?‘’åçëîñòšúß

Light Italic

abcdefghijklmnopqrstuvwxyz
ABCDEFGHIJKLMNOPQRSTUVWXYZ
1234567890&$£%.,:;-!?‘’åçëîñòšúß

Bold

abcdefghijklmnopqrstuvwxyz
ABCDEFGHIJKLMNOPQRSTUVWXYZ
1234567890&$£%.,:;-!?‘’åçëîñòšúß

Bold Italic

abcdefghijklmnopqrstuvwxyz
ABCDEFGHIJKLMNOPQRSTUVWXYZ
1234567890&$£%.,:;-!?‘’åçëîñòšúß

15 point

Bitstream is an independent digital typefoundry. Using the latest computer graphics tools, Bitstream's designers maintain the traditional essentials of good type design. Shape, weight and spacing rhythm are expertly controlled *to produce digitized letterforms of the highest quality in all font formats. In addition to making definitive versions of existing faces, Bitstream introduces creative new designs.*

9 point with 10 point lead

Bitstream is an independent digital typefoundry. Using the latest computer graphics tools, Bitstream's designers maintain the traditional essentials of good type design. Shape, weight and spacing rhythm ***are expertly controlled to produce digitized letterforms of the highest quality in all font formats. In addition to making definitive versions of existing faces, Bitstream introduces creative new designs.***

Charts

The Bitstream Cooper family of typefaces is used for its assertive yet approachable feeling and fine readability. Bitstream Cooper Bold remains very legible even when it is set small, as in the 1988 pie chart.

Note how the combined use of rules, type, and colored circles, set flush right in the key, serve to easily identify the elements in the pie charts.

Type specifications:
Text is set in 8/10 Bitstream Cooper Light. The title is set in Bitstream Cooper Light and Bold. Callouts in the pie charts are in 8-point Bitstream Cooper Light and Bold. Figures labeling the years for each chart are in 14-point Bitstream Cooper Bold.

Note: Charts need to be created on Charts/Graphs software program, then imported to a word processing or desktop publishing system.

Renculus International Corporation
Annual Report: Customer Support

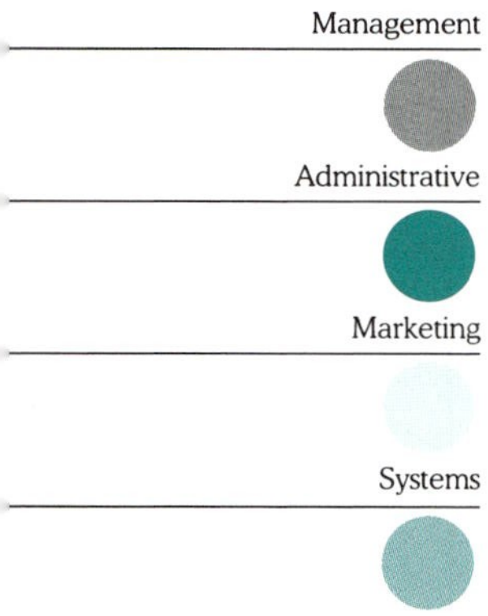

1986

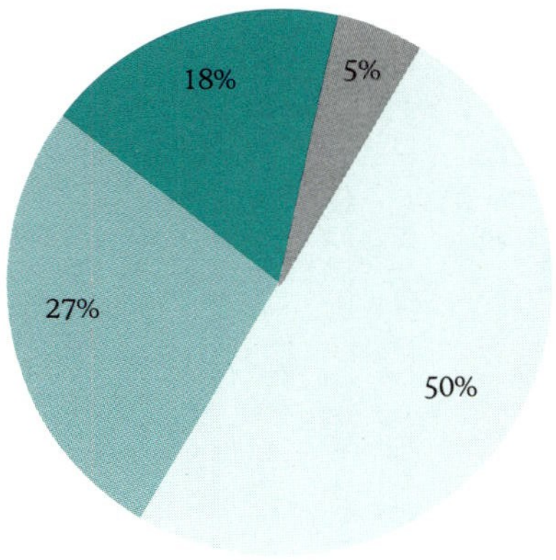

1987

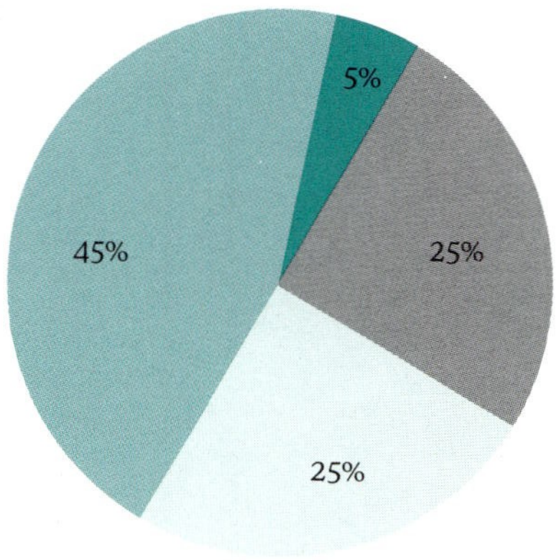

1988

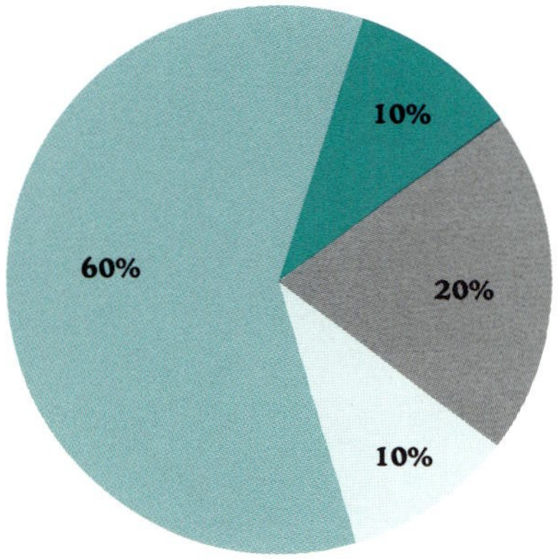

As the graphs indicate during the period of 1986–1988, Marketing involvement has decreased while Systems involvement has increased due to the implementation of the dealer communications system. Administrative and Marketing support have varied to meet the demands of the project.

Projections for 1989 indicate a continuation of these trends; therefore, additional funding for Systems support is required. Budgets will be revised to provide these funds. See detail on following page for additional justification.

Courier

Roman 10 Pitch

abcdefghijklmnopqrstuvwxyz
ABCDEFGHIJKLMNOPQRSTUVWXYZ
1234567890&$£%.,:;-!?''åçëîñòšúß

Italic

abcdefghijklmnopqrstuvwxyz
ABCDEFGHIJKLMNOPQRSTUVWXYZ
1234567890&$£%.,:;-!?''åçëîñòšúß

Bold

abcdefghijklmnopqrstuvwxyz
ABCDEFGHIJKLMNOPQRSTUVWXYZ
1234567890&$£%.,:;-!?''åçëîñòšúß

Bold Italic

abcdefghijklmnopqrstuvwxyz
ABCDEFGHIJKLMNOPQRSTUVWXYZ
1234567890&$£%.,:;-!?''åçëîñòšúß

15 point

Bitstream is an independent digital typefoundry. Using the latest computer graphics tools, Bitstream's designers maintain the traditional essentials of good type design. Shape, weight and spacing rhythm are expertly con- *trolled to produce digitized letterforms of the highest quality in all font formats. In addition to making definitive versions of existing faces, Bitstream introduces creative new designs.*

9 point with 10 point lead

Bitstream is an independent digital typefoundry. Using the latest computer graphics tools, Bitstream's designers maintain the traditional essentials of good type design. Shape, weight and spacing rhythm are expertly con- ***trolled to produce digitized letterforms of the highest quality in all font formats. In addition to making definitive versions of existing faces, Bitstream introduces creative new designs.***

Announcement

While Courier isn't normally considered a typeset face, it's used well here as a display face for the words "and change." Courier should not usually be used as body text like this, unless you want this kind of intentionally "unslick," austere look, reminiscent of something which might have been posted on a bulletin board in college. ITC American Typewriter would give it a more typeset look, but it also might be too *cute* for this serious subject.

If you wanted a more typeset look, Charter or Serifa would work well for body text while still not looking too formal or fancy.

This announcement is based on a three-column grid. The headline in the middle of the page crosses all three columns and is an example of type used in an evocative, illustrative way. The word *expansion* is set with progressively increased letterspacing to imply expansion.

Courier is also used throughout for text; headlines are emphasized by letterspacing; the seminar title is set in Courier Bold; the titles of the speakers are set in Courier Italic.

Line spaces serve to separate sections of text. The institution's name is letterspaced and reversed to become a strong visual element.

Type specifications:
Text is set in 10/12 Courier and Courier Italic; the reversed copy is in 10-point Courier Bold; the word *expansion* is in 80-point Franklin Gothic Extra Condensed; the words *and Change* are in 96-point Courier Roman and Italic.

Winter 1989 at **THE JOHNSON INSTITUTE**

World Economic Seminars on Expansion and Change

Weekly Topics

A Global Marketplace

World Economic Growth

South American Debt Finance

An American Common Market?

Market Forces in China

Perestroika and Agriculture

Bringing U.S. Jobs Home

expansion and *Change*

This week

An American Plan for World Economic Growth in the 1990s

Tuesday
February 14, 1989
3:30 pm

The Johnson Institute
Abrams Lecture Hall
860 Custis Circle NW
Washington, DC

Speakers

Diane Aronsson-Davies
Economic Advisor to the President

William Nutting, Jr.
Senior Economic Fellow, The Johnson Institute

Alice Darrow
Chair, Council on World Agricultural Affairs

Norman Bohannon
Professor of Economics, Commonwealth University

Dutch

The Bitstream version of the Times Roman® typeface.

Roman

abcdefghijklmnopqrstuvwxyz
ABCDEFGHIJKLMNOPQRSTUVWXYZ
1234567890&$£%.,:;-!?‘’åçëîñòšúß

Italic

abcdefghijklmnopqrstuvwxyz
ABCDEFGHIJKLMNOPQRSTUVWXYZ
1234567890&$£%.,:;-!?‘’åçëîñòšúß

Bold

abcdefghijklmnopqrstuvwxyz
ABCDEFGHIJKLMNOPQRSTUVWXYZ
1234567890&$£%.,:;-!?‘’åçëîñòšúß

Bold Italic

abcdefghijklmnopqrstuvwxyz
ABCDEFGHIJKLMNOPQRSTUVWXYZ
1234567890&$£%.,:;-!?‘’åçëîñòšúß

15 point

Bitstream is an independent digital type-foundry. Using the latest computer graphics tools, Bitstream's designers maintain the traditional essentials of good type design. Shape, weight and *spacing rhythm are expertly controlled to produce digitized letterforms of the highest quality in all font formats. In addition to making definitive versions of existing faces, Bitstream introduces creative new designs.*
9 point with 10 point lead

Bitstream is an independent digital type-foundry. Using the latest computer graphics tools, Bitstream's designers maintain the traditional essentials of good type design. Shape, weight and *spacing rhythm are expertly controlled to produce digitized letterforms of the highest quality in all font formats. In addition to making definitive versions of existing faces, Bitstream introduces creative new designs.*

Documentation

A clean, easy-to-read serif, Dutch is an appropriate face for this page from a Bitstream documentation manual. Dutch helps give this documentation a typographically neutral tone (and also helps display the typefaces which were included with the package).

This page is organized on a strong four-column grid. The horizontal white channel across the top provides space for illustrations of the computer screen and callouts.

A clear reading path exists, with numbered instruction paragraphs appearing in Dutch Bold, further emphasized with color. The supporting text is set in Dutch. Paragraphs are in block format, separated by a line space.

Two sizes of uppercase characters are combined in the running page footer to provide the look of large and small capitals. Note how *the* and *for* are set in upper- and lower-case Dutch Italic for added visual interest.

The illustration number and page folio are set in Swiss Condensed to contrast with the Dutch text. The keystrokes are set in Swiss to stand out from the descriptive text.

Type specifications:
The headline, *Setting Up*, is set in 12-point Dutch Bold Italic; numbered instructions are in 10/12 Dutch Bold; text is in 9/12 Dutch; commands appearing in text are set in 9-point Swiss Bold.

Type within the screen is 5-point Prestige; callouts are in 9-point Dutch Italic. This "screen shot" was created using a graphics program, but most screen shots are captured using special screen capture software. These programs make graphics files which can then be imported into word processing and page composition programs.

Options

Messages

Action
Help

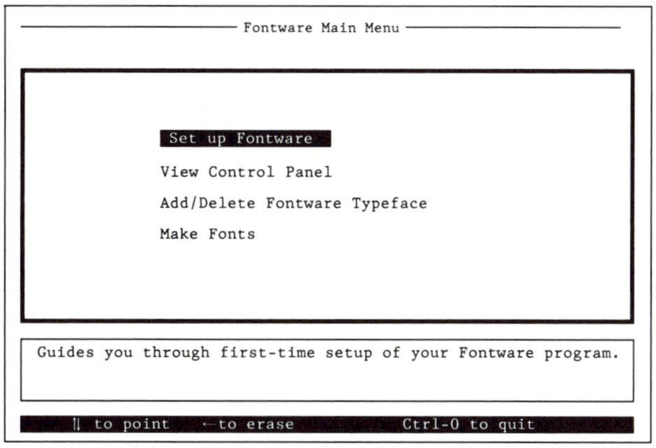

1-1. *Fontware Main Menu during setup*

Setting Up

Before you set up the Fontware Installation Kit on your system

- Make sure that Ventura Publisher is set up on your hard disk.
- If you have a Read Me First insert in your Fontware Installation Kit package, follow its instructions.
- If you are currently working in Ventura Publisher, return to the DOS prompt by choosing the *Quit* option.

1. With the PC turned on, insert Disk 1 of the Fontware Installation Kit into Drive A. Close the lever on the drive.

2. Type a: fontware and press < Enter > .

The copyright notice and Bitstream Fontware banner appear on your display.

The program asks whether to show menus in more than two colors. Type **Y** if you have a color monitor. Type **N** if you have a monochrome monitor.

The Fontware Main Menu, shown in Figure 1–1, appears on your display.

3. Press < Enter > to choose the Set Up Fontware option from the main menu.

You see the Fontware Control Panel.

The message window prompts you for the names of directories needed by Fontware, as well as for information about your display and printer.

If you need to, you can change the information in the control panel any time you use the Fontware Installation Kit.

Franklin Gothic®

Roman

abcdefghijklmnopqrstuvwxyz
ABCDEFGHIJKLMNOPQRSTUVWXYZ
1234567890&$£%.,:;-!?"åçëîñòšúß

Italic

abcdefghijklmnopqrstuvwxyz
ABCDEFGHIJKLMNOPQRSTUVWXYZ
1234567890&$£%.,:;-!?"åçëîñòšúß

Condensed

abcdefghijklmnopqrstuvwxyz
ABCDEFGHIJKLMNOPQRSTUVWXYZ
1234567890&$£%.,:;-!?"åçëîñòšúß

Extra Condensed

abcdefghijklmnopqrstuvwxyz
ABCDEFGHIJKLMNOPQRSTUVWXYZ
1234567890&$£%.,:;-!?"åçëîñòšúß

15 point

Bitstream is an independent digital typefoundry. Using the latest computer graphics tools, Bitstream's designers maintain the traditional essentials of good type design. Shape, weight and spacing rhythm ***are expertly controlled to produce digitized letterforms of the highest quality in all font formats. In addition to making definitive versions of existing faces, Bitstream introduces creative new designs.***

9 point with 10 point lead

Bitstream is an independent digital typefoundry. Using the latest computer graphics tools, Bitstream's designers maintain the traditional essentials of good type design. Shape, weight and spacing rhythm are expertly controlled to produce digitized letterforms of the highest quality in all font formats. In addition to making definitive versions of existing faces, Bitstream introduces creative new designs.

Rubber Stamps

The Franklin Gothic family of typefaces is used for this collection of rubber stamps. Century Schoolbook, used for the date on the *Received* stamp, mixes well with the bold Franklin Gothic Extra Condensed.

The commanding, easy-to-read Franklin Gothic type expresses a sense of weight and importance appropriate to rubber stamps. Notice how the Franklin Gothic Extra Condensed used on the *RUSH!* and *ARCHIVE* stamps allows maximum height in a narrow width. The pointing hand in the *Postage Due* stamp is from the ITC Zapf Dingbats collection available in the Bitstream *Symbols 1* typeface package.

ARCHIVE

RECEIVED
AUG 25 88

PROPRIETARY
INFORMATION

Stone's Throw Gardens
21 Ketchum Hill Road
Chilmark, MA 02535

HOLD

Dated Material

Disk Enclosed

PAID

URGENT

BOOK RATE

RUSH!

RECEIVED

Postage Due ____¢

Attn: Accounts Payable

DO NOT BEND!

FRAGILE

Please Remit!

ABCDEFGH

IJKLMNOPQ

RSTUVWXYZ

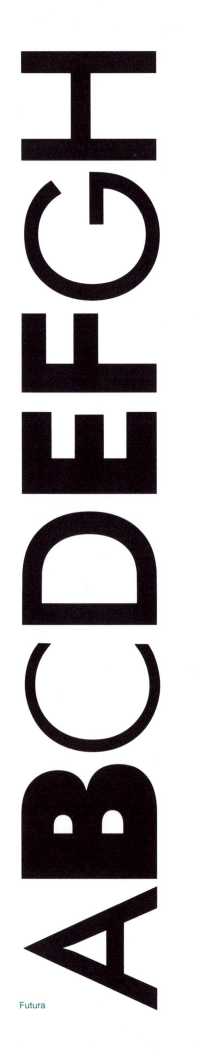

Futura

abcdefgh

ijklmnopq

rstuvwxyz

Futura®

Book

abcdefghijklmnopqrstuvwxyz
ABCDEFGHIJKLMNOPQRSTUVWXYZ
1234567890&$£%.,:;-!?"åçëîñòšúß

Book Italic

abcdefghijklmnopqrstuvwxyz
ABCDEFGHIJKLMNOPQRSTUVWXYZ
1234567890&$£%.,:;-!?"åçëîñòšúß

Heavy

abcdefghijklmnopqrstuvwxyz
ABCDEFGHIJKLMNOPQRSTUVWXYZ
1234567890&$£%.,:;-!?"åçëîñòšúß

Heavy Italic

abcdefghijklmnopqrstuvwxyz
ABCDEFGHIJKLMNOPQRSTUVWXYZ
1234567890&$£%.,:;-!?"åçëîñòšúß

15 point

Bitstream is an independent digital typefoundry. Using the latest computer graphics tools, Bitstream's designers maintain the traditional essentials of good type design. Shape, weight and spacing rhythm are expertly controlled *to produce digitized letterforms of the highest quality in all font formats. In addition to making definitive versions of existing faces, Bitstream introduces creative new designs.*

9 point with 10 point lead

Bitstream is an independent digital typefoundry. Using the latest computer graphics tools, Bitstream's designers maintain the traditional essentials of good type design. Shape, weight and spacing rhythm *are expertly controlled to produce digitized letterforms of the highest quality in all font formats. In addition to making definitive versions of existing faces, Bitstream introduces creative new designs.*

Business Plan

A clean, geometrically-based typeface, Futura is easy to read at both large and small sizes. The geometric quality is apparent in the logotype and works well to define the overall square shape of the logo.

Organized on a simple two-column grid, this brochure has a clear reading path. The developer's name is apparent but secondary to the property name. Text, located in the first column, relates easily to the floor plan in the second column.

Type specifications:
The logotype, *CHOATE WOODS SQUARE,* is set in 19/28 Futura Book; *Theurer and Associates* is set in 10-point Futura Heavy; the text is in 8/10 Futura Book; the floor plan callouts are in 6-point Futura Heavy.

Most page composition programs will directly accept files from architectural CAD programs for the best reproduction of details. If CAD files aren't available, the floorplan could also be scanned.

Theurer and Associates

CHOATE WOODS SQUARE

Features and Amenities

- Parking in enclosed garage within the building, or in secure area behing the school
- Extra large apartments, average sizes of:
  935 square feet—1 Bedroom
  1155 square feet—2 Bedrooms
  1370 square feet—3 Bedrooms
- Ceiling heights over ten feet
- Walk-in closets and eat-in kitchens with top-of-the-line appliances
- Extraordinary views out of oversized ''period'' windows, as large as 7'0" wide and 18'0" tall
- Original detailing preserved—inlaid panel wainscoting, triple-vaulted celings, Greek columns, arched windows, and wrought iron railings
- Storage and laundry areas
- Units available for the mobility-impaired
- Twenty-four-hour security system

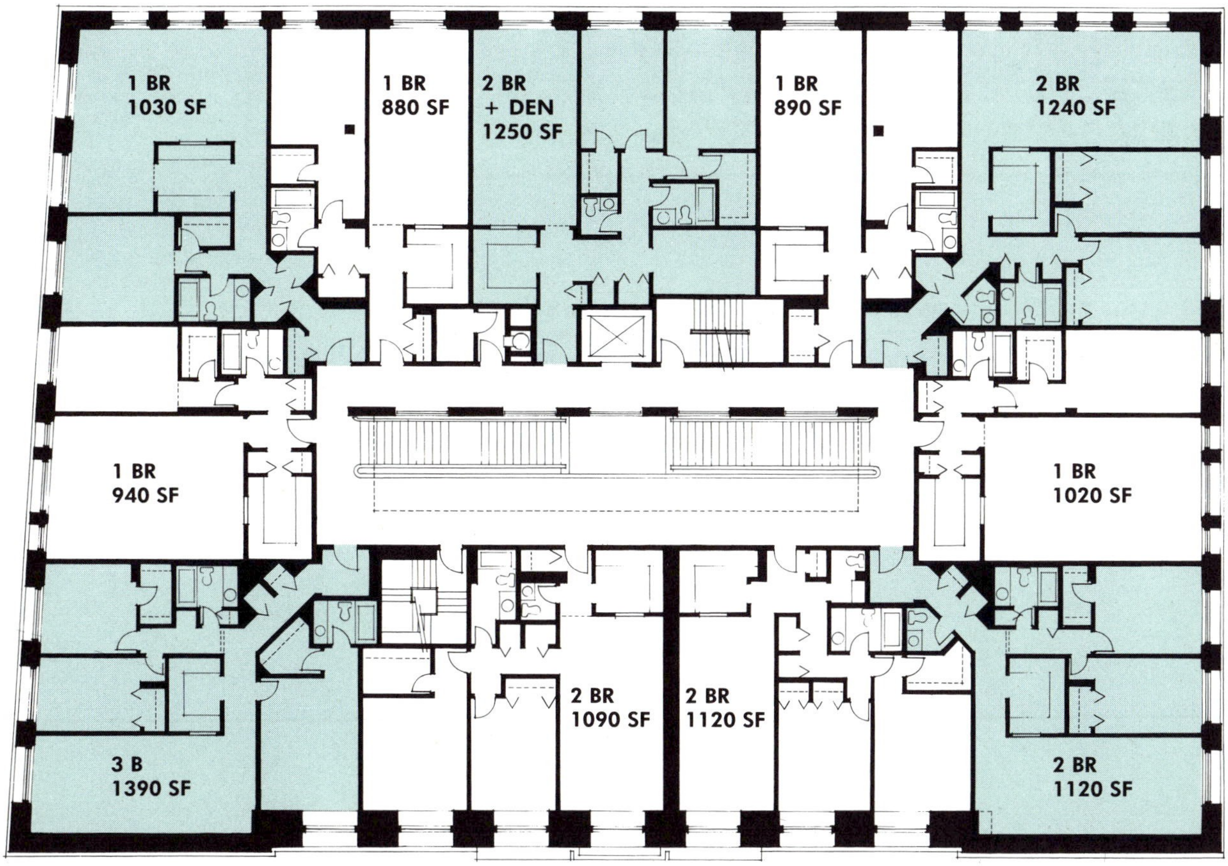

Futura Light

Light

abcdefghijklmnopqrstuvwxyz
ABCDEFGHIJKLMNOPQRSTUVWXYZ
1234567890&$£%.,:;-!?"åçëîñòšúß

Light Italic

abcdefghijklmnopqrstuvwxyz
ABCDEFGHIJKLMNOPQRSTUVWXYZ
1234567890&$£%.,:;-!?"åçëîñòšúß

Medium Condensed

abcdefghijklmnopqrstuvwxyz
ABCDEFGHIJKLMNOPQRSTUVWXYZ
1234567890&$£%.,:;-!?"åçëîñòšúß

Extra Black

abcdefghijklmnopqrstuvwxyz
ABCDEFGHIJKLMNOPQRSTUVWXYZ
1234567890&$£%.,:;-!?"åçëîñòšúß

15 point

Bitstream is an independent digital type-foundry. Using the latest computer graphics tools, Bitstream's designers maintain the traditional essentials of good type design. Shape, weight and spacing rhythm *are expertly controlled to produce digitized letterforms of the highest quality in all font formats. In addition to making definitive versions of existing faces, Bitstream introduces creative new designs.*
9 point with 10 point lead

Bitstream is an independent digital typefoundry. Using the latest computer graphics tools, Bitstream's designers maintain the traditional essentials of good type design. Shape, weight and spacing rhythm are expertly controlled to produce digitized letterforms of the highest quality in **all font formats. In addition to making definitive versions of existing faces, Bitstream introduces creative new designs.**

Menu

The Futura and Bernhard Modern typefaces, in contrasting serif and sanserif, roman and italic, light and bold, are combined in this menu to suggest the variety of the dishes.

Lowercase Futura Light, used for descriptions, has an airy feeling. Prices are set two sizes smaller to match the x-height of the lower case descriptions.

An easy-to-read two-column grid is used. Modulated white space is created by indenting the text under the subheads, reinforcing the composition of the logotype, *CAFE MAX.*

Setting the entire text in lowercase is acceptable for something short and trendy like this menu, but it *does* make it more difficult to read and should not be used for longer, running text.

Type specifications:
CAFE is set in 30-point Futura Medium Condensed. *APPETIZERS* and *DINNER* are set in 24-point Futura Medium Condensed. *MAX* and *WINES* in Bernhard Modern, 56- and 32-point; *Salads* and *Desserts* in 30-point Bernhard Modern Italic; *coffees* in 18-point Futura Extra Black; text in 10/14 Futura Light; prices in 8-point Futura Light.

CAFÉ MAX

APPETIZERS

chilled strawberry consommé 4.00
artichoke soup with hazelnuts and cognac 4.00
corn and wild mushroom pancakes 6.00
warm leek and vermont chèvre tart 4.00
crab cakes with celeriac rémoulade 5.00

DINNER

grilled yellow fin tuna with cilantro a
served with tomato, pecan couscou
chutney, green beans with parsley

chicken paillards with basil cream
vinegar served with wheat berry p
holland purple and yellow peppe

pan fried whole trout with creol
served with pine nut and red p
fiddlehead ferns with red cider

roast lamb with beach plum
served with minted new pota
baby carrots with caraway

Salads

pear salad with mixed greens and walnuts 5.00
christophene, hearts of palm and endive 6.00
arugula, shiitake mushroom salad with thai peanut sauce 6.00

Desserts

bittersweet chocolate te
strawberry rhubarb bre
hazelnut shortbread 4
blackberry cassis cobb
white cherry tart 6.0
poached pears in bit

WINES

maya sauvignon blanc, 1985 24.00
saint jean chardonnay, 1986 28.00
zinfandel point milou, 1985 32.00
château la rivaldière calvet 36.00
grand pommard chantilly, 1985 42.00
côte du petit cul de sac, 1984 38.00
gustavia méthode champenois, 1986 34.00
champagne haut village arrey, 1985 58.00

coffees

caffe latte espr
iced espresso
all 2.00

Futura Medium

Medium

abcdefghijklmnopqrstuvwxyz
ABCDEFGHIJKLMNOPQRSTUVWXYZ
1234567890&$£%.,:;-!?''åçëîñòšúß

Medium Italic

abcdefghijklmnopqrstuvwxyz
ABCDEFGHIJKLMNOPQRSTUVWXYZ
1234567890&$£%.,:;-!?''åçëîñòšúß

Bold

abcdefghijklmnopqrstuvwxyz
ABCDEFGHIJKLMNOPQRSTUVWXYZ
1234567890&$£%.,:;-!?''åçëîñòšúß

Bold Italic

abcdefghijklmnopqrstuvwxyz
ABCDEFGHIJKLMNOPQRSTUVWXYZ
1234567890&$£%.,:;-!?''åçëîñòšúß

15 point

Bitstream is an independent digital typefoundry. Using the latest computer graphics tools, Bitstream's designers maintain the traditional essentials of good type design. Shape, weight and spacing rhythm are expertly controlled *to produce digitized letterforms of the highest quality in all font formats. In addition to making definitive versions of existing faces, Bitstream introduces creative new designs.*

9 point with 10 point lead

Bitstream is an independent digital typefoundry. Using the latest computer graphics tools, Bitstream's designers maintain the traditional essentials of good type design. Shape, weight and spacing rhythm are expertly controlled to ***produce digitized letterforms of the highest quality in all font formats. In addition to making definitive versions of existing faces, Bitstream introduces creative new designs.***

Slide Presentation

Futura's high legibility holds up even when projected by slide. Varying weights of Futura are combined throughout for visual variety. In the logotype, *LUCENT*, the various weights suggest modulating dark and light, an image appropriate to a lighting company.

Type specifications:
The point sizes given here are the actual sizes they would appear in the transparency. When using some software you work on a large page and it is reduced to transparency size, in which case, the font sizes would all be large, from around 18 to 150 point. Text and heads are set in 7/8 Futura Medium Italic. Various weights of the Futura typeface family are used throughout: Light, Book, Medium Condensed, Bold and Extra Black. *ASSESS* is set in 9-point Futura Light; *DESIGN* in Medium and *INSTALL* in Extra Black. *Q* is set in 60-point Futura Bold.

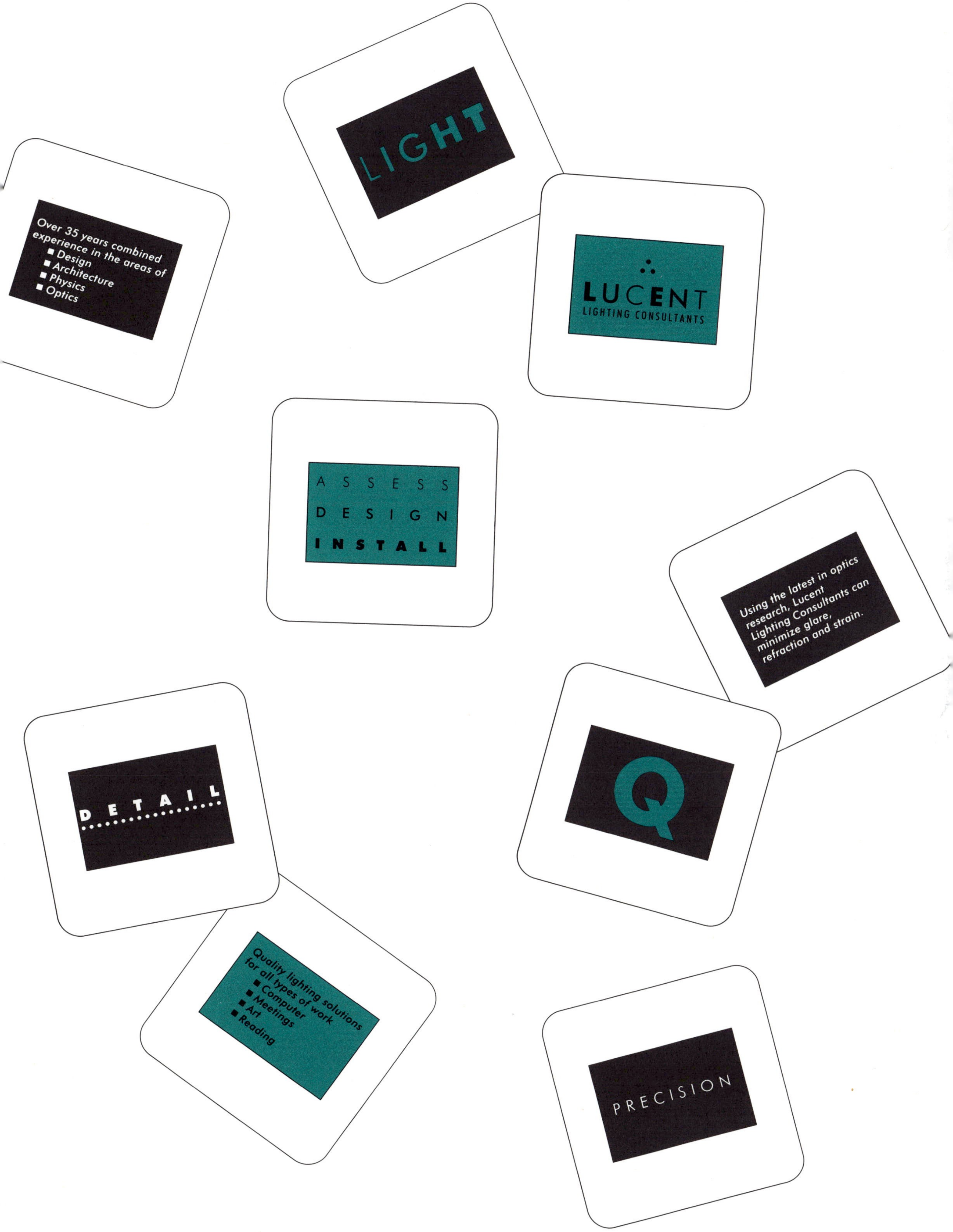
LIGHT
Over 35 years combined experience in the areas of
■ Design
■ Architecture
■ Physics
■ Optics
LUCENT
LIGHTING CONSULTANTS
ASSESS
DESIGN
INSTALL
Using the latest in optics research, Lucent Lighting Consultants can minimize glare, refraction and strain.
DETAIL
Q
Quality lighting solutions for all types of work
■ Computer
■ Meetings
■ Art
■ Reading
PRECISION

ITC Galliard®

Roman

abcdefghijklmnopqrstuvwxyz
ABCDEFGHIJKLMNOPQRSTUVWXYZ
1234567890&$£%.,:;-!?‘’åçëîñòšúß

Italic

abcdefghijklmnopqrstuvwxyz
ABCDEFGHIJKLMNOPQRSTUVWXYZ
1234567890&$£%.,:;-!?‘’åçëîñòšúß

Bold

abcdefghijklmnopqrstuvwxyz
ABCDEFGHIJKLMNOPQRSTUVWXYZ
1234567890&$£%.,:;-!?‘’åçëîñòšúß

Bold Italic

abcdefghijklmnopqrstuvwxyz
ABCDEFGHIJKLMNOPQRSTUVWXYZ
1234567890&$£%.,:;-!?‘’åçëîñòšúß

15 point

Bitstream is an independent digital typefoundry. Using the latest computer graphics tools, Bitstream's designers maintain the traditional essentials of good type design. Shape, weight and *spacing rhythm are expertly controlled to produce digitized letterforms of the highest quality in all font formats. In addition to making definitive versions of existing faces, Bitstream introduces creative new designs.*
9 point with 10 point lead

Bitstream is an independent digital typefoundry. Using the latest computer graphics tools, Bitstream's designers maintain the traditional essentials of good type design. Shape, weight and spacing rhythm are expertly ***controlled to produce digitized letterforms of the highest quality in all font formats. In addition to making definitive versions of existing faces, Bitstream introduces creative new designs.***

Manual

Complex information is logically organized to avoid monotony. The highly readable ITC Galliard, a classical serif face, is used for text and contrasts with the sanserif Swiss Condensed.

Rules and subheads break up the page and make it easier for readers to find the particular information they need. Note that the line above the headline is heavy, while the line below is light, which doesn't create too much separation between the subhead and the text which follows. Generous margins of white space further help to keep the page from overwhelming the reader.

Type specifications:
The chapter number, *3*, the head, *Data Definition*, and the folio, *21*, are set in 9-point Swiss Black Condensed; the section numbers *3.3* and *3.3.1* combine 9-point Swiss Black Condensed and Swiss Condensed. The section headings, *Dependencies* and *Specifying Dependencies*, are set in 9-point ITC Galliard Bold; text is in 9/12 ITC Galliard Roman. In the illustration, A, B, and C are set in 36-point ITC Galliard Italic; the captions are in 9/12 ITC Galliard Italic.

3.3 Dependencies

No process can begin until some other process completes (an event occurs). Even processes that occur daily depend on an event that occurs once each day, namely the change in the calendar date. An event upon which a process depends for its initiation is called a "*preceding dependency*," and a process can have any number of preceding dependencies. For example, the process that produces Purchase Orders has, as a preceding dependency, the successful execution of the Daily Inventory Update application.

3.3.1 Specifying Dependencies

Some scheduling systems provide only for the definition and display of a process's preceding dependencies, and thus provide only a one-way view of the relationships that exist between processes. For example, when process "B" is defined to these systems, it is defined as being dependent on the completion of process "A," but there is no facility to specify in the definition of "B" that it has any succeeding dependencies. If process "C" depends on the successful completion of "B," this relationship can only be specified in process "C's" definition, because the description of "B" will not contain any information about the relationship of "B" to "C" or to any other subsequent process. For the user to be able to answer the question,

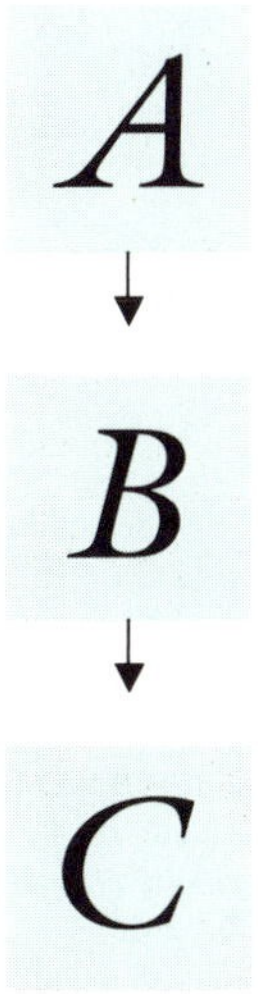

Has a calendar dependency of "Mondays."
*Has a succeeding dependency, which is "**B.**"*

*Has a preceding dependency, which is "**A.**"*
*Has a succeeding dependency, which is "**C.**"*

*Has a preceding dependency, which is "**B.**"*
Has no succeeding dependency.

ITC Garamond®

Book

abcdefghijklmnopqrstuvwxyz
ABCDEFGHIJKLMNOPQRSTUVWXYZ
1234567890&$£%.,:;-!?‘’åçëîñòšúß

Book Italic

abcdefghijklmnopqrstuvwxyz
ABCDEFGHIJKLMNOPQRSTUVWXYZ
1234567890&$£%.,:;-!?‘’åçëîñòšúß

Bold

abcdefghijklmnopqrstuvwxyz
ABCDEFGHIJKLMNOPQRSTUVWXYZ
1234567890&$£%.,:;-!?‘’åçëîñòšúß

Bold Italic

abcdefghijklmnopqrstuvwxyz
ABCDEFGHIJKLMNOPQRSTUVWXYZ
1234567890&$£%.,:;-!?‘’åçëîñòšúß

15 point

Bitstream is an independent digital typefoundry. Using the latest computer graphics tools, Bitstream's designers maintain the traditional essentials of good type design. Shape, weight and spacing rhythm are expertly controlled *to produce digitized letterforms of the highest quality in all font formats. In addition to making definitive versions of existing faces, Bitstream introduces creative new designs.*
9 point with 10 point lead

Bitstream is an independent digital typefoundry. Using the latest computer graphics tools, Bitstream's designers maintain the traditional essentials of good type design. Shape, weight and spacing rhythm ***are expertly controlled to produce digitized letterforms of the highest quality in all font formats. In addition to making definitive versions of existing faces, Bitstream introduces creative new designs.***

Commercial Catalog

A clear hierarchy is evident with the page header, *Furniture*, indicating the content of the page. A two-column grid is used: the narrow column on the left for illustrations, and the wider column on the right for text.

Rules emphasize each catalog number and enliven the page.

ITC Garamond Book, a classical old-style typeface, enhances the content of this auction catalog listing of antique furniture.

Type specifications:
Furniture is set in ITC Garamond Book Italic with a 42-point drop capital *F*; titles, text, and prices in 9/10 ITC Garamond Book with Book Italic; illustration numbers are set in 7-point Swiss Bold.

Note: Photos or illustrations must be scanned into the system or pasted on manually.

Furniture

1 1 5 6
SHAKER LADDER BACK CHAIR
19th century. Maple with five straight slats below a curved crest. Scrolled arm detail. Legs and stretchers have simple turnings. Exceptionally crafted. Signed by the artisan.

$425

32

1 1 5 7
AMERICAN WINDSOR CHAIR
Mid 18th century. Rare mahogany brace-back fan-back design. Nine spindles support the curved crest. Probably from Pennsylvania. Attributed to J.L. Gilbert. Excellent condition.

$550

33

1 1 5 8
WINDSOR ROCKING CHAIR
18th century. Walnut with comb-back design. Curved rail atop eight spindles. Light in proportion. Typical of chairs produced in New England during this period.

See illustration 32 $625

1 1 5 9
QUEEN ANNE SIDE CHAIR
Late 17th century. Walnut New York Colony style with curved crest and splat. Unusually turned cabriole legs supporting rush seat. Turned crest supports and stretchers suggest Dutch influence. One stretcher appears to have been replaced reducing its value slightly.

See illustration 33 $425

34

1 1 6 0
SHERATON CHAIR
Late 18th century. New England walnut with lattice back design. Intricate rosewood inlay. Padded seat supported by slightly curved legs set at an angle. Transitional style. Museum condition.

See illustration 34 $475

ITC Garamond Condensed

Book Condensed

abcdefghijklmnopqrstuvwxyz
ABCDEFGHIJKLMNOPQRSTUVWXYZ
1234567890&$£%.,:;-!?‘’åçëîñòšúß

Book Condensed Italic

abcdefghijklmnopqrstuvwxyz
ABCDEFGHIJKLMNOPQRSTUVWXYZ
1234567890&$£%.,:;-!?‘’åçëîñòšúß

Bold Condensed

abcdefghijklmnopqrstuvwxyz
ABCDEFGHIJKLMNOPQRSTUVWXYZ
1234567890&$£%.,:;-!?‘’åçëîñòšúß

Bold Condensed Italic

abcdefghijklmnopqrstuvwxyz
ABCDEFGHIJKLMNOPQRSTUVWXYZ
1234567890&$£%.,:;-!?‘’åçëîñòšúß

15 point

Bitstream is an independent digital typefoundry. Using the latest computer graphics tools, Bitstream's designers maintain the traditional essentials of good type design. Shape, weight and spacing *rhythm are expertly controlled to produce digitized letterforms of the highest quality in all font formats. In addition to making definitive versions of existing faces, Bitstream introduces creative new designs.*
9 point with 10 point lead

Bitstream is an independent digital typefoundry. Using the latest computer graphics tools, Bitstream's designers maintain the traditional essentials of good type design. Shape, weight and spacing rhythm are expertly con-***trolled to produce digitized letterforms of the highest quality in all font formats. In addition to making definitive versions of existing faces, Bitstream introduces creative new designs.***

Business Plan

An underlying three-column grid organizes this page. The ITC Garamond Book Condensed typeface projects a businesslike tone. Clean, even-weighted Swiss Bold Condensed, used in the graphs, page folio, and company name, offers an orderly counterpoint to the ITC Garamond Book Condensed.

The text provides a clear reading path and is related visually to the graphs below. The graphs are a good example of how to use rules and type together to display quantitative information so that it is easy to read. Notice how the graphs straddle two column widths.

The generous margins of white space provide relief for the text and space for additional graphic elements—the cents symbol and *OVERVIEW* passage—to contrast with the text and graphs.

Type specifications:
Text is set in 9/10 ITC Garamond Book Condensed; run-in headlines are set in 9/10 ITC Garamond Bold Condensed; *OVERVIEW* is in 11-point ITC Garamond Bold Condensed Italic. The page folio, graph callouts, and *Northwestern Gas* are set in Swiss Bold Condensed. The large cents symbol used as a graphic is set in 494-point ITC Garamond Book Condensed Italic.

O V E R V I E W

Northwestern is the largest independent natural gas distributor in the Northwest, one of America's leading growth markets for natural gas. The Company serves 250,000 customers in Washington and Oregon and has diversified into gas and oil exploration, gas pipeline transmission and retail sales of propane and energy conservation products. Northwestern and its predecessor companies have paid continuous dividends since 1901.

The economy in Northwestern's service area is thriving. Northwestern is positioned for strong growth in operations thanks to the expansion of high-technology and service companies. Although these companies use only small volumes of natural gas, they multiply gas demand by providing the additional jobs and increased personal income that promote the growth of retail and service businesses that also use gas. Meanwhile, the Northwest remains a very oil-dependent part of the nation. As a result, Northwestern's low market penetration and space-heating saturation provide an opportunity for customer growth not found elsewhere.

Northwestern increased its pipeline gas supply by 25 percent in 1984. Due to these long-term purchases of new Canadian and domestic supplies, as well as greater competition in the interstate natural gas market, Northwestern's wholesale and retail gas prices declined in 1984. The cost of gas home heating averaged about 20 percent less than fuel oil in the Company's Washington service area.

Because of its price advantage and marketing programs, the Company added 3,800 new customers in 1984. Northwestern converted 1,900 current customers to gas heating, while sales volume reached an all-time high. Northwestern expects that further retail price declines and expanded marketing programs in 1985 will contribute to a continuation of favorable conditions for growth.

**Facts based upon latest full year available at December 31, 1984.*

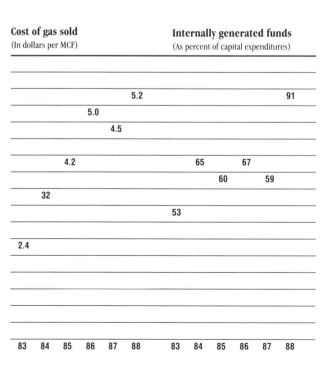

Cost of gas sold
(In dollars per MCF)

83	84	85	86	87	88
2.4	32	4.2	5.0	4.5	5.2

Internally generated funds
(As percent of capital expenditures)

83	84	85	86	87	88
53	65	60	67	59	91

Goudy Old Style®

Roman

abcdefghijklmnopqrstuvwxyz
ABCDEFGHIJKLMNOPQRSTUVWXYZ
1234567890&$£%.,:;-!?''åçëîñòšúß

Italic

abcdefghijklmnopqrstuvwxyz
ABCDEFGHIJKLMNOPQRSTUVWXYZ
1234567890&$£%.,:;-!?''åçëîñòšúß

Bold

abcdefghijklmnopqrstuvwxyz
ABCDEFGHIJKLMNOPQRSTUVWXYZ
1234567890&$£%.,:;-!?''åçëîñòšúß

Extra Bold

abcdefghijklmnopqrstuvwxyz
ABCDEFGHIJKLMNOPQRSTUVWXYZ
1234567890&$£%.,:;-!?''åçëîñòšúß

15 point

Bitstream is an independent digital typefoundry. Using the latest computer graphics tools, Bitstream's designers maintain the traditional essentials of good type design. Shape, weight and spacing rhythm are *expertly controlled to produce digitized letterforms of the highest quality in all font formats. In addition to making definitive versions of existing faces, Bitstream introduces creative new designs.*

9 point with 10 point lead

Bitstream is an independent digital typefoundry. Using the latest computer graphics tools, Bitstream's designers maintain the traditional essentials of good type design. Shape, weight and spacing rhythm are expertly controlled to produce digitized letterforms of the highest quality in all font formats. In addition to making definitive versions of existing faces, Bitstream introduces creative new designs.

Annual Report Financials

Goudy Old Style gives this annual report page a polished appearance. It is a typeface that projects tradition and stability without obscuring the content. A heavier typeface, Hammersmith Bold, is used for the letterspaced headline.

The horizontal rules lead the eye from the text to the figures. A heavier rule is used to underscore subtotals, while the totals are double ruled. Indents establish a visual hierarchy throughout the text.

Type specifications:
Title and folio are set in 9-point Hammersmith Bold; financial text is in 9-point Goudy Old Style; table notes are in Goudy Old Style Italic. 1988 figures are in Goudy Old Style Bold

L O A N   P O R T F O L I O

The following table presents the detail of the Corporation's consolidated loan portfolio on December 31, for the past five years.

(in thousands)	1988	1987	1986	1985	1984
Domestic					
Commercial, financial and agricultural	**$2,244,763**	$1,871,251	$1,620,038	$1,483,332	$1,301,934
Lease financing receivables	**149,385**	98,945	6,530	11,111	18,250
Real Estate —					
construction	**209,200**	159,262	115,460	89,515	70,572
mortgages (for investment)	**824,585**	619,909	569,714	596,871	588,301
mortgages held for resale	**154,713**	17,000	23,800	—	—
Consumer	**921,063**	793,291	654,920	631,148	519,508
Total domestic	**4,503,709**	3,559,658	2,990,462	2,811,977	2,498,565
Foreign					
Commercial and industrial	**78,870**	71,139	108,868	119,042	118,610
Financial institutions	**104,834**	110,535	114,566	110,684	103,902
Governments	**73,778**	83,436	69,930	42,995	33,565
Other	**—**	—	—	—	15,068
Total foreign	**257,482**	265,110	293,364	272,721	271,145
Loans, gross	**4,761,191**	3,824,768	3,283,826	3,084,698	2,769,710
Unearned discount	**(96,909)**	(77,304)	(53,559)	(56,351)	(60,872)
Reserve for loan losses	**(62,704)**	(52,059)	(42,845)	(40,953)	(36,112)
Loans, net	**$4,601,578**	$3,695,405	$3,187,422	$2,987,394	$2,672,726

The following table presents selected loan categories as of December 31, 1985, by maturity and interest rate sensitivity.

(in thousands)	One year or less	Over one through five years	Over five years	Total
Commercial, financial and agricultural	$1,231,579	$ 769,256	$ 243,928	$2,244,763
Lease financing receivables	43,444	102,984	2,957	149,385
Real estate —				
construction		95,019	10,435	209,200
Foreign	103,746	91,754	10,726	257,482
Total	155,002	$1,059,013	$ 268,046	
Interest sensitivity of above loans due after one year with				
predetermined rate		$ 490,877	$ 84,371	
floating rate		568,136	183,675	
Total		$1,059,013	$ 268,046	

fghi

Hammersmith Roman

Bitstream is an indepe
typefoundry. Using the
puter graphics tools,
designers maintain th
essentials of good typ
weight and spacing rh
pertly controlled to p
letterforms of the hig
all font formats. In ad
definitive versions of
Bitstream introduces

Hammersmith™

The Bitstream version of the Gill Sans® typeface.

Roman

abcdefghijklmnopqrstuvwxyz
ABCDEFGHIJKLMNOPQRSTUVWXYZ
1234567890&$£%.,:;-!?“åçëîñòšúß

Italic

abcdefghijklmnopqrstuvwxyz
ABCDEFGHIJKLMNOPQRSTUVWXYZ
1234567890&$£%.,:;-!?“åçëîñòšúß

Bold

abcdefghijklmnopqrstuvwxyz
ABCDEFGHIJKLMNOPQRSTUVWXYZ
1234567890&$£%.,:;-!?“åçëîñòšúß

Bold Italic

abcdefghijklmnopqrstuvwxyz
ABCDEFGHIJKLMNOPQRSTUVWXYZ
1234567890&$£%.,:;-!?“åçëîñòšúß

15 point

Bitstream is an independent digital typefoundry. Using the latest computer graphics tools, Bitstream's designers maintain the traditional essentials of good type design. Shape, weight and spacing rhythm are expertly *controlled to produce digitized letterforms of the highest quality in all font formats. In addition to making definitive versions of existing faces, Bitstream introduces creative new designs.*

9 point with 10 point lead

Bitstream is an independent digital typefoundry. Using the latest computer graphics tools, Bitstream's designers maintain the traditional essentials of good type design. Shape, weight and spacing rhythm are expertly controlled *to produce digitized letterforms of the highest quality in all font formats. In addition to making definitive versions of existing faces, Bitstream introduces creative new designs.*

Commercial Catalog

Hammersmith is a distinctive sanserif, well suited for use in this catalog. Not highly structured, it retains a hand-drawn look with its varying stroke widths. It combines clean elegance with an easy-to-read, neutral tone. The uppercase titles in Hammersmith have a solid, chiseled feeling.

The centered titles and captions in this catalog create a formal, elevated environment for the product, suggesting a high-quality retail store.

Type specifications:
The uppercase, reversed company name is set in 10-point Dutch Bold; *Fabric and Wallcovering Catalog* is set in 9.5 Hammersmith Italic; product names are in 11-point Hammersmith; text is in 9.5/11 Hammersmith; pattern numbers are in 9.5 Hammersmith Bold; page folio is in 12-point Dutch.

Note: Graphic images were scanned into the system. They might also be imported from a paint or draw program or added by means of manual paste-up.

CALAIS

This climbing pattern of delicate spring flowers with simple trailing foliage creates an easy, pretty design. Inspired by a nineteenth-century English cotton pattern, the freshness and understated sophistication of this design exemplify Sarah Kenyon design philosophy.

Pattern 7742

KALE ROSES

Combining grace and charm, this typically Victorian print endows the simple trailing floral motif with power and sophistication. Clusters of cabbage roses delicately climb the exquisitely detailed trellis, which echos the largers trellis made from the roses themselves.

Pattern 6601

CRAFTSBURY

Full-blown dog roses and bursting buds join to give this floral design the naturalistic and simple sophistication of bygone days. Trailing stems link throughout creating a unified, integrated pattern. Available in companion fabric.

Pattern 6602

LAUREL

Elegant and light, this early nineteenth-century English chintz offsets white lilies, carnations and roses on an off-white background. Cool, restful and sophisticated, this relatively simple design emanates dignity and charm.

Pattern 6604

You may order Sarah Kenyon Home Furnishings by telephone. Call 1-800-623-1326.

Headlines 1

Bitstream Cooper Black

abcdefghijklmnopqrstuvwxyz
ABCDEFGHIJKLMNOPQRSTUVWXYZ
1234567890&$£%.,:;-!?"åçëîñòšúß

University Roman

abcdefghijklmnopqrstuvwxyz
ABCDEFGHIJKLMNOPQRSTUVWXYZ
1234567890&$£%.,:;-!?"åçëîñòšúß

Cloister Black

abcdefghijklmnopqrstuvwxyz
ABCDEFGHIJKLMNOPQRSTUVWXYZ
1234567890&$£%.,:;-!?"åçëîñòšúß

Broadway

abcdefghijklmnopqrstuvwxyz
ABCDEFGHIJKLMNOPQRSTUVWXYZ
1234567890&$£%.,:;-!?"åçëîñòšúß

15 point

Bitstream Cooper Black

University Roman®

Cloister Black®

Broadway®

30 point

Shopping Bag

Used as an illustration, the *S* becomes a device representing the bookstore. Cloister Black suggests the elegant tradition of Gutenberg's early movable types, an especially suitable image for a store dealing in rare and antique books.

Steinheld Books is set in a letter-spaced sanserif to provide a modern contrast to the antique and ornamental "S."

Type specifications:
The *S* is set in Cloister Black at 864-point; *Steinheld Books* in Futura Medium Condensed.

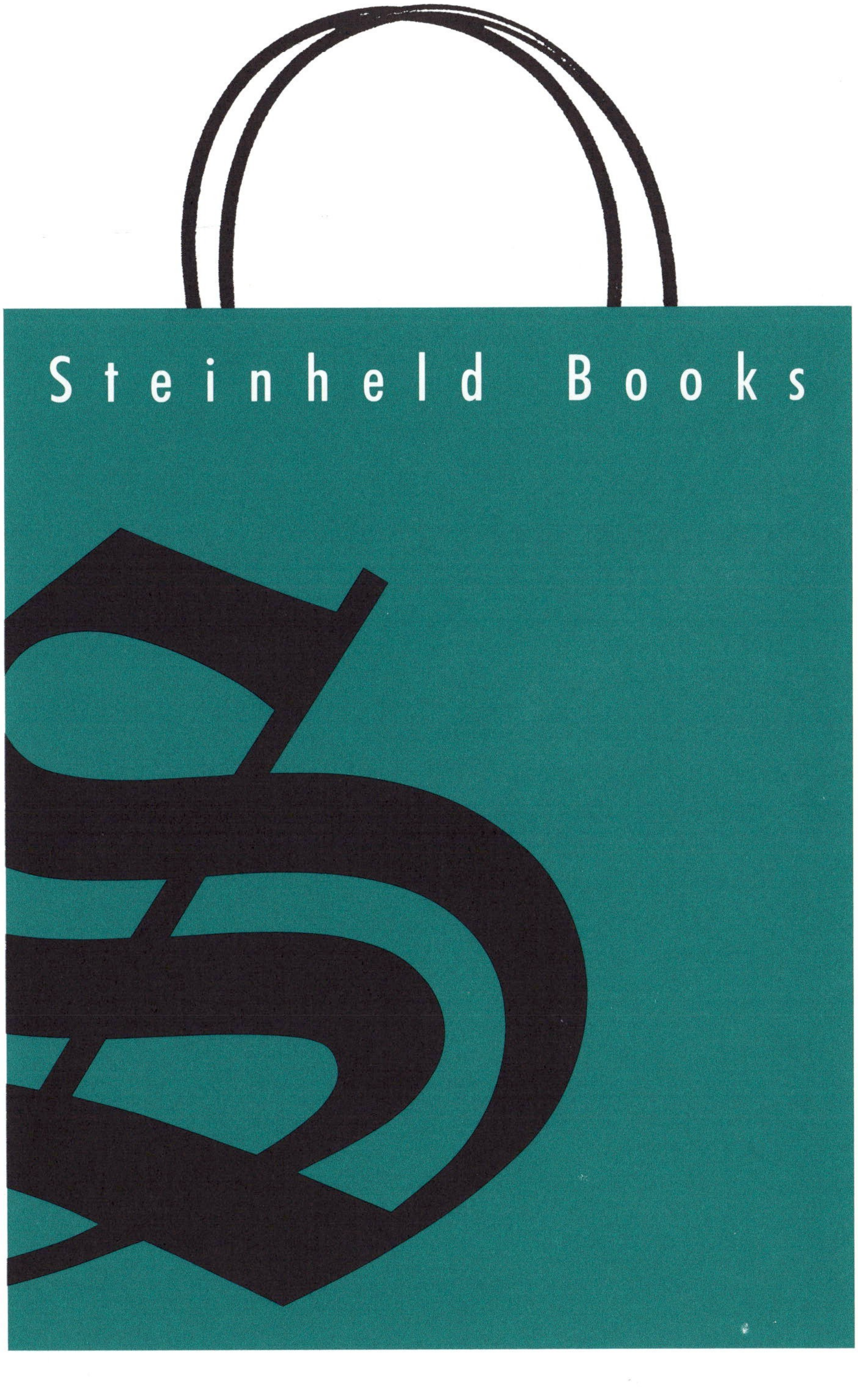
Steinheld Books

Headlines 2

Brush Script

abcdefghijklmnopqrstuvwxyz
ABCDEFGHIJKLMNOPQRSTUVWXYZ
1234567890&$£%.,:;-!?''åçëîñòšúß

Blippo Black

abcdefghijklmnopqrstuvwxyz
ABCDEFGHIJKLMNOPQRSTUVWXYZ
1234567890&$£%.,:;-!?''åçëîñòšúß

Hobo

abcdefghijklmnopqrstuvwxyz
ABCDEFGHIJKLMNOPQRSTUVWXYZ
1234567890&$£%.,:;-!?''åçëîñòšúß

Windsor

abcdefghijklmnopqrstuvwxyz
ABCDEFGHIJKLMNOPQRSTUVWXYZ
1234567890&$£%.,:;-!?''åçëîñòšúß

15 point

Brush® Script
Blippo® Black
Hobo®
Windsor®

30 point

Postcard

Contrasting typefaces from the Bitstream Headlines 2 and 3 packages are combined in this playful postcard announcement.

The store name, *DeVicES*, uses type in an illustrative manner, so that the word becomes the picture. Each character appears as a distinct object while forming a word.

The text, set in Swiss Bold Condensed, sets a businesslike tone that contrasts with the playful store name and is appropriate for the content of the announcement.

Type specifications:
In the word *DeVicES*, *D* and *E* are set in Swiss Extra Compressed; *e* is set in Brush Script; *V*, *i*, *c*, and *S* are set in Blippo Black. *ONE WEEK ONLY* is set in 10-point Swiss Black; text is set in 10/18 Swiss Bold Condensed.

ONE WEEK ONLY
215 EAST FIRST STREET NEW YORK 00170
25–35% Off
Store Wide
Clearance
Devices
Accessories
for the Home
and Office

Headlines 3

Swiss Compressed*

abcdefghijklmnopqrstuvwxyz
ABCDEFGHIJKLMNOPQRSTUVWXYZ
1234567890&$£%.,:;-!?"åçëîñòšúß

Swiss Extra Compressed*

abcdefghijklmnopqrstuvwxyz
ABCDEFGHIJKLMNOPQRSTUVWXYZ
1234567890&$£%.,:;-!?"åçëîñòšúß

Exotic Demi-Bold**

abcdefghijklmnopqrstuvwxyz
ABCDEFGHIJKLMNOPQRSTUVWXYZ
1234567890&$£%.,:;-!?''ÅÇËÎÑÒŠÚß

Exotic Bold**

abcdefghijklmnopqrstuvwxyz
ABCDEFGHIJKLMNOPQRSTUVWXYZ
1234567890&$£%.,:;-!?''ÅÇËÎÑÒŠÚß

15 point
*The Bitstream version of the Helvetica® Compressed and Extra Compressed typefaces.
**The Bitstream version of the Peignot® typeface.

Swiss Compressed

Swiss Extra Compressed

Exotic Demi-Bold

Exotic Bold

30 point

Direct Mail Brochure

Visual contrasts between large and small, serif and sanserif, light and bold illustrate the different kinds of theatrical works described in this brochure.

The large *A* letterform fills and bleeds off the first panel, becoming a symbol for the theater and a background for the overprinted text.

Color is used in a restrained, effective manner.

Type specifications:
A is set in 780-point Swiss Compressed; the headline reversed out of *A* is Swiss Compressed; *Shakespeare* is 140-point Swiss Extra Compressed; *Gilbert & Sullivan* is 84-point Baskerville; text is 11/12 Baskerville Bold Italic; type in form is 8-point Baskerville. *Reply Card* is set in 14-point Swiss Compressed.

Reply Card

From Gilbert and Sullivan to Shakespeare. Let the Astor bring a season of contrast to you. Mail in the reply card to learn more about the 1988-89 season at the Astor Theatre.

Name		
Address		
City	State	Zip
Company/Organization	Address	
State	Zip	

If this is a duplicate, please pass it on to a friend.

Shakespeare

Gilbert & Sullivan

A Spectacular Season of Contrast at the Astor Theatre

Headlines 4

ITC Zapf Chancery Medium Italic

abcdefghijklmnopqrstuvwxyz
ABCDEFGHIJKLMNOPQRSTUVWXYZ
1234567890&$£%.,:;-!?"åçëîñòšúß

Coronet Bold

abcdefghijklmnopqrstuvwxyz
ABCDEFGHIJKLMNOPQRSTUVWXYZ
1234567890&$£%.,:;-!?"åçëîñòšúß

Clarendon

abcdefghijklmnopqrstuvwxyz
ABCDEFGHIJKLMNOPQRSTUVWXYZ
1234567890&$£%.,:;-!?"åçëîñòšúß

Clarendon Bold

abcdefghijklmnopqrstuvwxyz
ABCDEFGHIJKLMNOPQRSTUVWXYZ
1234567890&$£%.,:;-!?"åçëîñòšúß

15 point

ITC Zapf Chancery® Med. It.

Coronet® Bold

Clarendon

Clarendon Bold

30 point

Flyer

In this example of illustrative typography, contrasting typefaces from the Bitstream Headlines 4 package are combined in the word *SuNDay* to express the eclectic variety of a new television show.

For added impact, the word *PICK* and the figure *6* are reversed in black bars to frame the word *SuNDay*.

Text is treated in a more sober manner, set in a three-column grid. White space at the bottom and at the left balance the density of the headline.

Type specifications:
WRLV is set in Swiss Extra Compressed; *6* is in Swiss Black; *Pick* is in Clarendon Bold. In the word *SuNDay*, *S* is set in Coronet Bold, *u* in Clarendon Bold, *N* in Swiss Condensed, *D* in Bitstream Cooper Bold, *a* in Futura Bold, *y* in ITC Zapf Chancery Medium Italic. The text is set in 10/15 Century Schoolbook.

Note: Triangular shape is clip art that was scanned into the system.

WRLV

Sunday Pick
Sundays, 9:00–10:00 a.m.

6

SuNDay PICK

You had planned to see "Our Times" for that Midwestern Spots segment featuring Summer on Lake Michigan, but you missed it. . . . you read that Diane Demeron was going to be interviewed on "What's Next," but you were at work and unable to watch . . . you wanted to see Tanya Brady's feature on Japan, but you were out. Well now you'll get a second chance on "Sunday Pick." Paul Stein hosts this encore presentation of some of the best segments from our locally produced weekly programs. Each week we'll show you the most popular segments and let you see what you may have missed.

We'll also give you the first news of the morning with a live news and weather update from "Newscenter 6." If you're too busy to see all the best during the week, give us an hour on Sunday and we'll give you "Sunday Pick!"

6 TV Place
Milwaukee, WI 53214

Headlines 5

Park Avenue

abcdefghijklmnopqrstuvwxyz
ABCDEFGHIJKLMNOPQRSTUVWXYZ
1234567890&$£%.,:;-!?"åçëîñòšúß

Handel Gothic

abcdefghijklmnopqrstuvwxyz
ABCDEFGHIJKLMNOPQRSTUVWXYZ
1234567890&$£%.,:;-!?"åçëîñòšúß

Futura Black

abcdefghijklmnopqrstuvwxyz
ABCDEFGHIJKLMNOPQRSTUVWXYZ
1234567890&$£%.,:;-!?"åçëîñòšúß

Dom Casual

abcdefghijklmnopqrstuvwxyz
ABCDEFGHIJKLMNOPQRSTUVWXYZ
1234567890&$£%.,:;-!?"åçëîñòšúß

15 point

Park Avenue™

Handel Gothic®

Futura® Black

Dom™ Casual

30 point

Poster

Type is used to create the main illustration for this poster. The large letterforms make a striking graphic statement. The black bar containing the text and the square below it create an exclamation point for the word *TyPe*.

All the characters are from the Headlines 5 package and offer the variety needed to creatively illustrate the word *TyPe*, which contains a stencil face, a script, a sanserif, and a brush script.

Type specifications:
T is set in 390-point Futura Black; *Y* in 420-point Park Avenue; *P* in 298-point Handel Gothic; *e* in 303-point Dom Casual; text is set in 11/13 Zurich Black. *T* in ring is from the ITC Zapf Dingbats collection available in the Bitstream *Symbols 1* typeface package.

An exhibition of typographic design
August 25 through October 3, 1989
Tuesday through Saturday 10am–6pm
Museum of Design 3 Palace Road Boston
By train: (T) Orange line to Ruggles station
Funded in part by a generous grant from Zero-zero Corporation Inc.

Mermaid*

abcdefghijklmnopqrstuvwxyz
ABCDEFGHIJKLMNOPQRSTUVWXYZ
1234567890&$£%.,:;-!?''åçëîñòšúß

ITC Bolt Bold

abcdefghijklmnopqrstuvwxyz
ABCDEFGHIJKLMNOPQRSTUVWXYZ
1234567890&$£%.,:;-!?''åçëîñòšúß

P.T. Barnum

abcdefghijklmnopqrstuvwxyz
ABCDEFGHIJKLMNOPQRSTUVWXYZ
1234567890&$£%.,:;-!?''åçëîñòšúß

Kaufmann Bold

abcdefghijklmnopqrstuvwxyz
ABCDEFGHIJKLMNOPQRSTUVWXYZ
1234567890&$£%.,:;-!?''åçëîñòšúß

15 point
*The Bitstream version of the Ondine™ typeface.

Mermaid™

ITC Bolt Bold®

P.T. Barnum™

Kaufmann® Bold

30 point

Tickets

These tickets provide examples of evocative typography. A typeface elicits a particular feeling: dignity, elegance, speed, or modernism, for example. Occasionally, a very particular image is evoked by the typeface—P.T. Barnum, used on the circus ticket, for example, is reminiscent of the playful faces used on circus broadsides.

Mermaid is used in setting *A 1001 Nights* because of its exotic calligraphic look, which is similar to Persian script.

The ballet ticket uses ITC Bolt Bold to contrast with the classical ITC Galliard. Note that rules have been used to create a Danish flag.

Type specifications:
A 1001 Nights is set in Mermaid; accompanying copy on the same ticket is in Swiss Extra Compressed; the figures *07861* are in Century Schoolbook. *HAY PENNY CIRCUS* and *Admit One* are set in P.T. Barnum; accompanying copy on the same ticket is in Franklin Gothic Extra Condensed; the figures *095252* are in Bodoni Bold. *Ballet, Denmark,* and *1989* are set in ITC Bolt Bold; copy on the same ticket is in ITC Galliard Roman, Italic and Bold. *DEC 21 8PM* and *G 23* are set in Letter Gothic 12 Pitch.

FRI. AUG. 25
BURKLYN COMMON
SCRIPPS MASON MEDICAL CENTER PRESENTS
A 1001 Nights
A FESTIVAL TO BENEFIT CHILDREN'S BURN UNIT
CHILD $3.00
07861
№ 095252
Sat., January 21, 8 P.M.
$12.00
HAY PENNEY CIRCUS
Alexander Twilight Amphitheater
Admit One
THE STATE
Ballet
OF
Denmark
WINTER TOUR
1989
Ivar Klint, Director
THE NUTCRACKER
RAFIN HALL
MINNEAPOLIS
DEC 21 8PM
ROW G
SEAT 23

ITC Korinna®

Regular

abcdefghijklmnopqrstuvwxyz
ABCDEFGHIJKLMNOPQRSTUVWXYZ
1234567890&$£%.,:;-!?"åçëîñòšúß

Kursiv Regular

abcdefghijklmnopqrstuvwxyz
ABCDEFGHIJKLMNOPQRSTUVWXYZ
1234567890&$£%.,:;-!?"åçëîñòšúß

Extra Bold

abcdefghijklmnopqrstuvwxyz
ABCDEFGHIJKLMNOPQRSTUVWXYZ
1234567890&$£%.,:;-!?"åçëîñòšúß

Kursiv Extra Bold

abcdefghijklmnopqrstuvwxyz
ABCDEFGHIJKLMNOPQRSTUVWXYZ
1234567890&$£%.,:;-!?"åçëîñòšúß

15 point

Bitstream is an independent digital typefoundry. Using the latest computer graphics tools, Bitstream's designers maintain the traditional essentials of good type design. Shape, weight and spacing rhythm are expertly controlled to *produce digitized letterforms of the highest quality in all font formats. In addition to making definitive versions of existing faces, Bitstream introduces creative new designs.*
9 point with 10 point lead

Bitstream is an independent digital typefoundry. Using the latest computer graphics tools, Bitstream's designers maintain the traditional essentials of good type design. Shape, weight and spacing rhythm *are expertly controlled to produce digitized letterforms of the highest quality in all font formats. In addition to making definitive versions of existing faces, Bitstream introduces creative new designs.*

Flyer

The ITC Korinna typeface projects a comfortable, yet slightly formal image. The excerpted reviews are set in the Extra Bold weight to assure clean reproduction when reversed.

Type specifications:
Varying Sizes of ITC Korinna Regular and ITC Korinna Kursiv Regular are combined in this flyer. Quotes are set in 9/10 ITC Korinna Extra Bold.

Author **Erin Eisenman**

will be here

Wednesday, October 2 3–5 pm

signing her new novel

The Garden Path

"I can see why it made the top ten best reading list."
—Henri Van Cline
The Standard

". . . filled with all the romantic details to keep you reading. It's so absorbing."
—Freedale Press

"Definitely Eisenman's best work to date. One of the top ten . . ."
—Port Flane Post

"The decade's best novel in this genre . . . clear, visionary, and memorable"
—N.Y. Register

Cloister Black

1234567890

abcdefghijklmn

opqrstuvwxyz

&åçëêñòšúß

Letter Gothic

Roman 12 Pitch

abcdefghijklmnopqrstuvwxyz
ABCDEFGHIJKLMNOPQRSTUVWXYZ
1234567890&$£%.,:;-!?''åçëîñòšúß

Italic

abcdefghijklmnopqrstuvwxyz
ABCDEFGHIJKLMNOPQRSTUVWXYZ
1234567890&$£%.,:;-!?''åçëîñòšúß

Bold

abcdefghijklmnopqrstuvwxyz
ABCDEFGHIJKLMNOPQRSTUVWXYZ
1234567890&$£%.,:;-!?''åçëîñòšúß

Bold Italic

abcdefghijklmnopqrstuvwxyz
ABCDEFGHIJKLMNOPQRSTUVWXYZ
1234567890&$£%.,:;-!?''åçëîñòšúß

15 point

Bitstream is an independent digital typefoundry. Using the latest computer graphics tools, Bitstream's designers maintain the traditional essentials of good type design. Shape, weight and spacing rhythm are *expertly controlled to produce digitized letterforms of the highest quality in all font formats. In addition to making definitive versions of existing faces, Bitstream introduces creative new designs.*

9 point with 10 point lead

Bitstream is an independent digital typefoundry. Using the latest computer graphics tools, Bitstream's designers maintain the traditional essentials of good type design. Shape, weight and spacing rhythm are ***expertly controlled to produce digitized letterforms of the highest quality in all font formats. In addition to making definitive versions of existing faces, Bitstream introduces creative new designs.***

Spreadsheet

Letter Gothic (12 pitch) is a monospaced typeface, suitable for applications which have difficulty working with proportional faces. In this case, however, where it is mixed with Charter, it is used to recall the simplicity of a mainframe computer-generated printout.

This wide, seventeen-column table is easy to read both horizontally and vertically. The horizontal bars serve to separate entries and guide the eye, left to right, across the page.

Type specifications:
Columns of figures are set in 8/11 Letter Gothic. Headline is set in 12-point Bitstream Charter Black with Bitstream Charter Italic. Company name is set in 12-point Bitstream Charter. Vendor list and descriptions are set in 10-point Bitstream Charter. Column heads are set in Bitstream Charter Italic.

Printing & Typesetting Expenses FV *1988*

Cameron Day Corporation

	Inv	*Vendor*	*Description*			*Department Description*										
						300	**320**	**330**	**340**	**350**	**370**	**380**	**600**	**610**	**640**	**650**
10/87	3192	Stanley Press	Licensee List	320	20	0	20	0	0	0	0	0	0	0	0	0
	3169	Stanley Press	Industry Standards List	610	48	0	0	0	0	0	0	0	0	48	0	0
	8944	Jansen Graphics	Industry Endorses	330	68	0	0	68	0	0	0	0	0	0	0	0
	3178	Typehouse	Dealership Agreements	350	129	0	0	0	0	129	0	0	0	0	0	0
	8943	Jansen Graphics	Top 20 Sheet	350	439	0	0	0	0	439	0	0	0	0	0	0
	8954	Jansen Graphics	Canton Press Releases	640	626	0	0	0	0	0	0	0	0	0	626	0
	5466	Grenda11 Graphics	Print Customer Stock	300	32	32	0	0	0	0	0	0	0	0	0	0
	8953	Jansen Graphics	Dear Dealer Letter	600	419	0	0	0	0	0	0	0	419	0	0	0
	8151	Typehouse	Original Composition for Business Cards	370	126	0	0	0	0	0	126	0	0	0	0	0
	8942	Jansen Graphics	Cameron Day Diecut Folders	340	2,170	0	0	0	2,170	0	0	0	0	0	0	0
	8200	Stanley Press	Cameron Day International Press Releases	380	606	0	0	0	0	0	0	606	0	0	0	0
11/87	3252	Stanley Press	Canton Document	650	57	0	0	0	0	0	0	0	0	0	0	57
	9172	Jansen Graphics	Printing + Collating Kits	340	1,621	0	0	0	1,621	0	0	0	0	0	0	0
	3238	Stanley Press	Customer Statistics	320	231	0	231	0	0	0	0	0	0	0	0	0
	3259	Stanley Press	Industry Breakdown	320	438	0	438	0	0	0	0	0	0	0	0	0
	9079	Jansen Graphics	Licensee List	370	828	0	0	0	0	0	828	0	0	0	0	0
	3343	Stanley Press	Convention Itinerary	640	114	0	0	0	0	0	0	0	0	0	114	0
	3357	Stanley Press	Press Kits–Collate + Staple	320	45	0	45	0	0	0	0	0	0	0	0	0
	3305	Typehouse	Composition for Agreement	330	47	0	0	47	0	0	0	0	0	0	0	0
	3299	Typehouse	Agreement Forms	350	37	0	0	0	0	37	0	0	0	0	0	0
	8985	Jansen Graphics	Collation of Dealer Kits	600	2,910	0	0	0	0	0	0	0	2,190	0	0	0
	9062	Jansen Graphics	Authorized Dealer Kits	610	1,418	0	0	0	0	0	0	0	0	1,418	0	0
	8989	Jansen Graphics	Corporate Profile	330	137	0	0	137	0	0	0	0	0	0	0	0
	9003	Jansen Graphics	Booklet Envelopes	300	189	189	0	0	0	0	0	0	0	0	0	0
	8830	Jansen Graphics	Business Cards–Wright	370	110	0	0	0	0	0	110	0	0	0	0	0
	8870	Jansen Graphics	Dealership Agreements	650	58	0	0	0	0	0	0	0	0	0	0	58
	9122	Jansen Graphics	Sales Order Forms + Invoices	330	2,186	0	0	2,186	0	0	0	0	0	0	0	0
	9126	Jansen Graphics	Return Merchandise Authorization Forms	350	504	0	0	0	0	504	0	0	0	0	0	0
	8867	Jansen Graphics	Ordersheets	380	189	0	0	0	0	0	0	189	0	0	0	0
	9285	Jansen Graphics	Booklet Envelopes	320	456	0	456	0	0	0	0	0	0	0	0	0
	9292	Jansen Graphics	Dealer Agreement Order Form	330	1,221	0	0	1,221	0	0	0	0	0	0	0	0
	9266	Jansen Graphics	Business Cards–McArthur, Gross	640	350	0	0	0	0	0	0	0	0	0	350	0
	3354	Stanley Press	Claim Forms	350	15	0	0	0	0	15	0	0	0	0	0	0
	3475	Typehouse	Original Composition for Miscellaneous	380	42	0	0	0	0	0	0	42	0	0	0	0
	3198	Typehouse	Composition for Dealer Kitforms	350	263	0	0	0	0	263	0	0	0	0	0	0
	9266	Jansen Graphics	Business Cards–Stevens	600	70	0	0	0	0	0	0	0	70	0	0	0
	9268	Jansen Graphics	Authorized Dealer Kits	350	3,975	0	0	0	0	3,975	0	0	0	0	0	0

ITC Lubalin Graph®

Book

abcdefghijklmnopqrstuvwxyz
ABCDEFGHIJKLMNOPQRSTUVWXYZ
1234567890&$£%.,:;-!?"åçëîñòšúß

Medium

abcdefghijklmnopqrstuvwxyz
ABCDEFGHIJKLMNOPQRSTUVWXYZ
1234567890&$£%.,:;-!?"åçëîñòšúß

Demi

abcdefghijklmnopqrstuvwxyz
ABCDEFGHIJKLMNOPQRSTUVWXYZ
1234567890&$£%.,:;-!?"åçëîñòšúß

Bold

abcdefghijklmnopqrstuvwxyz
ABCDEFGHIJKLMNOPQRSTUVWXYZ
1234567890&$£%.,:;-!?"åçëîñòšúß

15 point

Bitstream is an independent digital typefoundry. Using the latest computer graphics tools, Bitstream's designers maintain the traditional essentials of good type design. Shape, weight and spacing rhythm are expertly controlled to produce digitized letterforms of the highest quality in all font formats. In addition to making definitive versions of existing faces, Bitstream introduces creative new designs.

9 point with 10 point lead

Bitstream is an independent digital typefoundry. Using the latest computer graphics tools, Bitstream's designers maintain the traditional essentials of good type design. Shape, weight and spacing rhythm are expertly controlled to produce digitized letterforms of the highest quality in all font formats. In addition to making definitive versions of existing faces, Bitstream introduces creative new designs.

Flyer

This flyer shows how type can be used as an illustration. The headline is designed to resemble an eye chart, which is appropriate to the content, and centered to contrast with the text, set flush left.

Rather than increasing the size of the text to fill the space, the designer gave the more important headline added power by making sure that it did not visually compete with the text.

The *iscan* logotype is made more distinctive by the use of the heavier ITC Lubalin Graph Demi for the *i*, which reinforces the typographic word play: an *i* for an eye.

Type specifications:
The headline is set in 174-, 82-, 42-, 20-, and 14-point ITC Lubalin Graph Demi. Text is set in 9/18 Swiss. The logotype is set in 20-point ITC Lubalin Graph Book, the *i* in Demi.

C

A N

Y O U

R E A D

T H I S ?

Sign up
now
for vision
and
glaucoma
testing
Monday,
Dec. 8

iscan

Monospaced 1

Pica 10 Pitch

abcdefghijklmnopqrstuvwxyz
ABCDEFGHIJKLMNOPQRSTUVWXYZ
1234567890&$£%.,:;-!?‘’åçëîñòšúß

Script 12 Pitch

abcdefghijklmnopqrstuvwxyz
ABCDEFGHIJKLMNOPQRSTUVWXYZ
1234567890&$£%.,:;-!?''åçëîñòšúß

Orator 10 Pitch

abcdefghijklmnopqrstuvwxyz
ABCDEFGHIJKLMNOPQRSTUVWXYZ
1234567890&$£%.,:;-!?''åçëîñòšúß

Swiss Monospaced 10 Pitch

abcdefghijklmnopqrstuvwxyz
ABCDEFGHIJKLMNOPQRSTUVWXYZ
1234567890&$£%.,:;-!?‘’åçëîñòšúß

15 point

Bitstream is an independent digital typefoundry. Using the latest computer graphics tools, Bitstream's designers maintain the traditional essentials of good type design. Shape, weight and spacing *rhythm are expertly controlled to produce digitized letterforms of the highest quality in all font formats. In addition to making definitive versions of existing faces, Bitstream introduces creative new designs.*

9 point with 10 point lead

Bitstream is an independent digital typefoundry. Using the latest computer graphics tools, Bitstream's designers maintain the traditional essentials of good type design. Shape, weight and spacing rhythm are expertly controlled to produce digitized letterforms of the highest quality in all font formats. In addition to making definitive versions of existing faces, Bitstream introduces creative new designs.

Business Letters

Some people still prefer that their correspondence appear to be typewritten so it seems more "personal." I don't recommend this archaic approach in an age where efficient business practices warrant the use of word processing. Furthermore, monospaced typefaces are not nearly as readable as proportionally spaced faces.

Still, if you must use a monospaced typeface, Pica, Orator, or Swiss Monospaced are a better choice than Courier, which is standard in most laser printers. Script would be acceptable for personal communications, but is not very businesslike.

Serifa or Charter would provide a similar mechanical feeling, yet create a more attractive and readable letter, and ITC American Typewriter would create a whimsical "mock" typewritten feeling. For personal letters, Korinna is an excellent choice because of its casual and warm feeling.

Each letter is set in a flush left block format. Paragraphs are indicated by extra linespaces rather than indents. The closing, signature, name, and title are also set flush left, providing a clean, businesslike look.

Type specifications:
The four business letters, left to right, are set in 10/12 Pica, Script, Orator, and Swiss Monospaced. Futura Medium and Bold are combined in the company name, *ANTISTAT INC.*

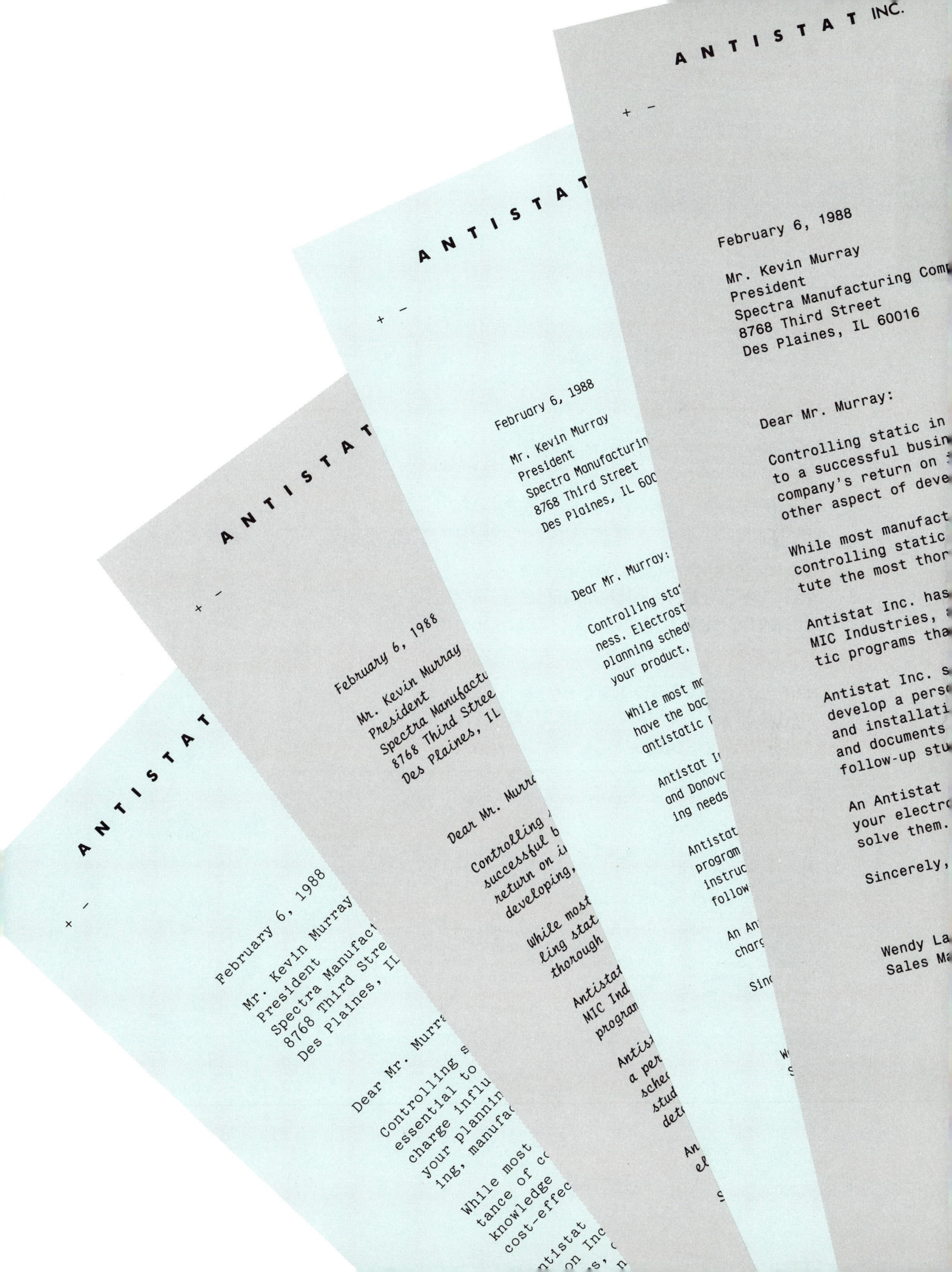
ANTISTAT INC.
+ –
February 6, 1988
Mr. Kevin Murray
President
Spectra Manufacturing Comp
8768 Third Street
Des Plaines, IL 60016
Dear Mr. Murray:
Controlling static in
to a successful busin
company's return on
other aspect of deve
While most manufact
controlling static
tute the most thor
Antistat Inc. has
MIC Industries,
tic programs tha
Antistat Inc. s
develop a pers
and installati
and documents
follow-up stu
An Antistat
your electr
solve them.
Sincerely,
Wendy La
Sales Ma

News Gothic

Roman

abcdefghijklmnopqrstuvwxyz
ABCDEFGHIJKLMNOPQRSTUVWXYZ
1234567890&$£%.,:;-!?"åçëîñòšúß

Italic

abcdefghijklmnopqrstuvwxyz
ABCDEFGHIJKLMNOPQRSTUVWXYZ
1234567890&$£%.,:;-!?"åçëîñòšúß

Bold

abcdefghijklmnopqrstuvwxyz
ABCDEFGHIJKLMNOPQRSTUVWXYZ
1234567890&$£%.,:;-!?"åçëîñòšúß

Bold Italic

abcdefghijklmnopqrstuvwxyz
ABCDEFGHIJKLMNOPQRSTUVWXYZ
1234567890&$£%.,:;-!?"åçëîñòšúß

15 point

Bitstream is an independent digital typefoundry. Using the latest computer graphics tools, Bitstream's designers maintain the traditional essentials of good type design. Shape, weight and spacing rhythm *are expertly controlled to produce digitized letterforms of the highest quality in all font formats. In addition to making definitive versions of existing faces, Bitstream introduces creative new designs.*
9 point with 10 point lead

Bitstream is an independent digital typefoundry. Using the latest computer graphics tools, Bitstream's designers maintain the traditional essentials of good type design. Shape, weight and spacing rhythm are expertly controlled ***to produce digitized letterforms of the highest quality in all font formats. In addition to making definitive versions of existing faces, Bitstream introduces creative new designs.***

Map

The high legibility of News Gothic even at small point sizes makes it appropriate for the callouts. The use of four type sizes creates an informational hierarchy.

The compass points are represented in a strong typographic manner. The large ITC Zapf Chancery Medium Italic *N* is used for its calligraphic quality, which suggests antique maps. Reversed figures set in Baskerville Bold serve to identify highway route numbers.

Type specifications:
Map callouts are set in three different sizes of News Gothic, News Gothic Italic and News Gothic Bold. The compass points *E*, *S*, and *W* are set in News Gothic Bold at 36-, 72-, and 86-point. The *N* is 340-point ITC Zapf Chancery Medium Italic. The figures reversed out of circles are in Baskerville Bold. News Gothic Italic is used to label landmarks.

Note: A map like this would be best created in a draw program which makes it easy to combine the graphic map and the text. Draw programs also allow the text to be rotated in one-degree increments, an important consideration for maps.

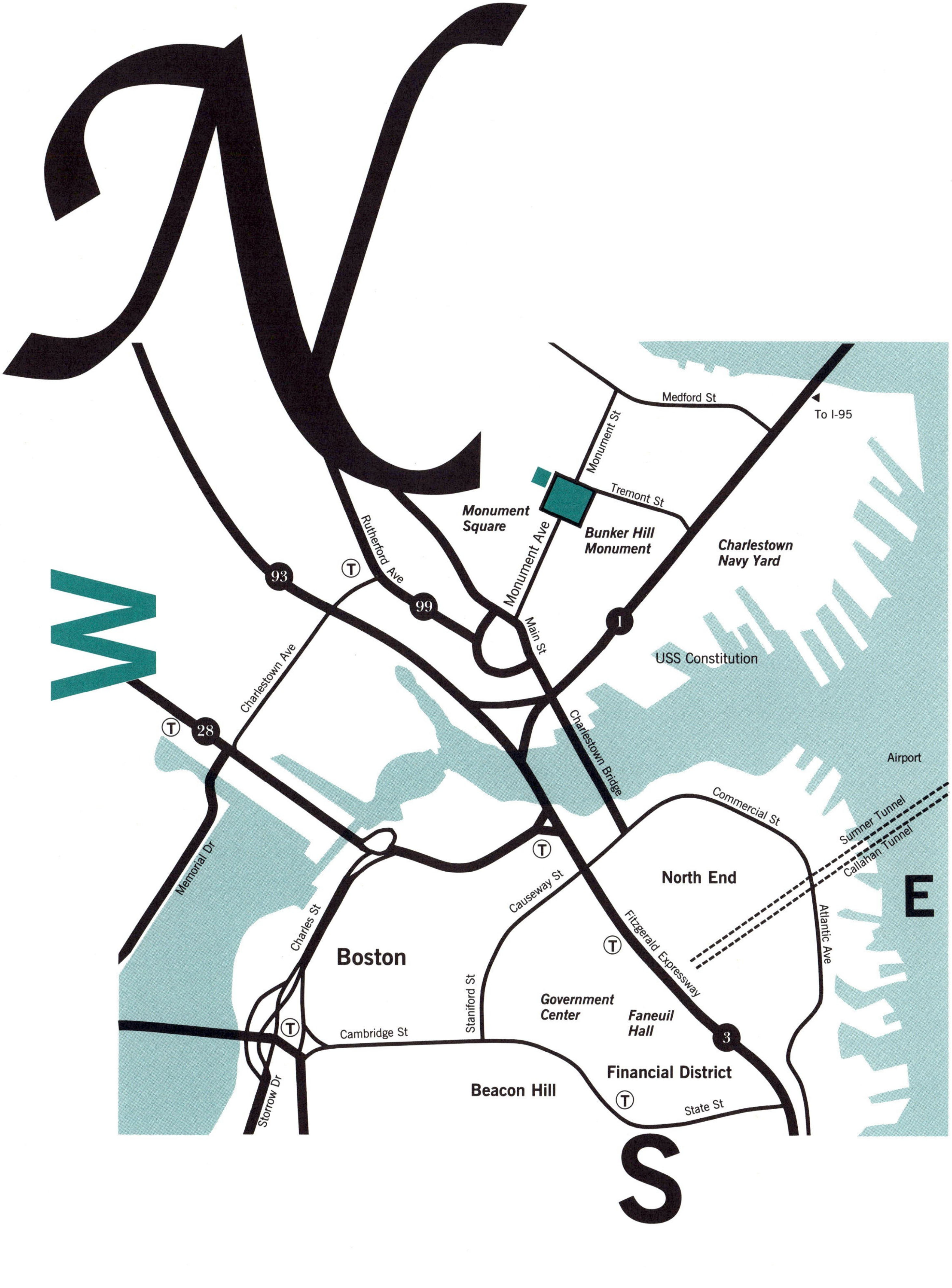

N
W
E
S
Medford St
To I-95
Monument St
Tremont St
Monument Square
Bunker Hill Monument
Charlestown Navy Yard
Rutherford Ave
Monument Ave
93
99
1
Main St
USS Constitution
Charlestown Ave
28
Charlestown Bridge
Airport
Commercial St
Sumner Tunnel
Callahan Tunnel
Memorial Dr
North End
Causeway St
Atlantic Ave
Fitzgerald Expressway
Charles St
Boston
Staniford St
Government Center
Faneuil Hall
3
Cambridge St
Financial District
Beacon Hill
State St
Storrow Dr

Prestige

Roman 12 Pitch

abcdefghijklmnopqrstuvwxyz
ABCDEFGHIJKLMNOPQRSTUVWXYZ
1234567890&$£%.,:;-!?‘’åçëîñòšúß

Italic

abcdefghijklmnopqrstuvwxyz
ABCDEFGHIJKLMNOPQRSTUVWXYZ
1234567890&$£%.,:;-!?‘’åçëîñòšúß

Bold

abcdefghijklmnopqrstuvwxyz
ABCDEFGHIJKLMNOPQRSTUVWXYZ
1234567890&$£%.,:;-!?‘’åçëîñòšúß

Bold Italic

abcdefghijklmnopqrstuvwxyz
ABCDEFGHIJKLMNOPQRSTUVWXYZ
1234567890&$£%.,:;-!?‘’åçëîñòšúß

15 point

Bitstream is an independent digital typefoundry. Using the latest computer graphics tools, Bitstream's designers maintain the traditional essentials of good type design. Shape, weight and spacing rhythm are expertly controlled *to produce digitized letterforms of the highest quality in all font formats. In addition to making definitive versions of existing faces, Bitstream introduces creative new designs.*

9 point with 10 point lead

Bitstream is an independent digital typefoundry. Using the latest computer graphics tools, Bitstream's designers maintain the traditional essentials of good type design. Shape, weight and spacing rhythm are expertly con-_**trolled to produce digitized letterforms of the highest quality in all font formats. In addition to making definitive versions of existing faces, Bitstream introduces creative new designs.**_

News Release

Just because releases *used* to be done in a typewriter font doesn't mean they *still* have to be. They're not easier to read that way, and they're not as attractive. So what's the point?

But for that "newsy" appearance, Prestige is perfect for the nameplate. Using it in a large size shows it off as a kind of "period piece," setting the tone, but not sacrificing the readability of the body text.

The nameplate is large, enabling it to stand out from competing releases. *News* is set large in upper and lowercase. *RELEASE* is set smaller in Prestige Bold. The wide letterspacing and vertical rules visually suggest the broadcasting of information.

Type specifications:
News is set in 120-point Prestige; *RELEASE* in 16-point Prestige Bold. *Quantum Research* is set in a combination of Swiss and Swiss Black; the address is set in 9/32 Swiss Bold Condensed. Text is set in 10/12 Century Schoolbook with Italic and Bold.

Quantum Research

266 State Street

Boston, MA 02111

617-555-8678

News

R E L E A S E

January 5, 1991

In 1945, the last of the warships for the British Royal Navy, built at the Hingham Shipyard in Massachusetts, were sent to England to defend the allies. In just a few weeks another ship, and most likely the last, will be launched at the Hingham Shipyard. And once again, this boat will sail under a British captain.

After five years, Mick Robson, originally from Yorkshire England, has completed the construction of the *Garrett Lee*, a sixty-four foot sloop named after his five-year-old son.

From the hull to the interior—the mast, sails and rigging—Mick has built his boat to show his wife, Dorinda, and their son the world.

On September 15, 1991, the *Garrett Lee* will begin her travels. Mick will sail to the Caribbean offering charters in the winter months and traveling the world the rest of the year.

Mick's interest in boats began as a boy when his dad bought him a small model boat he had seen in a store window. His love of the sea compelled him to become a merchant seaman. Having traveled the world himself, he wants his family to see it.

"The life on the sea is the best life. You meet people from all countries, you learn the culture of all lands . . . This is the school I want my boy to learn from," explains Mick in his heavily accented English.

Mick would like to talk to you and take you aboard his boat.

For more information, contact Betsy Wood at 617-555-8678.

Provence™

The Bitstream version of the Antique Olive® typeface.

Roman

abcdefghijklmnopqrstuvwxyz
ABCDEFGHIJKLMNOPQRSTUVWXYZ
1234567890&$£%.,:;-!?''åçëîñòšúß

Italic

abcdefghijklmnopqrstuvwxyz
ABCDEFGHIJKLMNOPQRSTUVWXYZ
1234567890&$£%.,:;-!?''åçëîñòšúß

Black

abcdefghijklmnopqrstuvwxyz
ABCDEFGHIJKLMNOPQRSTUVWXYZ
1234567890&$£%.,:;-!?''åçëîñòšúß

Compact

abcdefghijklmnopqrstuvwxyz
ABCDEFGHIJKLMNOPQRSTUVWXYZ
1234567890&$£%.,:;-!?''åçëîñòšúß

15 point

Bitstream is an independent digital typefoundry. Using the latest computer graphics tools, Bitstream's designers maintain the traditional essentials of good type design. Shape, weight and spacing rhythm *are expertly controlled to produce digitized letterforms of the highest quality in all font formats. In addition to making definitive versions of existing faces, Bitstream introduces creative new designs.*

9 point with 10 point lead

Bitstream is an independent digital typefoundry. Using the latest computer graphics tools, Bitstream's designers maintain the traditional essentials of good type design. Shape, weight and spacing rhythm are expertly controlled to produce digitized letterforms of the highest quality in all font formats. In addition to making definitive versions of existing faces, Bitstream introduces creative new designs.

Report Cover

The clean-cut lines and organic-looking letterforms of Provence create an appropriate image for a biogenetic engineering laboratory report. ITC Garamond Bold Condensed Italic offers a contrast to the sanserif Provence.

The background imagery of DNA was produced using a graphics program.

Type specifications:
The initial *O* in *Otis Langley Institute* is set in 18-point Provence Compact, the remainder of the company name in 18-point Provence. *1991* is set in ITC Garamond Bold Condensed Italic. *Report of the Director* is set in 11-point Provence, *Biogenetic* in Provence Black, *Engineering* in Provence Italic.

Note: Graphic image was scanned into the system. It might also be imported from a paint or draw program or added by means of manual paste-up.

Otis Langley Institute

Report of the Director

1 9 9 1

Biogenetic *Engineering*

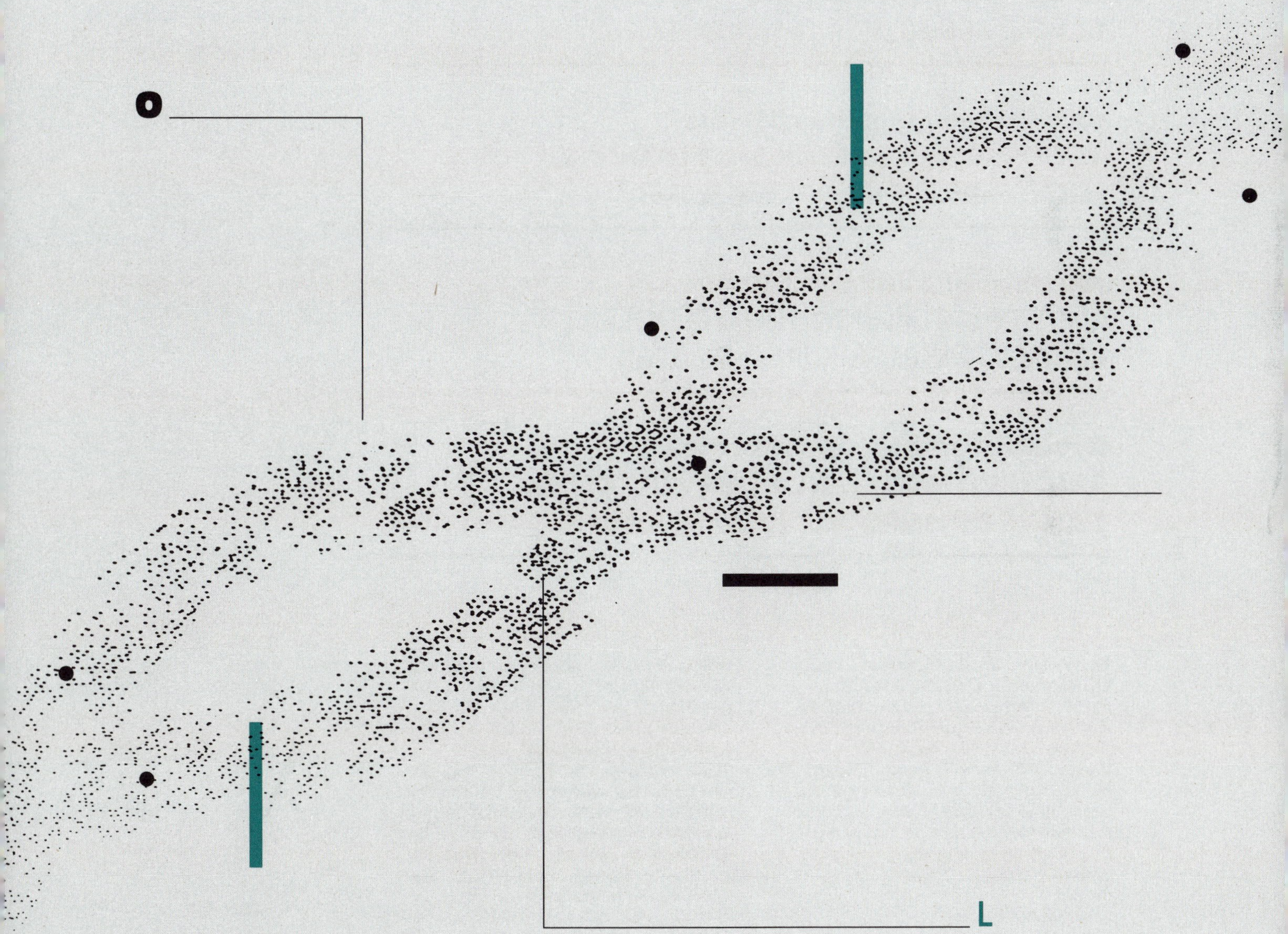

Serifa®

Roman

abcdefghijklmnopqrstuvwxyz
ABCDEFGHIJKLMNOPQRSTUVWXYZ
1234567890&$£%.,:;-!?''åçëîñòšúß

Italic

abcdefghijklmnopqrstuvwxyz
ABCDEFGHIJKLMNOPQRSTUVWXYZ
1234567890&$£%.,:;-!?''åçëîñòšúß

Bold

abcdefghijklmnopqrstuvwxyz
ABCDEFGHIJKLMNOPQRSTUVWXYZ
1234567890&$£%.,:;-!?''åçëîñòšúß

Black

abcdefghijklmnopqrstuvwxyz
ABCDEFGHIJKLMNOPQRSTUVWXYZ
1234567890&$£%.,:;-!?''åçëîñòšúß

15 point

Bitstream is an independent digital typefoundry. Using the latest computer graphics tools, Bitstream's designers maintain the traditional essentials of good type design. Shape, weight and spacing rhythm are ex*pertly controlled to produce digitized letterforms of the highest quality in all font formats. In addition to making definitive versions of existing faces, Bitstream introduces creative new designs.*

9 point with 10 point lead

Bitstream is an independent digital typefoundry. Using the latest computer graphics tools, Bitstream's designers maintain the traditional essentials of good type design. Shape, weight and spacing rhythm are expertly controlled to produce digitized letterforms of the highest quality in all font formats. In addition to making definitive versions of existing faces, Bitstream introduces creative new designs.

Letterhead

Elements in this example were placed at various points on the page, rather than centered at the top of the page, to help define the letter area. The single red typing dot to the right of *MECHANO* indicates the beginning of the letter and sets the left margin. Since most modern correspondence is going to be produced on a word processor rather than a typewriter, the first dot serves more as a visual cue to the reader than to help the typist.

The list of cities serves to reinforce the left margin and provides a vertical pointer to the salutation. The right margin is defined by the right edge of the address block.

The structured, machine-like character of the Serifa typeface is aptly used in the logotype for *MECHANO*, a company that works with machine systems. Three weights of Serifa are combined in the logotype to give a lively, rhythmic image and to create a more visually memorable mark than could be achieved by the use of a single weight.

The complete legal name of the company is set in Serifa Black to emphasize and distinguish it from the rest of the address block. The cities list, which constitutes secondary information, is set in Serifa Italic to differentiate it from the Serifa roman address.

The bullet to the right of *Boston* indicates where the letter originated. Charter is used for the body of the letter because of its slightly mechanical and very businesslike tone which contrasts with and compliments Serifa.

Type specifications:
The logotype, *MECHANO*, is set in a combination of 16-point Serifa, Serifa Bold, and Serifa Black. The company name is set in 8-point Serifa Black; the address block is in 8/10 Serifa; the cities list is in 8/10 Serifa Italic. The letter itself is set in 9/12 Charter.

Mechano Data Storage Systems, Inc.

300 Atlantic Center
Boston, Massachusetts
0 2 2 1 0

617 555-1236

MECHÄNO

Bonn
Boston •
Brussels
Canberra
Geneva
The Hague
Hong Kong
London
Munich
New York
Palo Alto
Paris
Rome
Santiago
Taipei
Tokyo
Toronto
Washington
Zurich

•
July 8, 1991

Mr. James Harwood
Rhode Island Bureau of Development
1901 Crown Road
Providence, RI 02850

Dear Mr. Harwood:

For 25 years, Mechano Data Storage Systems, Inc. has helped government agencies and corporations solve their data storage problems. Mechano converts paper to electronic rigid disk files allowing for compact, manageable files with easy accessibility.

By use of advanced computer systems and database management, Mechano can transfer and archive your files, thus eliminating paper build-up. Files can be cross-referenced and multiple-listed to provide the most advanced filing system.

Mechano Data Storage Systems has helped numerous agencies and corporations in New England including Massachusetts Protection Bureau, Vermont Educational Safety Board, Suffolk County Housing Offices, United Insurance Company and Nolan Inc.

The productivity of a company depends on the ability to efficiently access and handle information. The advanced systems of Mechano Data Storage can enable you to eliminate your data storage problem.

A Mechano representative will contact you next week to discuss the Mechano Data Storage System solution.

Sincerely,

David Thompson
Sales Manager

ABCDE

FGHIJK

LMNOP

QRSTU

VWXYZ

Slate Medium

B

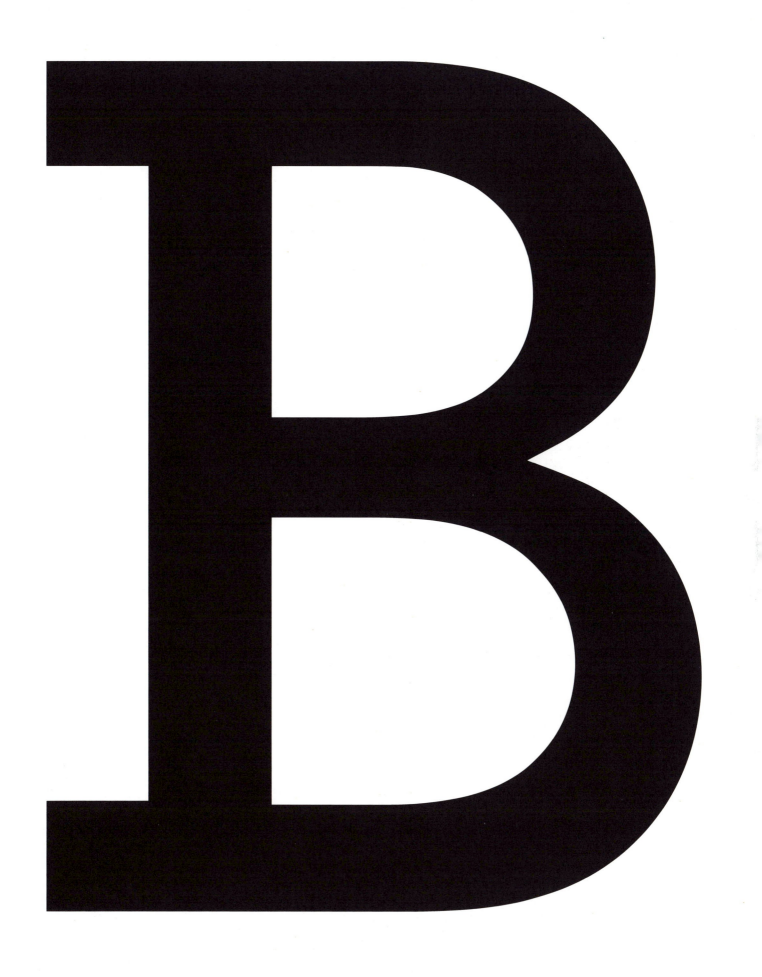

Slate™

The Bistream version of the Rockwell® typeface.

Medium

abcdefghijklmnopqrstuvwxyz
ABCDEFGHIJKLMNOPQRSTUVWXYZ
1234567890&$£%.,:;-!?"åçëîñòšúß

Medium Italic

abcdefghijklmnopqrstuvwxyz
ABCDEFGHIJKLMNOPQRSTUVWXYZ
1234567890&$£%.,:;-!?"åçëîñòšúß

Bold

abcdefghijklmnopqrstuvwxyz
ABCDEFGHIJKLMNOPQRSTUVWXYZ
1234567890&$£%.,:;-!?"åçëîñòšúß

Extra Bold

abcdefghijklmnopqrstuvwxyz
ABCDEFGHIJKLMNOPQRSTUVWXYZ
1234567890&$£%.,:;-!?"åçëîñòšúß

15 point

Bitstream is an independent digital typefoundry. Using the latest computer graphics tools, Bitstream's designers maintain the traditional essentials of good type design. Shape, weight and spacing rhythm are expertly controlled *to produce digitized letterforms of the highest quality in all font formats. In addition to making definitive versions of existing faces, Bitstream introduces creative new designs.*

9 point with 10 point lead

Bitstream is an independent digital typefoundry. Using the latest computer graphics tools, Bitstream's designers maintain the traditional essentials of good type design. Shape, weight and spacing rhythm are expertly controlled to produce digitized letterforms of the highest quality in all font formats. In addition to making definitive versions of existing faces, Bitstream introduces creative new designs.

Contract

Slate is used for its readability in lengthy copy at small point sizes and for its businesslike, modern look. The letterforms are clean and even-weighted with short, square serifs that help lead the eye from character to character for easy word recognition and reading.

The two-column format is easier to read than one very wide column. Slate Medium Italic and Slate Bold are used within the text to emphasize particular passages. The wide margin on the left separates the logotype from the contract copy, thus emphasizing the logotype.

Rather than setting *Signature, Name,* etc. on the same baseline as the rules in the form, the designer has chosen to center them vertically between the rules. The result is that the rules are not interrupted by type and are able to run the full column width, which gives a cleaner look.

Type specifications:
Text is set in 7.5/9 Slate Medium, Medium Italic, and Bold; the section numbers are set in Slate Bold; *Contract* is in Slate Extra Bold. In the logotype, *Quan* is in 19-point Baskerville bold; *Text* is in 17-point Zurich Black.

QuanText®

Contract Terms and Conditions

QuanText, Inc. (QuanText) and the Customer, by their acceptance of this Agreement, do agree to abide by the following terms and conditions:

1

QuanText does hereby grant to the customer a non-exclusive license to use at the location(s) described herein, and at the cost set forth and for the specified period, in accordance with this Agreement, the Product described herein.

2

QuanText will supply the Product on magnetic disk together with two copies of the Product documentation.

3

QuanText will provide additional copies of the Product documentation at the then prevailing cost.

4

QuanText has the right to terminate its obligation under this agreement if the requested Contract Date is more than ninety days (90) after the date the license is accepted by QuanText.

5

Payments will be made in full within twenty (20) days after the receipt by customer of invoice. A charge of 1½ percent per month or part-month will be assessed on late payments.

6

The Customer may obtain Special Features for the Product at any time at the then prevailing prices.

7

If the Customer sends QuanText a Registered Letter of Termination of this agreement within fourteen (14) days after the Contract Date then no license fees will be payable by the Customer and all obligations of QuanText under this Agreement will terminate.

8

The term of this Agreement shall commence on the Contract Date for the Product. QuanText may terminate this Agreement upon any material breach by the Customer if when notified the Customer does not promptly correct such breach. **Upon any such termination all the remaining payments committed under this agreement will be due and payable immediately.**

9

The Payments specified herein are net of taxes and are payable in full to QuanText; it is the Customer's responsibility to pay any taxes based on the Payment set forth in this Agreement.

10

All ownership rights and Title to the Product described herein remain with QuanText. The Product is agreed to be QuanText's proprietary information and trade secrets, whether or not any portion thereof is or may be copyrighted or patented. **The Customer will take all reasonable steps to protect the product and its documentation from disclosure to any other person, firm or corporation. The Customer will insure that all individuals having access to the Product be aware of and will observe and perform this non-disclosure covenant. The Customer will carry out this non-disclosure with no less efforts than those used to protect the Customer's own confidential and proprietary information.**

11

QuanText may assign this Agreement in whole or in part. The Customer's rights in and to the Product, as given by this Agreement, may not be assigned, licensed or otherwise without QuanText's prior written consent. QuanText will not unreasonably withhold consent to transfer this license to a division, subsidiary or holding company of the Customer for which a greater than 50% ownership exists.

12

Upon any termination of this Agreement for whatever reason, the Customer shall deliver to QuanText all materials, documentation and magnetic discs furnished by QuanText and pertaining to the Product and shall warrant in writing that all such materials have been returned or destroyed.

13

The Product may be used only for, by and on behalf of the Customer at the site(s) specified herein. The Customer may change the site location upon receiving QuanText's prior written consent, which shall not be unreasonably withheld. Notwithstanding the preceding, the Customer may use the System on a temporary basis in an emergency backup installation. Reasonable security measures must be maintained by the Customer during the transfer of all materials relating to the Product.

14

QuanText shall provide product maintenance and support in accordance with its then current support policies. This shall include correcting any program errors as may occur in the Product from time to time.

15

QuanText warrants that the Product as delivered by QuanText will perform in accordance with the latest Reference Manuals for the Product and warrants that QuanText has the right to authorize the use of the Product. However, QuanText's sole obligation under this warranty shall be to correct the Product so that it will so perform or to refund the Product payments upon return of all product materials if such authorization be invalid; and QuanText shall not be liable for any loss caused by any failure of the Product to perform or the ineffectiveness of the authorization for any reason. QuanText will, in addition, hold harmless and defend Customer against suits based on any claim that the Product infringes on any existing patent or property right. This warranty is in lieu of all other warranties, expressed or implied. *No other warranty is expressed and none shall be implied, including without limitation, warranty of merchantability or fitness for a particular purpose.*

16

No waiver of any breach of any provision of this Agreement shall constitute a waiver of any other breach of any provision hereof and no waiver is effective unless made in writing. In the event that any provision of this Agreement shall be illegal or otherwise unenforceable, such provision shall be served and the entire Agreement shall not fail on account thereof and the remainder of the Agreement shall continue in full force and effect.

17

All written notices required hereunder shall be sent by registered or certified mail to the addresses set forth in this agreement. Such notices will become effective on the sixth (6) day following the mailing date.

18

This Agreement shall be governed by the laws of the Commonwealth of Virginia, and constitutes the entire agreement between QuanText and the Customer with respect to the Product and supercedes all proposals, oral or written, and may be modified or supplemented only by a written document signed by an authorized representative of each party.

19

If any action or proceeding is brought in connection with this Agreement, the prevailing party shall be entitled to recover its costs and reasonable attorney fees.

Accepted by: QuanText

Signature

Name

Title

Date

Accepted by: Customer

Signature

Name

Title

Date

ITC Souvenir®

Light

abcdefghijklmnopqrstuvwxyz
ABCDEFGHIJKLMNOPQRSTUVWXYZ
1234567890&$£%.,:;-!?"åçëîñòšúß

Light Italic

abcdefghijklmnopqrstuvwxyz
ABCDEFGHIJKLMNOPQRSTUVWXYZ
1234567890&$£%.,:;-!?"åçëîñòšúß

Demi

abcdefghijklmnopqrstuvwxyz
ABCDEFGHIJKLMNOPQRSTUVWXYZ
1234567890&$£%.,:;-!?"åçëîñòšúß

Demi Italic

abcdefghijklmnopqrstuvwxyz
ABCDEFGHIJKLMNOPQRSTUVWXYZ
1234567890&$£%.,:;-!?"åçëîñòšúß

15 point

Bitstream is an independent digital typefoundry. Using the latest computer graphics tools, Bitstream's designers maintain the traditional essentials of good type design. Shape, weight and spacing rhythm are expertly controlled to *produce digitized letterforms of the highest quality in all font formats. In addition to making definitive versions of existing faces, Bitstream introduces creative new designs.*
9 point with 10 point lead

Bitstream is an independent digital typefoundry. Using the latest computer graphics tools, Bitstream's designers maintain the traditional essentials of good type design. Shape, weight and spacing rhythm ***are expertly controlled to produce digitized letterforms of the highest quality in all font formats. In addition to making definitive versions of existing faces, Bitstream introduces creative new designs.***

Conference Schedule

The ITC Souvenir typeface family is highly readable with a friendly, informal feeling.

The three-column table is well-organized to produce a simple, inviting page without overpowering it. Generous leading ensures that each event is easy to read as a distinct horizontal unit.

Dates are set in caps with wide letterspacing, as in the company logotype at the top of the page. The large rose illustration adds color and quietly enlivens the page without competing with the content.

Type specifications:
COLONAE BEAUTÉ is set in 12-point Swiss Extra Compressed; text is in 9/22 ITC Souvenir Light with Light Italic; the leaf ornament is from the ITC Zapf Dingbats collection available in the Bitstream *Symbols 1* typeface package.

COLONAE BEAUTÉ

1988 International Conference
Amsterdam, the Netherlands

SEPTEMBER 26

9:30	Coffee and Danish	Salon E
10:00	Welcome/Objectives	Louise Wallis, U.S.A.
10:30	Where We've Been/Where We're Going	Samuel Vedisan, U.S.A.
11:30	Introduction to Colonae International	Francis Dubré, France
12:15	Lunch	Almaar
2:00	Colonae Beauté Shades	Istan Mechin, Egypt
3:30	Colonae Beauté Demonstration I	Inger Stuvan, Sweden
5:00	Cocktails	Salon D
6:30	Dinner	Voltendam

SEPTEMBER 27

9:30	Opening Statements	Louise Wallis, U.S.A.
10:00	New Advances in Skin Care	Kathleen Fontaine, U.S.A.
12:00	Marketing Colonae Beauté	Hana Wordeman, Germany
1:00	Lunch	Kamaaram
2:30	Color System Demonstration	Tristan Royce, Great Britain
3:30	Promotional Activities	Salina Biondi, Italy
4:00	Colonae Beauté Demonstration II	Pauline Trivine, Switzerland
6:00	Cocktails	Salon D
7:00	Dinner	Edam

Swiss

The Bitstream version of the Helvetica® typeface.

Roman

abcdefghijklmnopqrstuvwxyz
ABCDEFGHIJKLMNOPQRSTUVWXYZ
1234567890&$£%.,:;-!?"åçëîñòšúß

Italic

abcdefghijklmnopqrstuvwxyz
ABCDEFGHIJKLMNOPQRSTUVWXYZ
1234567890&$£%.,:;-!?"åçëîñòšúß

Bold

abcdefghijklmnopqrstuvwxyz
ABCDEFGHIJKLMNOPQRSTUVWXYZ
1234567890&$£%.,:;-!?"åçëîñòšúß

Bold Italic

abcdefghijklmnopqrstuvwxyz
ABCDEFGHIJKLMNOPQRSTUVWXYZ
1234567890&$£%.,:;-!?"åçëîñòšúß

15 point

Bitstream is an independent digital typefoundry. Using the latest computer graphics tools, Bitstream's designers maintain the traditional essentials of good type design. Shape, weight and spacing rhythm are expertly controlled *to produce digitized letterforms of the highest quality in all font formats. In addition to making definitive versions of existing faces, Bitstream introduces creative new designs.*

9 point with 10 point lead

Bitstream is an independent digital typefoundry. Using the latest computer graphics tools, Bitstream's designers maintain the traditional essentials of good type design. Shape, weight and spacing rhythm ***are expertly controlled to produce digitized letterforms of the highest quality in all font formats. In addition to making definitive versions of existing faces, Bitstream introduces creative new designs.***

Signage

Swiss Bold's clean, directive quality is appropriate for use in signage. The use of all uppercase characters provides maximum legibility at a distance.

Type specifications:
NO is set in 60-point Swiss Bold Condensed; *SMOKING* is 100-point Swiss Bold; *please* is 72-point Swiss Condensed.

NO

SMOKING

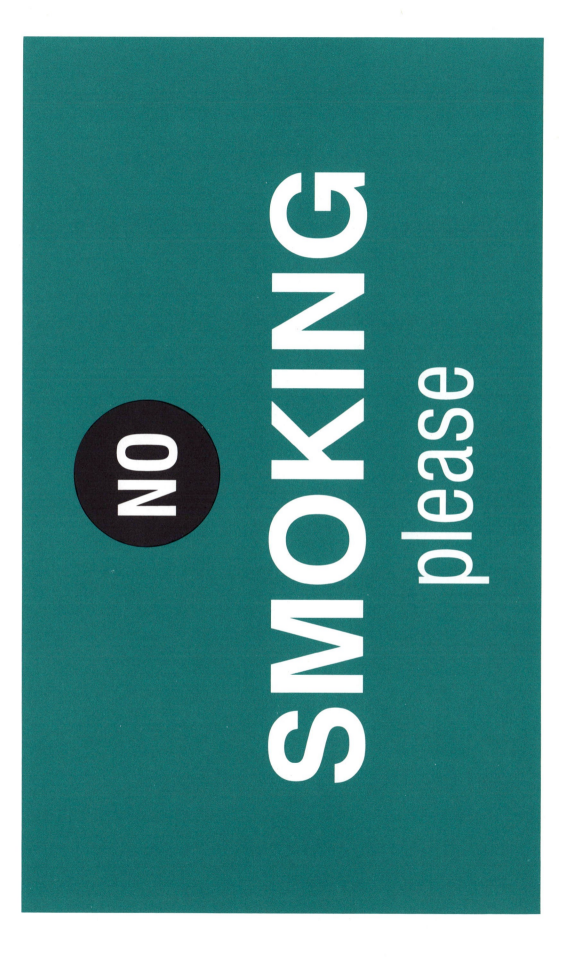

please

Swiss Condensed

The Bitstream version of the
Helvetica® Condensed typeface.

Condensed

abcdefghijklmnopqrstuvwxyz
ABCDEFGHIJKLMNOPQRSTUVWXYZ
1234567890&$£%.,:;-!?‘‘åçëîñòšúß

Condensed Italic

abcdefghijklmnopqrstuvwxyz
ABCDEFGHIJKLMNOPQRSTUVWXYZ
1234567890&$£%.,:;-!?‘‘åçëîñòšúß

Bold Condensed

abcdefghijklmnopqrstuvwxyz
ABCDEFGHIJKLMNOPQRSTUVWXYZ
1234567890&$£%.,:;-!?‘‘åçëîñòšúß

Black Condensed

abcdefghijklmnopqrstuvwxyz
ABCDEFGHIJKLMNOPQRSTUVWXYZ
1234567890&$£%.,:;-!?‘‘åçëîñòšúß

15 point

Bitstream is an independent digital typefoundry. Using the latest computer graphics tools, Bitstream's designers maintain the traditional essentials of good type design. Shape, weight and spacing rhythm are ex-*pertly controlled to produce digitized letterforms of the highest quality in all font formats. In addition to making definitive versions of existing faces, Bitstream introduces creative new designs.*

9 point with 10 point lead

Bitstream is an independent digital typefoundry. Using the latest computer graphics tools, Bitstream's designers maintain the traditional essentials of good type design. Shape, weight and spacing rhythm are expertly controlled to produce digitized letterforms of the highest quality in all font formats. In addition to making definitive versions of existing faces, Bitstream introduces creative new designs.

Directory

Swiss Condensed is used for its high legibility and compact width, allowing more characters per line. This membership directory is based on an easy-to-read, two-column grid.

A line space separates individual entries. Names are emphasized by the use of Swiss Bold Condensed. A dotted line separates the letters of the alphabet.

The large *E* serves to identify the alphabetical order of the directory.

Type specifications:
Names are set in 8-point Swiss Bold Condensed; address in 8/9 Swiss Condensed; telephone numbers in 8/9 Swiss Condensed Italic. The large *E* is set in 96-point Swiss Extra Compressed; the subhead, *F*, in 12-point Swiss Black Condensed.

Eldridge, Jerald
President
Full Research
414 Orleans Ave.
Huntington Station, NY 11746
(516) 555-1269

Elliot, Jan
President
Mesna Institute
P.O. Box 1072
Grand Junction, CO 81502
(303) 555-5250

Ellis, Jill
President
Epstein Quantitative Research
523 South Third St.
New York, NY 10016
(212) 555-0483

Ellis, Thomas
Principal
Norcross Marketing Research
701 Fifth St.
Norcross, GA 30092
(404) 555-3491

Ema, Donald
President
Allo Ema Associates
1940 Broadway
New York, NY 10001
(212) 555-0222

Emery, Donna
Owner
Emery Research
35 Roosevelt Rd.
Green Bay, WI 54305
(414) 555-9410

Emley, Joshua
President
Alexandria Enterprises Inc.
53 Lexington Ave.
New York, NY 10010
(212) 555-0216

Eng, Beth
Director
Vandegeer Associates
1403 Executive Dr.
Fort Washington, PA 19034
(215) 555-1430

Engel, Wendy
President
New England Strategy Inc.
115 West Church St.
Nashua, NH 03063
(603) 555-5389

Enger, Mark
President
Enger Associates
58 Korman Dr.
New Rochelle, NY 10801
(914) 555-4422

Enomoto, Bud
Field Manager
Egyptian Service Bureau
86 Mohamed Komein St.
Heliopolis-Cairo, Egypt
669835
81 (3) 555-5081

Erickson, Vivian
Director
Computer Strategy Inc.
3209 Mannheim Rd.
Napa Valley, CA 94558
(707) 555-5069

Esposito, Lisa
Partner
Esposito & Thomas
Associates
588 Goodwin St.
Scarsdale, NY 10583
(914) 555-8080

Etan, Edwin
President
Communications Analysts Inc.
584 Park Ave.
New York, NY 10010
(212) 555-8693

Ewry, Julie
Director
Spaulding & Associates
578 Sutter St.
Kansas City, MO 64199
(816) 555-7575

F

Faber, Deborah
President
Eastern Data Inc.
211 Eastern Ave.
Hicksville, NY 11801
(516) 555-2770

Fairchild, Michael
Partner
F & F Market Research Inc.
180 Michigan Ave.
Charleston, SC 29407
(803) 555-7620

Swiss Light

The Bitstream version of the Helvetica® Light typeface.

Light

abcdefghijklmnopqrstuvwxyz
ABCDEFGHIJKLMNOPQRSTUVWXYZ
1234567890&$£%.,:;-!?''åçëîñòšúß

Light Italic

abcdefghijklmnopqrstuvwxyz
ABCDEFGHIJKLMNOPQRSTUVWXYZ
1234567890&$£%.,:;-!?''åçëîñòšúß

Black

abcdefghijklmnopqrstuvwxyz
ABCDEFGHIJKLMNOPQRSTUVWXYZ
1234567890&$£%.,:;-!?''åçëîñòšúß

Black Italic

abcdefghijklmnopqrstuvwxyz
ABCDEFGHIJKLMNOPQRSTUVWXYZ
1234567890&$£%.,:;-!?''åçëîñòšúß

15 point

Bitstream is an independent digital typefoundry. Using the latest computer graphics tools, Bitstream's designers maintain the traditional essentials of good type design. Shape, weight and spacing rhythm are expertly controlled to *produce digitized letterforms of the highest quality in all font formats. In addition to making definitive versions of existing faces, Bitstream introduces creative new designs.*
9 point with 10 point lead

Bitstream is an independent digital typefoundry. Using the latest computer graphics tools, Bitstream's designers maintain the traditional essentials of good type design. Shape, weight and spacing rhythm are expertly *controlled to produce digitized letterforms of the highest quality in all font formats. In addition to making definitive versions of existing faces, Bitstream introduces creative new designs.*

Overhead Transparency

The Swiss typeface family is used in this overhead transparency because its clean legibility and contemporary feeling hold up even when projected on a screen.

Complex information is organized in a rational manner. A clear reading path exists from headline to text and then through the chart. Rules and arrows lead the eye through two levels of information.

Type specifications:
*The headline is set in 14-point Swiss Black; text in 14/18 Swiss Light. Callouts in the chart are 11/14 Swiss Bold. Arrows are from the ITC Zapf Dingbats collection available in the Bitstream *Symbols 1* typeface package.

*Note: Overhead transparency shown here has been reduced to 64% of the original.

4.1 Marketing Flow Chart

In order to develop a successful marketing piece, a well-defined system is necessary. This system will ease the flow of information, eliminate redundant actions, track progress and create a more lucid piece. The flow chart presented here shows a system that is well organized and easy to follow.

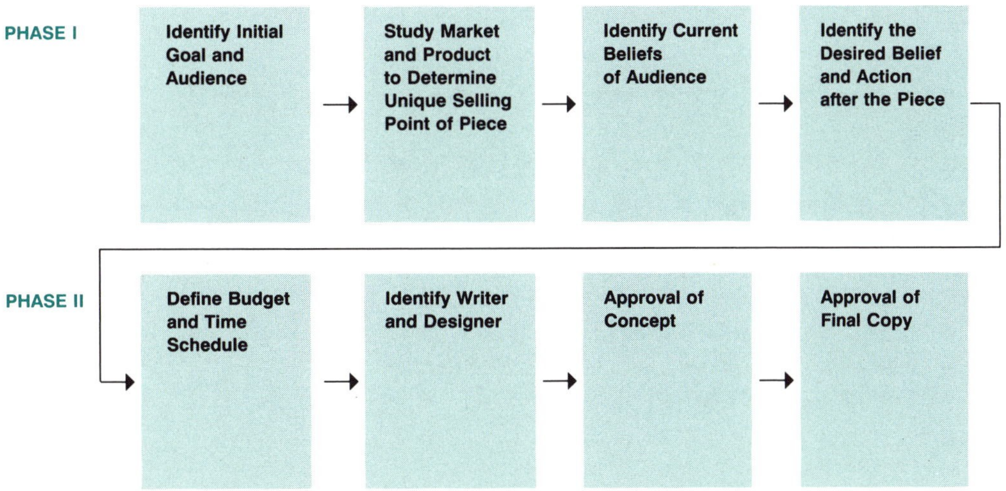

Symbols 1

Symbol A Proportional

! ∀ # ∃ % & ∍ ( ) ∗ + , − . / 0 1 2 3 4 5 6 7 8 9 : ; < = > ? ≅ A B
Χ Δ Ε Φ Γ Η Ι ϑ Κ Λ Μ Ν Ο Π Θ Ρ Σ Τ Υ ς Ω Ξ Ψ Ζ [∴] ⊥ _
‾ α β χ δ ε ϕ γ η ι φ κ λ μ ν ο π θ ρ σ τ υ ϖ ω ξ ψ ζ { | } ~ ϒ ′ ≤
⁄ ∞ ƒ ♣ ♦ ♥ ♠ ↔ ← ↑ → ↓ ° ± ″ ≥ × ∝ ∂ • ÷ ≠ ≡ ≈ … | —
↵ ∴ ℵ ℑ ℜ ℘ ⊗ ⊕ ∅ ∩ ∪ ⊃ ⊇ ⊄ ⊂ ⊆ ∈ ∉ ∠ ∇ ® © ™ ∏ √ · ¬
∧ ∨ ⇔ ⇐ ⇑ ⇒ ⇓ ◊ 〈 ® © ™ ∑ ⎛ ⎜ ⎝ ⎡ ⎢ ⎣ ⎧ ⎨ ⎩ ⎪ 〉 ∫ ⌠ ⎮ ⌡
⎞ ⎟ ⎠ ⎤ ⎥ ⎦ ⎫ ⎬ ⎭

Symbol A Monospaced

! ∀ # ∃ % & ∍ ( ) ∗ + , − . / 0 1 2 3 4 5 6 7 8 9 : ; <
= > ? ≅ A B X Δ E Φ Γ H I ϑ K Λ M N O Π Θ P Σ T Y ς Ω Ξ
Ψ Z [∴] ⊥ _ ‾ α β χ δ ε ϕ γ η ι φ κ λ μ ν ο π θ ρ σ τ
υ ϖ ω ξ ψ ζ { | } ~ ϒ ′ ≤ ⁄ ∞ ƒ ♣ ♦ ♥ ♠ ↔ ← ↑ → ↓ ° ± ″
≥ × ∝ ∂ • ÷ ≠ ≡ ≈ … | — ↵ ∴ ℵ ℑ ℜ ℘ ⊗ ⊕ ∅ ∩ ∪ ⊃ ⊇ ⊄ ⊂ ⊆
∈ ∉ ∠ ∇ ® © ™ ∏ √ · ¬ ∧ ∨ ⇔ ⇐ ⇑ ⇒ ⇓ ◊ 〈 ® © ™ ∑ ⎛ ⎜ ⎝ ⎡
⎢ ⎣ ⎧ ⎨ ⎩ ⎪ 〉 ∫ ⌠ ⎮ ⌡ ⎞ ⎟ ⎠ ⎤ ⎥ ⎦ ⎫ ⎬ ⎭

ITC Zapf Dingbats®

✁ ✂ ✃ ✄ ☎ ✆ ✇ ✈ ✉ ☛ ☞ ✌ ✍ ✎ ✏ ✐ ✑ ✒ ✓ ✔ ✕ ✖ ✗
✘ ✙ ✚ ✛ ✜ ✝ ✞ ✟ ✠ ✡ ✢ ✣ ✤ ✥ ✦ ✧ ★ ☆ ✪ ✫ ✬ ✭ ✮ ✯
✰ ✱ ✲ ✳ ✴ ✵ ✶ ✷ ✸ ✹ ✺ ✻ ✼ ✽ ✾ ✿ ❀ ❁ ❂ ❃ ❄ ❅ ❆ ❇ ❈ ❉
❊ ● ❍ ■ ❏ ❐ ❑ ❒ ▲ ▼ ◆ ❖ ◗ ❘ ❙ ❚ ❛ ❜ ❝ ❞ ❡ ❢ ❣ ❤ ❥ ❦
❧ ♣ ♦ ♥ ♠ ① ② ③ ④ ⑤ ⑥ ⑦ ⑧ ⑨ ⑩ ❶ ❷ ❸ ❹ ❺ ❻ ❼ ❽ ❾ ❿ ✱
➀ ➁ ➂ ➃ ➄ ➅ ➆ ➇ ➈ ➉ ➊ ➋ ➌ ➍ ➎ ➏ ➐ ➑ ➒ ➓ ➔ → ↔ ↕ ➘ ➙
➚ ➛ ➜ ➝ ➞ ➟ ➠ ➡ ➢ ➣ ➤ ➥ ➦ ➧ ➨ ➩ ➪ ➫ ➬ ➭ ➮ ➯ ➱
➲ ➳ ➴ ➵ ➶ ➷ ➸ ➹ ➺ ➻ ➼ ➽ ➾

Coupon

Symbols are used here to highlight key information and add visual interest. The hand, a symbol from the ITC Zapf Dingbats collection, points to the most important copy. The numbered round bullets, from the same face, visually reference related elements. The envelope and telephone images draw attention to the mailing address and telephone number. The scissors and broken rule quickly tell the reader that the coupon must be clipped out and returned.

Baskerville was selected to convey a formal look. It contrasts nicely with the sanserif Franklin Gothic used for the company logotype. The 2-point and hairline rules define the structure of the form. The solid black bar with reversed type emphasizes the headline.

Type specifications:
The headline, *6-MONTH CERTIFICATE*, is set in 10-point Franklin Gothic Extra Condensed. Text is set in 9/11 Baskerville with Baskerville Italic. Text within the form is 6-point Baskerville. The rate, *9.75%*, is set in 72-point Baskerville. The address and phone number are in 8-point Baskerville. *Miami Bank* and *Savings* are set in 13-point Franklin Gothic; *for* is set in Zurich Italic.

6-MONTH CERTIFICATE

From now until December 17, 1991, MBS is offering 6-month certificates of deposit at this outstanding rate (*minimum $10,000 deposit*). Mail your check with this ad to Miami Bank for Savings at the address below. For additional information call us at (305) 555-0096.

9.75% Annual Rate

◯ Single Account

◯ Joint Account

Name	1	
	2	
Social Sec. No.	1	
	2	
Date of Birth	1	
	2	
Telephone		
Address		
City	State	Zip
Signature	1	
	2	

12 Cardinelle Avenue, Miami, Florida 33152
305-555-0096

Miami Bank *for* Savings

Mr. and M

reque

marriage of the

Emily A

Coronet Bold

rs. Gerome La

st the honor of y

r daughter

en

ITC Tiffany

Medium

abcdefghijklmnopqrstuvwxyz
ABCDEFGHIJKLMNOPQRSTUVWXYZ
1234567890&$£%.,:;-!?''åçëîñòšúß

Medium Italic

abcdefghijklmnopqrstuvwxyz
ABCDEFGHIJKLMNOPQRSTUVWXYZ
1234567890&$£%.,:;-!?''åçëîñòšúß

Heavy

abcdefghijklmnopqrstuvwxyz
ABCDEFGHIJKLMNOPQRSTUVWXYZ
1234567890&$£%.,:;-!?''åçëîñòšúß

Heavy Italic

abcdefghijklmnopqrstuvwxyz
ABCDEFGHIJKLMNOPQRSTUVWXYZ
1234567890&$£%.,:;-!?''åçëîñòšúß

15 point

Bitstream is an independent digital typefoundry. Using the latest computer graphics tools, Bitstream's designers maintain the traditional essentials of good type design. Shape, weight and spacing rhythm *are expertly controlled to produce digitized letterforms of the highest quality in all font formats. In addition to making definitive versions of existing faces, Bitstream introduces creative new designs.*

9 point with 10 point lead

Bitstream is an independent digital typefoundry. Using the latest computer graphics tools, Bitstream's designers maintain the traditional essentials of good type design. Shape, weight and spacing rhythm are ***expertly controlled to produce digitized letterforms of the highest quality in all font formats. In addition to making definitive versions of existing faces, Bitstream introduces creative new designs.***

Greeting Card

Expressive and ornate, ITC Tiffany is well used in this holiday card. Type is used as illustration in the large *LA* initials. The heavy italic letterforms give a sense of energy that is heightened by bleeding them off the card.

The 8-point copy sprinkled across the page projects a quieter but cheerful message.

Type specifications:
LA is set in 406-point ITC Tiffany Heavy Italic; text in 8-point ITC Tiffany Medium and Heavy Italic.

Laser printers cannot print to the edge of the paper and create a bleed. To create this effect you must print to a larger piece of paper and have the print shop trim the edges.

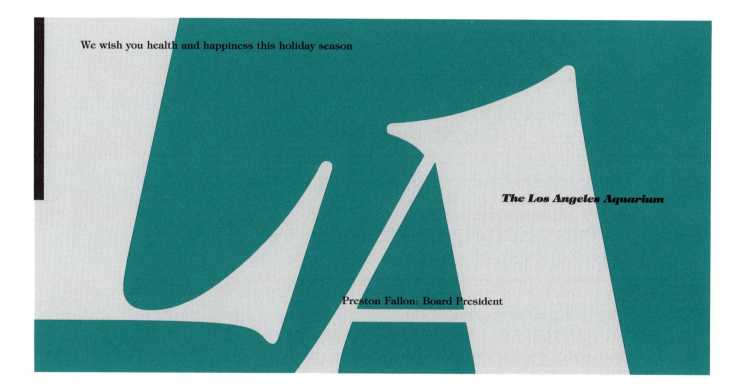

We wish you health and happiness this holiday season

The Los Angeles Aquarium

Preston Fallon: Board President

Zapf Calligraphic

The Bitstream version of the Palatino® typeface.

Roman

abcdefghijklmnopqrstuvwxyz
ABCDEFGHIJKLMNOPQRSTUVWXYZ
1234567890&$£%.,:;-!?'' åçëîñòšúß

Italic

abcdefghijklmnopqrstuvwxyz
ABCDEFGHIJKLMNOPQRSTUVWXYZ
1234567890&$£%.,:;-!?'' åçëîñòšúß

Bold

abcdefghijklmnopqrstuvwxyz
ABCDEFGHIJKLMNOPQRSTUVWXYZ
1234567890&$£%.,:;-!?'' åçëîñòšúß

Bold Italic

abcdefghijklmnopqrstuvwxyz
ABCDEFGHIJKLMNOPQRSTUVWXYZ
1234567890&$£%.,:;-!?'' åçëîñòšúß

15 point

Bitstream is an independent digital typefoundry. Using the latest computer graphics tools, Bitstream's designers maintain the traditional essentials of good type design. Shape, weight and spacing rhythm are expertly controlled *to produce digitized letterforms of the highest quality in all font formats. In addition to making definitive versions of existing faces, Bitstream introduces creative new designs.*
9 point with 10 point lead

Bitstream is an independent digital typefoundry. Using the latest computer graphics tools, Bitstream's designers maintain the traditional essentials of good type design. Shape, weight and spacing rhythm are ex- ***pertly controlled to produce digitized letterforms of the highest quality in all font formats. In addition to making definitive versions of existing faces, Bitstream introduces creative new designs.***

Letter of Transmittal

A good example of information design, this transmittal demonstrates that business forms do not necessarily have to be set in a sanserif typeface.

Given that the company logotype is set in Zapf Calligraphic, it was logical to use the same typeface family throughout the form. The classical feeling created in the letterspaced logotype is reinforced throughout the form, especially in the reversed letterspaced title.

A rational, easy-to-use appearance has been achieved by eliminating extraneous elements. Text is consistently kept upper- and lowercase, in a single point size. Emphasis is given with bolder type. Horizontal rules clearly define the writing areas. Columns are defined by breaking the horizontal rule as shown in the *Quantity* and *Description* columns. Vertical rules were not used because they would only serve to constrain the text.

Type specifications:
The company name is set in 9-point Zapf Calligraphic; the large ampersand is in Zapf Calligraphic Italic; remaining copy is in 7/18 Zapf Calligraphic and Zapf Calligraphic Bold.

P E D E R S O N & A S S O C I A T E S

177 Connecticut Ave.

Bethesda, Maryland 20816

301-555-0650

T R A N S M I T T A L

Project **Project No.**

Date

To

Enclosed you will find

- ☐ copy
- ☐ specifications
- ☐ galleys
- ☐ corrections
- ☐ samples
- ☐ photographs
- ☐ camera ready
- ☐

for your

- ☐ comments
- ☐ verification
- ☐ signature
- ☐ information
- ☐ records
- ☐ use
- ☐ distribution
- ☐ please return
- ☐

Quantity	Description

Notes

Copies to

Zapf Elliptical

The Bitstream version of the Melior™ typeface.

Roman

abcdefghijklmnopqrstuvwxyz
ABCDEFGHIJKLMNOPQRSTUVWXYZ
1234567890&$£%.,:;-!?‘’åçëîñòšúß

Italic

abcdefghijklmnopqrstuvwxyz
ABCDEFGHIJKLMNOPQRSTUVWXYZ
1234567890&$£%.,:;-!?‘’åçëîñòšúß

Bold

abcdefghijklmnopqrstuvwxyz
ABCDEFGHIJKLMNOPQRSTUVWXYZ
1234567890&$£%.,:;-!?‘’åçëîñòšúß

Bold Italic

abcdefghijklmnopqrstuvwxyz
ABCDEFGHIJKLMNOPQRSTUVWXYZ
1234567890&$£%.,:;-!?‘’åçëîñòšúß

15 point

Bitstream is an independent digital typefoundry. Using the latest computer graphics tools, Bitstream's designers maintain the traditional essentials of good type design. Shape, weight and spacing rhythm are expertly controlled *to produce digitized letterforms of the highest quality in all font formats. In addition to making definitive versions of existing faces, Bitstream introduces creative new designs.*
9 point with 10 point lead

Bitstream is an independent digital typefoundry. Using the latest computer graphics tools, Bitstream's designers maintain the traditional essentials of good type design. Shape, weight and spacing rhythm are ex- ***pertly controlled to produce digitized letterforms of the highest quality in all font formats. In addition to making definitive versions of existing faces, Bitstream introduces creative new designs.***

Journal

This journal page demonstrates how text and headlines alone can be visually exciting and attract the reader's interest. A serif typeface, Zapf Elliptical, was chosen as the primary text face for its readability and traditional tone. This face contrasts with the sanserif Swiss Black, which is used for the indented text.

The clean, even stroke width and heavy weight of the Swiss Black provide a distinct contrast to the serif text. The two-column grid is easy to read, and the wide indents emphasize particular passages.

The indents also serve to introduce white space and break up the monotony of solid text. The large initial cap *M* provides a clear starting point for the reader.

Type specifications:
The headline for the article is set in 16-point Zapf Elliptical Bold; text is set in 9/13 Zapf Elliptical, with the indented passage set in 8/13 Swiss Black. The author's name is set in 9-point Swiss Black, the initial cap *M* in 36-point Swiss Black.

Monet: The Basin at Argenteuil

Adrienne Cash

Introduction

Monet's landscape of Argenteuil was painted some time around 1874. As in earlier landscapes and seascapes, Monet retains the high overhead viewpoint to flatten the elements in the painting. He also employs a surface geometry to organize the painting. His palette consists of pure, intense color as it has since he painted with Renoir in 1869. As always, Monet is interested in the motif as a purely optical spectacle.

Bella Kunin notes a purpose in Monet's tendency to create situations where space is expected and implied but never developed past a rudimentary form:

> **The comprehension of a reality behind the painting depends on a release from an enclosed world. The formal relations define the interest and intentions of Monet clearly: the natural scene exists as a stimulus for artistic expression.**

The landscape divides naturally into four zones. In the foreground, nondescript foliage extends across most of the width of the painting, stopping abruptly at the lower left corner. The second area of water fills a large proportion of the canvas and creates a flat, impenetrable link between foreground and shore. Two sails cut from the water into the third zone of shoreline and connect the two areas visually. The shoreline extends across the canvas and is filled with a band of trees, which are uninterrupted except for a small house. A strip of hazy, blue-green sky completes the scene. The foreground and background both function as the sides of a box, within which Monet plays with the idea of an enclosed space.

Although he chose to paint this scene many times, Monet always dominated it by reducing it to serve his needs. The color, for example, is based in reality and does not deviate from the range of observable color. It is intensified color, however, which builds light into every part of the canvas while rejecting shadows or exact replication of local color. Kunin has noted the significance of Monet's treatment of space:

> **For Monet the creation of space is no essential act, but the matter occupies much of his attention in this painting. Whether implying, denying, or subverting space, Monet uses it in this painting. Just as the canvas provides a surface for the paint, space provides a background for expression.**

The foreground foliage is painted with rough, dry strokes of varying sizes and directions which suggest rather than describe different kinds of plant growth. Multiple color contrasts occur more here than elsewhere, and the range of colors is extensive. Greens, ochres, salmon, black, cream, and even a few rose flecks vibrate optically without defining the area specifically. Neither space nor mass is allowed to develop; the general effect is that of a two-dimensional screen cut away jaggedly to expose a view of the lake. This flatness varies, however, in different places. In the upper part, thick cream swirls almost achieve a spatial separation from the water, while in the lower corner, the two areas confusedly enter each other through overlapping brushstrokes. In the middle, the water and land are joined along a clear dividing line.

Zapf Humanist

The Bitstream version of the Optima® typeface.

Roman

abcdefghijklmnopqrstuvwxyz
ABCDEFGHIJKLMNOPQRSTUVWXYZ
1234567890&$£%.,:;-!?''åçëîñòšúß

Italic

abcdefghijklmnopqrstuvwxyz
ABCDEFGHIJKLMNOPQRSTUVWXYZ
1234567890&$£%.,:;-!?''åçëîñòšúß

Bold

abcdefghijklmnopqrstuvwxyz
ABCDEFGHIJKLMNOPQRSTUVWXYZ
1234567890&$£%.,:;-!?''åçëîñòšúß

Bold Italic

abcdefghijklmnopqrstuvwxyz
ABCDEFGHIJKLMNOPQRSTUVWXYZ
1234567890&$£%.,:;-!?''åçëîñòšúß

15 point

Bitstream is an independent digital typefoundry. Using the latest computer graphics tools, Bitstream's designers maintain the traditional essentials of good type design. Shape, weight and spacing rhythm *are expertly controlled to produce digitized letterforms of the highest quality in all font formats. In addition to making definitive versions of existing faces, Bitstream introduces creative new designs.*
9 point with 10 point lead

Bitstream is an independent digital typefoundry. Using the latest computer graphics tools, Bitstream's designers maintain the traditional essentials of good type design. Shape, weight and spacing rhythm are expertly controlled ***to produce digitized letterforms of the highest quality in all font formats. In addition to making definitive versions of existing faces, Bitstream introduces creative new designs.***

Certificate of Merit

The uppercase Zapf Humanist characters have a monumental feeling that is appropriate to an award such as this. The *5* and large triangle create a strong graphic image. The large triangle also serves as a pointer to move the eye down to the text.

While many certificates of this kind have ornate, old-fashioned borders, the extensive use of white space gives this award a more modern and elegant look.

Type specifications:
The *5* is set in 120-point Zapf Humanist Bold; *YEARS* in 10-point Zapf Humanist Bold; *CERTIFICATE* and *MERIT* in 13-point Zapf Humanist; *of* in 13-point Bodoni Book Italic; text in 10/26 Zapf Humanist. The triangle and stars are from the ITC Zapf Dingbats collection available in the Bitstream *Symbols 1* typeface package.

CERTIFICATE *of* MERIT

5

YEARS

THEODORE RUSK GROVES

is awarded

this certificate

in recognition

of 5 years

service with

Meridien Corporation

presented

December 12, 1987

* * * * *

David C. Gampfer

Zurich™

The Bitstream version of the Univers® typeface.

Roman

abcdefghijklmnopqrstuvwxyz
ABCDEFGHIJKLMNOPQRSTUVWXYZ
1234567890&$£%.,:;-!?"åçëîñòšúß

Italic

abcdefghijklmnopqrstuvwxyz
ABCDEFGHIJKLMNOPQRSTUVWXYZ
1234567890&$£%.,:;-!?"åçëîñòšúß

Black

abcdefghijklmnopqrstuvwxyz
ABCDEFGHIJKLMNOPQRSTUVWXYZ
1234567890&$£%.,:;-!?"åçëîñòšúß

Black Italic

abcdefghijklmnopqrstuvwxyz
ABCDEFGHIJKLMNOPQRSTUVWXYZ
1234567890&$£%.,:;-!?"åçëîñòšúß

15 point

Bitstream is an independent digital typefoundry. Using the latest computer graphics tools, Bitstream's designers maintain the traditional essentials of good type design. Shape, weight and spacing rhythm are expertly *controlled to produce digitized letterforms of the highest quality in all font formats. In addition to making definitive versions of existing faces, Bitstream introduces creative new designs.*

9 point with 10 point lead

Bitstream is an independent digital typefoundry. Using the latest computer graphics tools, Bitstream's designers maintain the traditional essentials of good type design. Shape, weight and spacing rhythm are expertly controlled ***to produce digitized letterforms of the highest quality in all font formats. In addition to making definitive versions of existing faces, Bitstream introduces creative new designs.***

Business Form

This time sheet shows how even very complex tabular information can be organized in a clean, rational manner. Zurich and Zurich Black are used for their simple structure, which does not compete with the information to be written on the form. Hairline and 3-point rules provide organizational structure. Note that vertical rules are used minimally and that a break in the horizontal rules serves to separate columns. Both these elements further reinforce a clean image that doesn't overwhelm the reader.

The minimal use of color for the company name, address, and monogram separates that information from the material below.

Type specifications:
The company name is set in 9.5/11 Serifa Black; the address in 9.5/11 Serifa. *EPG* is set in 22-point Serifa Black. The form title, *Weekly Time Sheet,* is set in 16-point Zurich Black. Text of the form is in 8-point Zurich and Zurich Black. The days of the week and *Total* are set in 8-point Zurich Black Italic. The arrows are from the ITC Zapf Dingbats collection available in the Bitstream *Symbols 1* typeface package.

EPG

The Environmental Planning Group, P.C.

Two Harbor Place
Burlington, Vermont
0 5 4 0 1
802 555-4074

Weekly Time Sheet

Name ▶

Week ending Sunday ▶

Project hours

Project number	Sub-code	Project	M	T	W	Th	F	S	S	Total
		Total billable hours ▶								

Office hours

0001	Holiday								
0002	Vacation								
0003	Sick								
0004	Office overhead								
0005	Personal								
0006	Computer overhead								
0007	General promotion								
0008	Specific promotion								
0009	Professional development								
	Total unbillable hours ▶								
	Total hours								

Employee signature ▶

Approved by ▶

Zurich Condensed

The Bitstream version of the
Univers® Condensed typeface

Condensed

abcdefghijklmnopqrstuvwxyz
ABCDEFGHIJKLMNOPQRSTUVWXYZ
1234567890&$£%.,:;-!?"åçëîñòšúß

Condensed Italic

abcdefghijklmnopqrstuvwxyz
ABCDEFGHIJKLMNOPQRSTUVWXYZ
1234567890&$£%.,:;-!?"åçëîñòšúß

Bold Extended

abcdefghijklmnopqrstuvwxyz
ABCDEFGHIJKLMNOPQRSTUVWXYZ
1234567890&$£%.,:;-!?''åçëîñòšúß

Black Extended

abcdefghijklmnopqrstuvwxyz
ABCDEFGHIJKLMNOPQRSTUVWXYZ
1234567890&$£%.,:;-!?''åçëîñòšúß

15 point

Bitstream is an independent digital typefoundry. Using the latest computer graphics tools, Bitstream's designers maintain the traditional essentials of good type design. Shape, weight and spacing rhythm are expertly controlled to *produce digitized letterforms of the highest quality in all font formats. In addition to making definitive versions of existing faces, Bitstream introduces creative new designs.*
9 point with 10 point lead

Bitstream is an independent digital typefoundry. Using the latest computer graphics tools, Bitstream's designers maintain the traditional essentials of good type design. Shape, weight and spacing rhythm are expertly controlled to produce digitized letterforms of the highest quality in all font formats. In addition to making definitive versions of existing faces, Bitstream introduces creative new designs.

Announcement

Three intersecting columns of text and city names create an active, exciting composition using type alone. The announcement illustrates how various weights and widths of the Zurich typeface family can be combined for variety while maintaining a unified look.

The columns of text, though intersecting, are easily distinguished by the color break.

In the airlines logotype, *Air* is set in Zurich Light to suggest air and lightness; *Benelux* is set in Zurich Black for a contrasting feeling of stability. The word *AIR* is set diagonally to contrast with the strong vertical/horizontal composition below and to visually imply the trajectory of flight.

Type specifications:
Text in the left columns is 10/48 Zurich Condensed Italic; text in the middle column is in 10/48 Zurich Condensed; the list of cities is in 14/48 Zurich Black Extended. In the logotype, *Air* is set in 14-point Zurich Light; *Benelux* in 14-point Zurich Black.

R

I

AirBenelux, the airline of Belgium, the

Belgrade

Netherlands, and Luxembourg is happy to

Boston

announce eleven new international destina-

Chicago

tions in North America, western Europe and

Dresden

the central and eastern European nations.

Helsinki

AirBenelux will now have Europe's only daily

Service begins Monday, November 21, 1991. **Leningrad**

flight to the Soviet Union, with nonstop

For timetable and ticket information in North **Montréal**

service form Brussels to Leningrad.

America call 1-800-555-5865. **Munich**

AirBenelux, Europe's door to the world.

Prague

Sarajevo

Warsaw

Air**Benelux**

Zurich Light

The Bitstream version of the Univers® Light typeface.

Light

abcdefghijklmnopqrstuvwxyz
ABCDEFGHIJKLMNOPQRSTUVWXYZ
1234567890&$£%.,:;-!?"åçëîñòšúß

Light Italic

abcdefghijklmnopqrstuvwxyz
ABCDEFGHIJKLMNOPQRSTUVWXYZ
1234567890&$£%.,:;-!?"åçëîñòšúß

Bold

abcdefghijklmnopqrstuvwxyz
ABCDEFGHIJKLMNOPQRSTUVWXYZ
1234567890&$£%.,:;-!?"åçëîñòšúß

Bold Italic

abcdefghijklmnopqrstuvwxyz
ABCDEFGHIJKLMNOPQRSTUVWXYZ
1234567890&$£%.,:;-!?"åçëîñòšúß

15 point

Bitstream is an independent digital typefoundry. Using the latest computer graphics tools, Bitstream's designers maintain the traditional essentials of good type design. Shape, weight and spacing rhythm are expertly controlled *to produce digitized letterforms of the highest quality in all font formats. In addition to making definitive versions of existing faces, Bitstream introduces creative new designs.*
9 point with 10 point lead

Bitstream is an independent digital typefoundry. Using the latest computer graphics tools, Bitstream's designers maintain the traditional essentials of good type design. Shape, weight and spacing rhythm ***are expertly controlled to produce digitized letterforms of the highest quality in all font formats. In addition to making definitive versions of existing faces, Bitstream introduces creative new designs.***

Employee Manual

A straightforward and stylish typeface, Zurich does not compete with the content of the message, thus making it appropriate for use in this manual.

By using two different weights of Zurich—Bold for headlines and Light for text—a clear hierarchy is established in the two-column table. This hierarchy is reinforced by the use of two rule weights: 1-point between entries and a hairline between sub-sections.

The square with reversed headline and page folio provide visual interest and make reference to the square page shape.

Type specifications:
The headline is set in 14/16 Zurich Bold; text is in 8/9 Zurich Light and Bold; the page folio is in 8-point Zurich Bold.

Retirement Benefits

Your Normal Retirement Date	At age 65
A projection of your estimated retirement benefit at age 65 based on a life annuity payment method	From the Retirement Plan
	From social security
	Total monthly benefit
	A dependent spouse age 65 is eligible for additional social security benefit equal to half of yours.
Early retirement benefit based on a life annuity payment method	Early retirement at a reduced benefit is available starting at age 55, with 15 or more years of service. Benefits are not reduced if you retire after reaching age 62 with at least 15 years of service.
Vested Benefit	If you leave the company after becoming vested, but before retirement, you are eligible for a deferred retirement benefit.

Credits for Chapter 15
Setting a good example

Studio
Forsythe Design
Cambridge, Massachusetts

Design Director
Kathleen Forsythe

Designers
Kathleen Forsythe
Julie Steinhilber
Jim Hood
Jane Cuthbertson

Contributing Designers
Julie Curtis Reed
Irene Cagney
Wallace Marozek

Production
Jane Cuthbertson
Phyllis Siccardi
Christine Amisano

Typesetting Output
Publication Services
Wrightson Typographers

Editor
Daniel Will-Harris

&

Appendix

Glossary

Type terminology

Glossary

Alley. The space between columns of type on a page. See *Gutter.*

Alignment. Designation regarding the ends of lines of type, such as flush right, flush left, justified, or centered.

Ampersand. Name of the type character "&," used in place of "and."

Ascender. The part of a lowercase letter that rises above the body of the letter, as in b, d, f, h, k, l, and t.

Baselines. Invisible lines on which the bottom of characters rest.

BF. Copyreader's abbreviation indicating that the copy should be set in boldface type.

Bleed. Printing that extends off the edge of a sheet or page after trimming.

Block. A standard paragraph in which the first character of the first line is not indented. Block paragraphs should be set with a blank line between paragraphs.

Blurb. A short summary of a book's contents to be used on the jacket copy. May also refer to a longish caption or a short block of text treated as a *readout.*

Boards. In traditional printing, the typeset copy is pasted up on a board. In desktop publishing, if you are not going to use a laser printer for your final output, you may still need to employ paste up boards for the printer to use in preparation for duplicating.

Body copy. The bulk of text in a publication. The stories and articles are the body of your publication. Headlines are not body copy, they are *display type.*

Body type. The type used for body copy, usually set in 9- to 12-point.

Boldface. A heavier, darker version of a regular typeface.

Boxed. Material enclosed by rules or borders.

Bullet. A large dot or box used as a graphic element in body copy. See *Dingbat.*

Byline. A line telling the reader who wrote the article. The byline is usually set in boldface type.

Camera-ready copy. Finished pages prepared for the printer's camera. The camera is a *copy* camera, which photographs pages so that they can be used with the printing press. The whole idea behind desktop publishing is the ability to produce these completely ready-to-go-to-the-printer pages.

Capitals. The large letters of the alphabet. Also know as "caps" or "uppercase letters."

Captions (or cut-lines). Sentences or paragraphs of descriptive text accompanying illustrations. They are usually set in a different typestyle (often italics or boldface) to distinguish them from body copy.

Characters. Individual letters, figures, punctuation marks, etc., of the alphabet.

Clay-coated paper. A paper with an especially smooth surface, recommended for use in laser printers because the toner doesn't smudge on it. It is heavier than regular copy paper and can easily be sprayed with adhesive or glued with rubber cement for manual pasteup.

Clip art. Illustrations, usually black and white, which can be used without securing permission from the artist or paying royalties.

Columns. Vertically-oriented sections of text. The purpose of a column is to make reading easier by keeping lines of text shorter, while allowing you to print a lot of text on a page.

Comp. The abbreviation for *comprehensive,* an accurate layout displaying type and illustrations in position on a page. Mainly used in advertising agencies to show clients various layouts.

Condensed type. Narrow version of a regular typeface.

Copy. All the text on your page. Available in various "flavors," the most plentiful of which is body copy.

Copyfitting. The calculation of how much space a given amount of copy will occupy in a given size and typeface. Also, the adjustment of the type size to make it fit in a given amount of space.

Deckhead or deckline. The lines following the headline and preceding the byline, usually imparting more information about the article. See *Headline* and *Subhead.*

Descenders. The part of lowercase letters that falls below the baseline, as in g, j, p, q, and y.

Dingbat. The collective name for all symbols and ornaments, such as stars, pointing fingers, and arrows. *ITC Zapf Dingbats* is a specific typeface containing dingbats, and is the most popular and widely available for desktop publishing. Dingbats are often used as bullet characters.

Display type. Type (usually 14-point or larger) that by virtue of its design is used to attract attention in headlines, pull quotes, subheads, etc. Ornate, attention-grabbing display typefaces are employed for effect in advertisements, promotional materials, etc.

Drop cap. Display letter that is inset into the text. May also be raised.

Dummy. A "blueprint" for page layouts. You mark sections of a page where stories or artwork will be placed later. Dummies are a quick and efficient way to decide what goes on each page.

Editing. The process of checking copy for accuracy, stylistic consistency, spelling, grammar, and punctuation prior to typesetting.

Em. A printer's unit of measurement, refers to the width of the letter "M."

Em space. A blank space representing the square of a given point-size of type, used as a measure for indenting and spacing (the width of the letter "M").

En. Another printer's unit of measurement, which refers to the width of the letter "N," used for inserting white space in a line of type. Sometimes called a *thin space.*

Extended. A wide version of a typeface.

Face (also Typeface). A specific design of a set of letters, numbers, and symbols, such as Dutch, Baskerville, etc.

Family of type. A series of typefaces that are consistent in style but different in weight and width (roman, italic, bold, condensed, expanded, etc.); a major division of typefaces (e.g., Dutch, Bodoni).

Flop. To turn an image over so it faces the opposite way. This is usually done with portraits so that they face the correct direction on the page. A mirror image.

Folio. Page numbers.

Font. Complete assortment of all the characters (upper- and lowercase letters, numerals, punctuation marks, etc.) of one size and one typeface.

Footer. Text appearing at the bottom of a page, such as a page number or chapter title.

Formatting. The process of designing pages on the computer.

Galley. A long sheet of typeset text not yet in page format, often used to proofread text.

Graphics. Art and other elements (including type) used on a page as a visual statement.

Grid. A network of horizontal and vertical lines, usually not printed, used to guide the placement of elements on the page layout.

Gutter. The blank space where two pages meet at the publication's binding, or the blank space between columns of type.

Hairline. A fine line or rule, the finest that can be reproduced in printing. The next largest size in many systems is a half-point line, followed by a one-point line.

Halftone. The process of reproducing photographs so they can be printed on a large press. Photos have a "continuous tone" that is converted into a "halftone" by photographing the original through a fine cross-line screen. This is necessary for quality reproduction of the photos. Halftoning is performed at the printer's before plates are produced for printing.

Hanging indent (outdent). A style in which the first line of copy is set full measure, and all the lines that follow are indented.

Hard copy. Type that is printed on a piece of paper, as opposed to type on the screen of a computer. It is useful to print out a hard copy of a page as a rough draft for proofing before you print out a final version.

Header. A line of text (such as the title of a publication, name of article or chapter) appearing at the top of a page.

Headlines. Lines of type (set in a display type, a larger size than body copy), telling readers what stories or articles are about. They are often accompanied by subheads (or deckheads), which are smaller headlines. Also abbreviated as "hed."

Hung initial. A display letter set in the left-hand margin.

Indent. An indented paragraph is the most common style. The first line of each paragraph is indented, usually one em, with no blank lines between paragraphs. The indent can be longer or shorter, depending on the desired effect.

Initial cap. The first letter of a body of copy, set in a display type for decoration or emphasis. Often used to begin each chapter of a book, it may be either dropped into a paragraph or raised above it.

Insert. A separately prepared and printed piece that is inserted into another printed piece or a publication.

Italic. A letterform that slants to the right or is cursive. Italics are usually companions to, and distinct from, roman (upright) typefaces. *Italics look like this*.

Jumphead. The headline appearing above an article continued from another page. The jumphead may only contain one or two words of the original headline.

Jumpline. The line at the end of a column of text, stating the page to which the article jumps. Also at the top of the column, under the *jumphead,* stating where the article was continued from.

Justified type. Lines of type that align on both the left and the right of a column's full measure (the width of the entire column).

Kerning. Adjusting the space between letters (usually moving them closer together) to improve the apparent regularity of the spacing.

Kicker. The words positioned just above the headline. Usually in a smaller typesize, flush left, sometimes underlined. Also called a "teaser."

Landscape. A horizontal page, printed so that the width of the page is greater than its height. A vertical page is called *portrait.* Type can also be landscape or portrait.

Layout (or make-up). The placement of all elements, including text and graphics, on a page. Layout is the design process, while *make-up* involves the physical paste-up of the elements. In desktop publishing, layout is also referred to as page composition or page processing. A layout specifies the sizes and styles of type, the positions of illustrations, spacing, and general style.

Leading (pronounced ledding). The term originates from a time when thin strips of lead were inserted between lines of type to achieve proper spacing. Leading determines the amount of white space between lines of type, and can be expressed as "10/11," or "10 on 11,"(10-point type with 11-point leading).

Letterspacing. Adding space between individual letters in order to fill out a line of type and improve appearance.

Ligatures. A ligature refers to two connected characters, like the "ae" in *Encyclopædia Britannica.* Kerned pairs of letters, such as the "ff" and "fi," may fit so closely together that they resemble ligatures. Not all software supports ligatures, as they are not included in all fonts.

Line drawing. Any artwork created by solid black lines, usually with pen and ink.

Logotype. "Logo" for short. Two or more type characters joined together for use as a trademark or company signature. Can also refer to any type and artwork combined to represent a single graphic element or distinctive symbol.

Lowercase. The small letters, as opposed to the capitals.

Measure. The length of a line of type, normally expressed in picas, or in picas and points.

Mechanical. The camera-ready pasted-up assembly of all type and design elements located in exact position on artboard or illustration boards; instructions for the platemaker are contained either in the outside margins or on an overlay.

Monospaced. A typeface in which all characters occupy the same amount of horizontal space, such as a fixed-pitch typewriter face.

Non-repro blue. A light blue pencil or pen used especially for marking camera-ready copy or paste-up boards because the marks will not reproduce when photographed.

Oblique. Roman characters that have been slanted to the right. Not true italics.

Offset printing. A system that uses special printing plates created directly from photographs of the original pages. Your camera-ready copy is used as the original page.

Outdent. Text on the first line of a paragraph that prints to the left of the paragraph margin.

Orphan. The last word or line of a paragraph stranded at the top of a column of text. Or the first line of a paragraph stranded at the very bottom of a column of text. This is undesirable and should be adjusted whenever possible. See also *Widow.*

Page composition. Identical to layout. The design and placement of all the elements on a page. Also called *page processing*.

Pagination. The process of putting pages into consecutive order. In page composition programs, *batch pagination* is a process in which text is automatically flowed onto pages in consecutive order. Some programs require you to paginate manually by using a mouse to place the text on each individual page.

Paste-up. The process of placing the type and graphic elements on the pasteboard to create camera-ready copy. When the paste-up is completed it is called a *mechanical.*

Photomechanical. The complete assembly of type, line art, and halftone art in the form of film positives. Used for checking proofs and monitoring the production of printing plates.

Pica. A typographic unit of measurement equal to one-sixth of an inch. Column width is measured in picas.

Pi characters. Special characters of a font, such as arrows, bullets, stars, and the copyright symbols. (® © ™ ⇐ ⇒).

Point. Smallest typographical unit of measurement, approximately 1/72 of an inch. Type is measured in terms of points, the standard sizes being 6, 8, 10, 12, 14, 18, 24, 30, 36, 42, 48, 60, and 72.

Point size. The size of a particular font.

Portrait. A vertical page, printed so that the width of the page is less than its height. A horizontal page is called *landscape.*

Printing plate. A surface, usually composed of metal, that has been treated to carry an image. The plate is inked, and the ink is transferred to the paper by a printing press.

Production artist. A person who performs paste-up.

Proofreader. A person who checks for accuracy by reading set type against original copy. Proofreaders may also read for consistency, fact, and style.

Proofs. A trial print or sheet of printed material that is checked against the original manuscript, and then subsequently used for corrections.

Pull quote (or callouts or readouts). A pull quote is a section of text set apart from the body copy as a graphic element. It pulls out an important quote or statement from the text, and is set in a larger typesize than the body copy.

Raised cap. Display letter that is set above the text. The "R" at the beginning of this entry is a raised cap. May also be dropped into the text.

Ream. A unit of measure for paper of any size: 500 sheets of paper.

Reverse type. Type that drops out of the background and assumes the color of the paper or image behind it. Normally white type on a black background.

Rules. Black lines, used for a variety of effects, including borders and boxes. They come in a range of thicknesses or *weights* that are measured in point sizes, the thinnest of which is called *hairline.* Rules may be dotted, dashed, or contain a number of lines of various weights.

Running head or foot. Title or other information at the top or bottom of every page of a publication.

Sans serif. Without serifs. A clean, modern typeface, such as Swiss (Helvetica).

Scanner. A device, connected to a computer, which can convert a typewritten page or artwork (such as a photograph or line drawing), from the printed page into data that the computer can use.

Serifs. Small cross-bars (or finishing strokes) that end the main strokes of letters. Dutch (Times Roman) is a serif typestyle.

Sidebar. A shorter story than the primary one it supports, containing specific information relating to one aspect of the main article. Used to highlight a particular point, or to present related or background information.

Signature. A printer's term referring to a single sheet of paper with several pages printed on each side. The sheet is then folded into "booklets" from which books and magazines are assembled.

Subheads. Can be placed directly after a headline or above certain paragraphs to highlight specific areas of body copy. Subheads stand out and so help the reader find specific topics.

Text. The body copy on a page or in a book, as opposed to the headings.

Thumbnails. Small, rough sketches used to explore designs for page layout.

Typeface. A specific design of a set of letters, numbers, and symbols, such as Dutch, Baskerville, Goudy, etc.

Type family. The various weights and styles of a typeface. Baskerville roman, italic, bold, and bold italic together are a typeface family. Some families include only two styles, others contain 12 or more variations.

Typestyle. A variation of weight or width within a typeface family. Standard typestyles include roman, italic, bold, condensed, or extended but there are many different weights and widths, and each one is a typestyle.

Typography. The art and process of working with and printing from type.

X-height. A typesetting term used to represent the height of the main body of the lowercase letters of a typeface, excluding the ascenders and descenders.

White space. Refers to the blank space that frames or sets off text and graphics. Also called *negative space*.

Widow. A relative of the orphan: a single word on a line by itself at the end of a paragraph. It's unattractive and makes the text harder to read. Many software programs automatically help you eliminate these outcasts of the type world.

Wordspacing. Adding space between words to fill out a line of type and improve appearance.

WYSIWYG. What You See Is What You Get (printed). Pronounced "wissywig" or "wizzywig," depending on how you pronounce *Caribbean*. Refers to the ability to display a close representation of the printed page on the computer screen.

Bibliography

Read more about it

Bibliography: Read more about it

There are many books that deal specifically with type, and a few of them that address both design and electronic publishing techniques. Here are a few I consider to be the best.

Graphic Design

Editing by Design, Jan White (R. R. Bowker), 1982. A useful book for the editor who wants to learn more about communicating effectively in print. Also helpful for the art director who wants an improved understanding of how to effectively present written material. Covers all the basics, including type specifications, cropping photos, and numerous design alternatives. The author spent 22 years as an art director for major magazines and what he doesn't know about graphic design isn't worth knowing. $34.95.

Graphic Design for the Electronic Age, Jan White (Watson-Guptill), 1988. The subtitle for this book is "the manual for traditional and desktop publishing," but the emphasis is on graphic design rather than desktop publishing specifics. No particular software or hardware is referred to, although electronic typographic considerations are dealt with extensively. This book draws on material from several of White's other informative and useful books, and is well worth the price. If you can only afford one of White's books, this is the one. $34.95.

Graphic Idea Notebook: *Inventive techniques for designing printed pages,* Jan White (Watson-Guptill), 1980. Another work by the master of the genre, Jan White. With this book, transforming ordinary material into provocative publications looks easy. A book to stimulate your imagination and open your eyes to the many possibilities by which you can enhance your publications with special handling of graphics. $22.50.

Graphics Handbook, Howard Munce (North Light), 1982. A book about design not written by Jan White? How did this wind up in here? Well, this is a good book, too. Not as detailed as White's, but excellent for the beginner. This book attempts to take the fright and mystery out of the design and preparation of simple printed pieces, and it really does simplify some of the mechanics. Illustrated with hundreds of graphic examples of the most popular applications. $14.95.

A History of Graphic Design, Philip B. Meggs (Van Nostrand Reinhold), 1983. Generously illustrated, this book covers all forms of design and typography. $34.95.

Typography

The Art of Typography: *Understanding contemporary type design through classic typography,* Martin Solomon (Watson-Guptill), 1988. This book explores aesthetic elements and contains numerous examples to illustrate attractive composition and design. Includes a variety of problem-solving ideas and a comprehensive directory of typefaces. $29.95.

Decorative Letters, *Copyright-free designs,* Carol Belanger Grafton (Dover Publications), 1986. Over 800 decorative letters of the alphabet to add spice to a variety of publications. For standard LaserJet users, these ornamental letters are especially effective when used as large dropped or raised capitals. $3.50.

Designing With Type, *a basic course in typography,* James Craig (Watson-Guptill). Often used as a textbook for design students, this manual thoroughly examines five popular typefaces and demonstrates how they can be applied to a multitude of publications. Also includes a type gallery of over 120 faces. The author has written several other books about design and typography, and is well-equipped to share his vast knowledge with readers. $24.95.

Photo Typography, Allan Haley (Scribner's Sons), 1982. The author is a vice president at ITC (International Typeface Corporation), and his book offers valuable guidelines and insight into effective typesetting and design standards. If you need more in-depth information about specific fonts, including their history, distinct characteristics, and usage, read this book. $18.95.

Printing Types: Their History, Forms, and Use: *In Two Volumes,* Daniel Berkeley Updike (Dover Publications), 1980. This standard history of printing types is more than worth its low price. $5.95.

Rookledge's International Typefinder, *the essential handbook of typeface recognition and selection,* Christopher Perfect & Gordon Rookledge (PCB International), 1983. An absolute classic. Although essential is an appropriate word, the subtitle could easily have been "the *perfect* handbook of typeface recognition," because that's what it is. The volume is well-structured, dividing 700 typefaces into a logical progression and highlighting the special identifying characteristics of each font. For anyone interested in type, this book is an Aladdin's cave, full of wondrous treasures. $24.95.

Twentieth Century Type Designers, Sebastian Carter (Taplinger Publishing Company), 1987. Profiles of type designers and examples of their work provide a lively history of type design. $18.95.

Type: Design, Color, Character & Use, Michael Beaumont (North Light), 1987. Full of color examples, this book provides inspiration and instructive commentary. $24.95.

Typographic Communications Today, Edward M. Gottschall (International Typeface Corporation and MIT Press), 1989. Over 500 color illustrations fill this critical review of the past hundred years of typographic design. This 14- by 11-inch book is illustrated with more than 200 full alphabet examples. $55.

Producing Newsletters

Editing Your Newsletter, 3rd Edition, Mark Beach (Van Nostrand Reinhold), 1988. Practical information on the writing, editing, design, and layout of newsletters. $18.50.

Slinging Ink, Jan Sutter (William Kaufman), 1982. All about newsletters, from start to finish. $12.95.

Offset Printing

Getting It Printed, Mark Beach (Coast to Coast), 1986. A how-to book on working with print shops and graphic artists, with an emphasis on the basics of getting the job done. $29.50.

Printing It, Clifford Burke (Wingbow Press), 1972. Written by a printer, this books offers sound advice on how to get a print shop to produce a publication to your satisfaction. $12.95.

Periodicals

Desktop Communications, an IDC publication. This magazine is useful for anyone who wants to improve their business by using computers and desktop publishing. Full of detailed, practical articles and the latest trends in this ever-growing field. Subscriptions are $24 a year. IDC, PO Box 941745, Atlanta, GA 30431.

EC & I (Electronic Composition & Imaging), published by Youngblood Publishing. A relatively new publication, *EC & I* approaches desktop publishing with an enthusiasm that is lacking in some of the established DTP magazines. A fresh perspective and an attention to detail make it well worth the subscription price. This high quality and comprehensive journal has proved to be valuable reading. Subscriptions are $42 (US) a year for six bimonthly issues. Youngblood, 505 Consumers Rd., Suite 102, Willowdale, ON, Canada M2J 4V8, 416-492-5777.

Step-By-Step Graphics, published by Dynamic Graphics. This magazine is jam-packed with informative articles about specific design techniques, with special focus on how to improve the visual communication process. Subscriptions are $42 a year for six bimonthly issues. Step-By-Step Graphics, 6000 N. Forest Park Dr., Peoria, IL 61614-3592, 800-255-8800.

Index

A

B

C

G

H

I

J

K

L

M

N

O

P

Q

R

S

Colophon

Bitstream typefaces were used exclusively in the body of the book and all examples. Body text was set in Bitstream Baskerville. Titles, heads, and subheads were set in Bitstream Hammersmith.

All illustrations for Chapters 1 through 14 were created by Daniel Will-Harris using GEM Artline, Arts & Letters, Corel Draw, and Micrographx Designer.

Final text pages were formatted with Ventura Publisher and output on a LaserMaster LM1000 plain paper typesetting laser printer at 1000 dpi.

Chapter 15 was printed on a Tegra XM72 at 2000 dpi.

Ventura Publisher, WordPerfect, ArtBeats, DesignClips, Metro ImageBase, and T-Maker's ClickArt EPS were also used in this book's production.

The book was written, edited, and produced on IBM-PC compatible computers. Camera-ready pages were created entirely on PCs without any manual paste-up. The computers used in the production of the book were from Zeos Corporation in St. Paul, Minnesota, Victor Technologies in Malvern, Pennsylvania, and Toshiba America in Tustin, California. The LaserMaster GlassPage 1280 monitor, with all fonts displaying perfectly on screen, helped speed the production of this book (LaserMaster, Eden Prairie, Minnesota).

Production by Toni and Daniel Will-Harris.

About the author

Daniel Will-Harris has always been interested in any form of communication, from playing with press-on type in his crib to being editor-in-chief of his college paper. It was on that paper that he met his first (and hopefully only) wife, Toni, who is responsible for the majority of the production of this book and that last parenthetical. Since escaping Los Angeles, they now live in the Northern California woods with their pet sheep, Selsdon, and his pet chipmunks.

For many years Daniel worked as a writer for television and the musical theater. When he discovered what computers offered a writer, he was hooked and has been a slave to technology ever since. He has written for many magazines and is in demand as a lecturer and speaker at seminars about desktop publishing, design, and writing with a computer.

As a consultant and designer, Daniel deals primarily with people in the entertainment industry and the media, such as Gene Roddenberry, William F. Buckley, Disney Studios, KUSC, Hanna-Barbera, the *LA Weekly*, and Time/Design. Daniel and Toni have served as editors on several books and have designed and desktop published many books, including Daniel's best-selling *WordPerfect: Desktop Publishing in Style, 2nd Edition for 5.1*. They have also developed their own line of *Designer Disk Style Sheets* for Ventura Publisher and WordPerfect.

Daniel has served as a consultant on feature films, most recently for *Half Moon Street* director Bob Swaim. Living proof of the "it's all who you know school," he's also appeared in several motion pictures, including *Love Letters* with Jamie Lee Curtis, *The Mae West Story* with Ann Jillian, and *Saturday the 14th* with Ray Walston.

In his spare time, Daniel likes to collect anything art deco or stuffed, and to get away for dinner at his favorite restaurant in Belgium. He is currently at work on his first novel, a pseudo-autobiography.

◆ The Little Mac Book

Robin Williams

This concise, handy, friendly book provides everything that a new Macintosh user needs for basic Macintosh literacy. Chapters include Ks, Megs, and Disks; Starting Up; The Desktop; The Mouse; Using Menus; Important Keys; Windows; Icons; Folders; Fonts; Saving; Printing; Ejecting Disks; Shutting Down; Desk Accessories; A Few Extra Tips.

(112 pages / ISBN 0-938151-21-5 / $12.95)

➢ *"Accessible, interesting, simple, and clear."*
—Jan White

◆ The Mac is Not a Typewriter

Robin Williams

Most users don't appreciate—or may be even ignorant of—the difference between typing and typography. More's the pity, for it means they are wasting some of the most impressive and valuable capabilities of their systems. This book explains the techniques and rules for creating aesthetically pleasing type, such as the proper use of quotation marks, how to combine typefaces, and proper use of underlining.

(72 pages / ISBN 0- 938151-31-2 / $9.95)

➢ *"Delightful! Valuable, practical information in an exceptionally palatable package."*
—Allan Haley, VP, International Typeface Corporation

◆ PageMaker 4: An Easy Desk Reference

Robin Williams, November 1990

This is a reference book rather than a tutorial. It is organized to answer any PageMaker question as quickly as possible. Three columns are labeled, respectively, "If You Want to Do This," "Then Follow These Steps," and "OR: Shortcuts/Notes/Hints." Includes a tear-out keyboard chart (printed on card stock) and an industrial-strength index.

(400 pages / ISBN 0- 938151-28-2 / $27.95)

◆ Canned Art: Clip Art for the Macintosh

Erfert Fenton and Christine Morrissett

This fully-indexed encyclopedia shows over 15,000 pieces of clip art available from 35 different companies. Arranged by vendor, the samples are accompanied by ordering and pricing information. The book also contains tips on clip art file formats and utilities for managing a clip art collection. Tear-out coupons provide over $1,000 in discounts on commercial clip art packages.

(825 pages / ISBN 0-938151-18-5 / $29.95)

➢ *"Nobody using clip art should be without a copy."*
—MacWeek

◆ The Macintosh Font Book

Erfert Fenton

This book begins by grounding you in the terminology of type and goes on to help you build, install, and manage your font collection. You'll learn how to choose among the many tools for organizing fonts, modify existing fonts, or create new ones. The book covers design considerations in using fonts, explains font ID numbers, and provides practical tips on printing special characters, fractions, and foreign language characters.

(271 pages / ISBN 0-938151-05-3 / $23.95)

➢ *"Best Books of 1989" award* *—Computer Currents*

◆ Learning PostScript: A Visual Approach

Ross Smith

This book meets the needs of graphic artists, desktop publishers, and others who require a clear and comprehensive but not burdensome introduction to the PostScript page description language. The book uses a unique "show-and-tell" format. Each left-facing page offers a new PostScript concept, including a short demonstration program; each right-facing page shows the printed result.

(426 pages / ISBN 0-938151-12-6 / $22.95)

➢ *"A fresh, effective approach to learning PostScript."*
—John Warnock, President, Adobe Systems

◆ LASERJET UNLIMITED Edition III

Nace, Gardner, and Cummings, December 1990

The definitive guide to HP's family of laser printers (including the LaserJet III), this book covers the use of these printers with word processors, spreadsheets, databases, and desktop publishing programs, as well as special subjects like font downloading, form design, envelope printing, printer upgrades, and LaserJet programming. The appendices include answers to common questions, a troubleshooting guide, and a font directory.

(560 pages / ISBN 0-938151-17-7 / $24.95)

➢ *"A wonderful book."* —*PC Week*

➢ *"A gold mine."* —*New York Times*

◆ DESKJET UNLIMITED

Steve Cummings

An in-depth guide to the HP DeskJet and DeskJet PLUS printers. The book explains how to use these printers with major word processing, spreadsheet, graphics, and desktop publishing programs. It also includes extensive information on fonts (including downloading and converting from LaserJet format), troubleshooting, and DeskJet programming, and tips on practical tasks such as printing envelopes and label sheets.

(428 pages / ISBN 0-938151-11-8 / $21.95)

➢ *Endorsed by Hewlett-Packard*

◆ SCANJET UNLIMITED

Roth, Dickman, and Parascandolo

This book takes you from scanning to final output with the HP ScanJet or ScanJet PLUS. Topics include autotracing, importing scans into other programs, optical character recognition, Linotronic output, halftone screens, and scanning utilities. A special 16-page section on coated stock shows images created using dozens of different scanner settings, output methods, and halftone screens.

(290 pages / ISBN 0-938151-09-6 / $24.95)

➢ *Endorsed by Hewlett-Packard*

◆ THE QUARKXPRESS BOOK

David Blatner, Steve Roth, & Keith Stimely
December 1990

In less than three years, QuarkXPress has come to rival PageMaker as the favorite layout program of serious Macintosh desktop publishers. Sponsored by Quark, Inc., this book provides both users and experienced users with a comprehensive reference to QuarkXPress 3 and QuarkStyle. It also explains QuarkXPress's capability to work in coordination with third-party extensions to the program.

(500 pages / ISBN 0-938151-24-X / $24.95)

➢ *Endorsed by Quark Inc.*

◆ MASTERING COREL DRAW

Dickman and Altman

This book provides beginning lessons and advanced tips and tricks on using this remarkable new drawing program. Tutorials include manipulating and grouping graphics, text shapes and paths, fills and color. Appendices cover file exports, slide creation, and techniques for speeding up the program. A special section displays award-winning drawings along with tips by their creators.

(240 pages / ISBN 0-938151-13-4 / $21.95)

➢ *Endorsed by Corel Systems Corporation*

◆ HELP! THE ART OF COMPUTER TECHNICAL SUPPORT

Ralph Wilson

The first book devoted to "helping the helpers." It overviews the $6 billion tech support industry, analyzes the dialog between the tech support worker and the user in trouble, explains how to set up and manage a tech support operation, discusses the technology of technical support (phone systems, online help, tracking systems), and provides profiles of successful support operations.

(210 pages / ISBN 0-938151-14-2 / $19.95)

➢ *The first guide for hundreds of thousands of technical support workers and managers*

Order Form: 800/283-9444

Quantity	Book Title	Price	Total
	Canned Art: Clip Art for the Macintosh	$29.95	
	DeskJet Unlimited	$21.95	
	The Easy Ventura Book (with disk)	$29.95	
	HELP! The Art Of Computer Technical Support	$19.95	
	Inside PostScript	$37.50	
	LaserJet IIP Essentials	$19.95	
	The LaserJet Font Book	$24.95	
	LaserJet Unlimited, Edition III	$24.95	
	Learning PostScript: A Visual Approach	$22.95	
	The Little Mac Book	$12.95	
	The Little Windows Book	$12.95	
	The Mac is Not a Typewriter	$9.95	
	The Macintosh Font Book	$23.95	
	Mastering Corel Draw	$21.95	
	PageMaker 4: an Easy Desk Reference	$27.95	
	The QuarkXpress Book	$24.95	
	ScanJet Unlimited	$24.95	
	TYPE*Style* — How to Choose and Use Type on a Personal Computer	$24.95	
	Ventura 3 By Example, Windows 3.0 Edition	$24.95	
	Ventura Tips & Tricks, 3rd Edition	$27.95	
	WORDPERFECT: Desktop Publishing In Style, 2nd Edition (5.1 & 5.0)	$23.95	

Tax of 6.5% applies to California residents only.
UPS ground shipping: $3 for first item, $1 for each additional item. UPS 2nd day air: $6 for first item, $2 each additional.
Air mail to Canada: $5 first item, $3 each additional.
Air mail overseas: $14 each item.

Subtotal	
6.5% Tax	
Shipping	
TOTAL	

Name	
Company	
Address	
City	
State	Zip
☐ Check ☐ Visa ☐ MasterCard	
☐ Company Purchase Order#	
Credit Card Number	
Card Holder Name	
Expiration Date	Phone #

Peachpit Press ➢ 1085 Keith Ave. ➢ Berkeley, CA 94708
800-283-9444 or 415/527-8555 ➢ Fax: 415/524-9775
Satisfaction Guaranteed or Your Money Refunded

Return this form for free information on Bitstream type products.

There's so much we could tell you about what Bitstream® type can do for you and your documents. But instead of busting the binding of this book, we'll be glad to send you information about the type and technology that has made Bitstream the leader in type for the PC.

Yes! I want to know more. Please send me information on the following:

☐ Bitstream FaceLift™ product line

☐ The Bitstream Typeface Library for the Macintosh® (over 1000 faces for all PostScript devices)

☐ Bitstream Fontware® product line

Name ____________________

Title ____________________ Department ____________________

Company ____________________

Address ____________________

City ____________________ State ____________________ Zip/Postal Code ____________________

Phone ____________________ Province ____________________ Country ____________________

To help us help you better, please answer these brief questions.

What make and model computer do you use? ____________________

What make and model monitor do you use? ____________________

What make and model printer do you use? ____________________

Which software programs do you use most often? ____________________

Do you use Microsoft® Windows™? ☐ *yes* ☐ *no*

Do you presently use Bitstream type? ☐ *yes* ☐ *no*

fax this form to: **1-617-868-4732**

or send to:

Bitstream Inc.
215 First Street
Cambridge, MA 02142-1270

for more information call:

1-800-522-FONT PC products

1-800-237-3335 Macintosh products